THE JEWS
BIOGRAPHY OF A PEOPLE
BY JUDD TELLER

To Faygele, who is descended from some
of the dynasties that made this history

DS
118
.T35
1966

THE JEWS: BIOGRAPHY OF A PEOPLE
A Bantam Book / published April 1966
2nd printing

Library of Congress Catalog Card Number: 66-15961

Published simultaneously in the United States and Canada

Bantam Books are published by Bantam Books, Inc., a subsidiary
of Grosset & Dunlap, Inc. Its trade-mark, consisting of the words
"Bantam Books" and the portrayal of a bantam, is registered in the
United States Patent Office and in other countries. Marca Registrada.
Bantam Books, Inc., 271 Madison Avenue, New York, N. Y. 10016.

PRINTED IN THE UNITED STATES OF AMERICA

PREFACE

THIS IS A PROFILE, NOT A HISTORY, OF THE JEWS. IT DELETES more than it includes. Yet the author hopes that it presents the quintessence of the collective Jewish personality. Like all profiles, it is subjective. It is not a likeness, but the author's impression. He is not a historian. His primary experience has been in the field of contemporary Jewish affairs, as reporter, editor, and lecturer on Jewish current events and as an executive of international Jewish organizations concerned with the shape and substance of such events. The result has been his fascination with the interaction between the Jew and his environment. In four thousand years of history, the Jew has lived in many and diverse environments. The author has tried to pursue and identify those elements in the long, collective Jewish experience that have survived the Jews' migrations from continent to continent and from civilization to civilization and have endured to this day, influencing both the Jew and those among whom he lives.

Along with the Indians and the Chinese, with whom he has had but slight and ephemeral contact, the Jew is among the oldest surviving peoples on earth. Most of his history unfolded in so-called pagan civilizations. His experience with Christian society represents only a fragment of his rich-tapestried history. It represented until very recently the most painful segment of his experience. The Ecumenical Council's schema is the most recent Christian effort to rectify the past. The Protestant theologian Reinhold Niebuhr, a decade earlier, dealt not with myth but with the living Jewish collectivity. "We should not ask this

particular miracle (the Jews) to fit into any kind of logic or conform to some historical analogy," he wrote. "It must be appreciated for what it is."

For the Jews, Christ's divinity is a myth, like the charge itself. Their only interest in the decree is its practical effect on Christian-Jewish relations. Unfortunately, it has been issued at least two decades too late. Then, more than one-third of the Jewish people resided in Catholic countries. That one-third perished in Hitler's gas chambers.

Better than one-half of the Jewish people live in Protestant lands. Among Protestants, the deicide myth has its most vigorous effect upon Fundamentalists, and they will be persuaded least by Catholic pronouncements. The fact is that contemporary anti-Semitism is secular. Its immediate impulses are economic and political.

In the words of some Christian theologians, we now live in a post-Christian era. The Ecumenical Council's decree on deicide is a further effort, one of many, by the Church to accommodate itself to the circumstances of the new era.

The Jew has less reason than most to be apprehensive about the post-Christian era. In the pre-Christian era, he enjoyed political sovereignty, interrupted periodically by the misadventures that befall all small nations. He also enjoyed great freedom, individually and as a member of the Jewish collectivity, outside the borders of his state—in Babylonia, Persia, Alexandria, and Rome. Pagan and Jewish cultures were involved in several fateful collisions, but irrational religious persecution of the Jew was rare in pre-Christian times. The present, post-Christian era bears considerable resemblance to that earlier time. Jewish statehood and communication between Jewry and the so-called pagan nations have been restored. The Jew enjoys greatest freedom in those Protestant lands that are most secularized, most firmly rooted in the post-Christian era.

It is in this context, viewing Christian-Jewish relations as a parenthesis in a larger Jewish history, that this profile is presented. It skirts the customary emphases on the Jewish faith and on Jewry's agony. Its concern is the collective Jewish experience which began in the East and has now, in appreciable and impressive measure, reverted to the East.

CONTENTS

GENERAL READINGS

Baron, Salo W. *A Social and Religious History of the Jews.* New York: Columbia University Press, 1937, 1952.

Finkelstein, Louis (ed.). *The Jews: Their History, Culture and Religion.* 2 vols. New York: Harper and Bros., 1949.

Freehof, Solomon B. *The Responsa Literature.* Philadelphia: Jewish Publication Society, 1955.

—— *A Treasury of Jewish Responsa.* Philadelphia: Jewish Publication Society, 1963.

Graetz, Heinrich. *History of the Jews.* 2 vols. Philadelphia: Jewish Publication Society, 1898.

Grayzel, Solomon. *A History of the Contemporary Jews from 1900 to the Present.* New York: Meridian Books, 1960.

—— *A History of the Jews from the Babylonian Exile to the End of World War II.* Philadelphia: Jewish Publication Society, 1947.

Lowenthal, Marvin. *The Jews of Germany.* Philadelphia: Jewish Publication Society, 1936.

Margolis, Max L. and Marx, Alexander. *A History of the Jewish People.* Philadelphia: Jewish Publication Society, 1927.

Reitlinger, Gerald. *The Final Solution.* 2 vols. New York: Beechhurst Press, 1953.

Roth, Cecil. *A Short History of the Jewish People.* London: East and West Library, 1953.

Sachar, Howard M. *The Course of Modern Jewish History Since 1781.* Cleveland: World Publishing Co., 1958.

Schwartz, Leo (ed.). *Great Ages and Ideas of the Jewish People.* New York: Random House, 1956.

Chapter ONE

EUPHRATES AND CANAAN

THE HISTORY OF NO OTHER KNOWN ANCIENT PEOPLE HAS HAD such nonapocalyptic beginnings as that of the Jews. That of other peoples is enshrouded in mythology, and, at later stages, evolves around kings and warriors. No such encumbrances clutter the biblical narrative of the Jews' origin. It is all human history, and its progenitors, the patriarchs, albeit extraordinary men, are of common breed —herdsmen, tillers of the soil, fruit-pickers, and nomads.

Yet the patriarchs are placed from the very outset at the vortex of mankind. The distinct patriarchal Hebrew personality—Abraham, Isaac, and Jacob—evolves from an amorphous interrelated humanity of many tongues and colors.

The word Hebrew, or "Ivri," is probably derived from "Ever," meaning Across. Hebrews had traveled across long distances, in a wide arc, between the Euphrates and the Nile, before they laid claim to Canaan, the Promised Land. The Bible is the only record containing their names, but archeology nonetheless confirms the route and chronology of their wanderings. There had at that time been great mass migrations within the region and in the same direction. The word Hebrew may also be related to "Habiru," which seems to have been the common name for displaced persons whom disaster or the wrath of the warders of the established order had set adrift in the world. The Habiru hired themselves out as seasonal laborers, or were seized as slaves and fled to become mercenaries and highwaymen, or, like the patriarchs, eventually settled down somewhere and established tribal dynasties.

1

The history of the Jews begins around the middle of the twentieth century B.C.E. with Abraham, whose family came north from the vicitiny of Ur, a city at the mouth of the Euphrates River, in Mesopotamia, today's Iraq. He then crossed into Syria, and again south into Canaan, which approximates today's Israel, where he acquired holdings and settled permanently. He had come from the metropolis of an advanced civilization and introduced some of its agricultural methods to Canaan. He had come from a region governed by law. Codes which originated there predate the law of Moses by some six hundred years and Roman law by at least fifteen hundred years. The effect of this culture was evident in Abraham's conduct. He was not a nomad who raided, carried away, or claimed squatter's rights. He negotiated leaseholds in the lands in which he tarried, paid for the right to draw water from their wells, and dealt with princes as their peer. He was evidently a man of known station, related by blood or marriage to important clans along the route.

His reputation for eccentricity may have preceded him. It is unlikely that the patriarchs were monotheists. Monotheism did not yet exist in their day. Nonetheless, Abraham's faith was sufficiently different to set him apart from others. He did not acknowledge the divinity of human rulers. His was a familial God, but it was perhaps the first God not confined to a specific locality. His God moved with Abraham, and Abraham was a wanderer on the face of the earth. He signed a covenant in the blood of circumcision with his deity, and the covenant was incised successively by the males of his clan through the generations.

The covenant forcefully introduced the moral and reduced the mythical element in the relationship between man and God. It was a contract, placing both parties under mutual obligation. "The Hebrews cried unto the Lord" whenever they felt He had breached their contract. The Hebrew synonyms suggest shouts, protest, as well as supplication. Abraham also demonstratively renounced human sacrifice. In obedience to God's command he had placed Isaac, his son, on an altar, but an angel stayed his hand, the Biblical narrative relates, and Abraham sacrificed a

THE WORLD OF THE PATRIARCHS
(c. 2000-1700 B.C.)

Main Patriarchal centers   Haran   Names in parentheses for orientation only

HITTITE EMPIRE

Haran

Ugarit

Tadmor
Damascus
Hazor
Shechem
Tyros
Jerusalem
Beersheba
Mamre
Gerar
EGYPT

(ASIA)

Nineveh
ASSYRIA
Asshur
BABYLONIA
Erech
Babylon
Susa
Ur

ALASHIA
Great Sea

(INDIA)

Early Bronze Age Culture

(EUROPE)

Khattushash
HITTITE EMPIRE
Ilium (Troy)
SICILY
Great Sea
LIBYA
Memphis
Heliopolis
Heracleopolis
EGYPT
Thebes
Elephantine

CUSH

(ARABIA)

(AFRICA)

Late Stone Age Survivors
Bronze Age

ram instead. One thousand years later, the Hebrews' Canaanite neighbors still sacrificed their first born to placate the Gods, and buried human beings alive under the foundations of new homes to ward off evil.

Abraham begot Isaac, and Isaac begot Jacob, and when their eyes dimmed, they assembled their children and blessed them and were foregathered unto their ancestors. The record telescopes time. Each patriarch probably denotes the passage of an era.

The first great crisis in the Hebrews' early history begins with Joseph. It was not at all impossible then for a Hebrew to have risen from slave to chief economic minister at Pharaoh's court, deviser of controls which transformed Egypt into a granary for all her neighbors when seven ample harvests were succeeded by seven years of drought.

JOSEPH IN EGYPT

Egypt was the victor in a protracted struggle with Babylonia for control of the region west of Mesopotamia. The princes of the Canaanite city-states were dutifully delivering their annual tribute to the Pharaohs, but as so often happens in history, the conquered seduced their conquerors. Semites now formed a majority of the population of her northern province, directly on the frontier of the Sinai peninsula. Many had been brought there as slave labor for construction work; many others—merchants, scholars, mercenaries—were attracted to the area by the imperial glamor. Their rituals were absorbed into Egyptian worship; Hebrew and Canaanite vocabulary seeped into the Egyptian language; the country's civil service lists included men with Hebrew names, Semites not necessarily descended from the Biblical patriarchs.

Pharaoh had use for men of wide Asian experience, who spoke the tongues of his newly acquired subjects, understood their psychology, and could negotiate with them. Jacob's favorite son, Joseph, was tailor-made for a career at the court.

The Biblical account describes Joseph's sojourn in Egypt as reluctant. He had been sold into bondage by his brothers. Yet when he daydreamed while his brothers

worked in the fields, it may have been Egypt he was dreaming of. Once there, he evidently found it attractive. To anyone possessed of talent and ambition it offered the refinements of cosmopolitan life and a share in the exercise of power. Joseph adapts himself quickly. He is relaxed with the felons in Pharaoh's dungeons and at ease with princes at Pharaoh's court. He is the archetype of the assimilationist Jew.

This archetypal Jew is presented with a prototypal situation. Both his type and the situation will be repeated throughout Jewish history. He has become worldly and Egyptianized, his brothers are parochial and awkward. They have come to Egypt to purchase grain, for there is a famine at home in Canaan. They are shown in to Joseph, the king's chief economic steward in charge of the granaries. He recognizes them at a glance, these sullen and curt tribesmen, bearing on their garments the dust and sweat of their long journey across the desert. Dare he reveal himself? He no doubt has enemies at court, and association with these Canaanites might compromise his station. This apprehensiveness of older assimilated settlers that the new unassimilated arrivals of their faith or ethnic origin might embarrass and imperil their own position is familiar to all migrating peoples. It has been traumatic with the Jews since the days of Joseph. The ancestral pull prevails. Joseph is overcome. He is concerned with the fate of his father and of his own younger brother, Benjamin, born of the same mother whom he might still be able to save from the tribal stranglehold and bring up in the cosmopolitanism of the Egyptian court. This attitude, too, concern succeeding apprehension, has been the traditional attitude of the assimilated Jew since Joseph's day.

UPHEAVALS IN EGYPT

Several generations passed. The Jews had become well established in Egypt. Their assimilation was evidently more or less complete when another prototypal situation presented itself. Sometime in the eighteenth century B.C.E. the Hyksos, a Semitic tribe, probably allied with the Canaanite city-states, seized the northern region of Egypt and proclaimed it a Semitic empire. In a brilliant campaign in

the sixteenth century, Egyptian forces regained the territory, shattering the Hyksos. A purge of Semites from all office in Egypt followed. The xenophobic mood permitted no distinction between the brethren of Joseph, the House of Jacob, who had contributed to Egypt's economy, and the Hyksos who had tried to destroy her.

Archeologists are of divided opinion as to who precisely, in the long succession of Pharaohs, cast the Jews into slavery and ordered the destruction of their new-born males. Whichever ruler it was, he drew heavily on Semitic slave labor. The House of Jacob had suffered all manner of affliction in its wanderings from the Euphrates to the Nile, but never before had it lost its freedom. This was its first experience with bondage.

There was at this time great restiveness at the heart of Pharaoh's empire, and in its most remote provinces. Groans rose from the vassal states of Canaan, which were ruled by an alien nobility that squeezed the peasants without mercy to sustain its bacchanalian entertainments and to fill the coffers of the splendorous Egyptian court. And worse still were the cries from Goshen whose Hebrew slave population contained descendants from those who had been members of the elite in Joseph's day.

MOSES FOLLOWS THE PATTERN

For the second time in their history, one of their brethren, holding high rank in Pharaoh's court, delivers the Hebrews from disaster. The assimilated Jew returned to his people, the sophisticated penitent, is the kind of leader who would repeatedly reveal himself to the Jews in crises and repeatedly be treated with ambivalence. Joseph delivered them from famine, Moses from bondage. Joseph had to overcome a rankling memory of their meanness toward him. Moses, raised as an Egyptian prince, faced them in complete innocence. He intrudes between a Hebrew slave and his tormentor, and slays the Egyptian. But when on the next day he interposes himself between two Hebrew slaves, he is turned upon in fury and threatened with exposure of yesterday's crime.

Moses fled to the Sinai peninsula, probably not because

he feared exposure. A member of the royal household could slay an inferior with impunity, and no one would accept the testimony against him of a Hebrew slave. He fled perhaps to recover from the shock of his first encounter with the Hebrews' ambivalence.

Sinai was the home of nomads and herdsmen, a sanctuary for fugitive slaves from Canaan and Goshen, for brigands and assassins, for visionaries, and for preachers of illicit doctrines. Moses' Sinai experience spoiled him completely for life at the court. He returned with new teachings that mixed freedom with innocence. These teachings seemed uniquely designed at that stage in history for the Hebrews, the most unique of all bondsmen in Egypt. They had tussled with Babylonian law, Canaanite sensual perversion, and richly embellished Egyptian polytheism, yet doggedly persisted in their own tribal puritanism.

Polytheism at that time, and even later in the Greek era, was local; the writ of the gods, like that of a governor or royal tax collector, was restricted to a single province, town, or even hamlet. The Hebrew could worship none of these. He had no land which could honorably accommodate them, and which they could decently protect. A wanderer, he required a transcendental God. The gods, like man, were captives of esoteric dark forces that could be ordered by magical deeds and words. The Hebrew could not respect a captive god. He could not worship gods no more sovereign than himself. He snorted his disbelief in the godliness of Pharaoh. Nor could he worship the multitude of nature gods. He had been a farmer, but also a herdsman and a nomad. Unlike the peasant, he did not feel dependent on the weather; in his wanderings, he moved against the elements, overwhelmed them, and survived. He could only scorn the gods of fertility who writhed in the agony of excessive sexualism; man in the desert would quickly perish from such lack of restraint; and when Pharaoh ordered the extinction of the Ivrim by drowning their new-born males, the Hebrews multiplied nonetheless and without the intervention of geneologic gods.

THE NEW LAW

The Hebrew needed a god who was with man in all his wanderings—a great, imageless, weightless god who would not slow down a caravan in the desert. Islam, nearly two thousand years later, also ministering to a mobile population of nomads and merchants, similarly never acquired ikons. Christianity, conversely, which unfolded amid the squalor and splendor of Greco-Roman cities, and addressed itself to urban populations, appointed its church with images to contest the allure of heathen temples.

The ancestral God of Abraham, redefined by Moses, had been ubiquitous, hence universal, from the very beginning. He had accompanied the patriarchs across East Asia into Africa, had been with Joseph in the dungeon and at the palace, with the foundling in the bulrushes, and with his mother in congested Goshen. Moses announced him simultaneously to his brethren and to Pharaoh, and surely did not deny his insights to the Sinai peoples with whom he had intermarried. His father-in-law was Jethro, a Midianite priest who advised Moses on judicial administration, and charted the logistics of the Hebrews' long march across the desert to Canaan. Thus, the Hebrews who finally entered the Promised Land were probably the entire Near East in microcosm.

All evidence disproves the contentions of an earlier generation of biblical scholars that Moses' monotheism was adapted from Atenism, the short-lived faith of an Egyptian reform monarch of nearly a century earlier. Atenism conceived of god as a presiding deity, not the only deity. It did not impugn the ruler's claim to divinity. It reinforced that claim. It was the private god of the royal family, like Abraham's familial god; unlike Abraham's god, it imposed no ethical obligations.

Moses' god differed from all others not only in his aloneness, but also in his substantive nature. Abraham's covenant, or contractual agreement, was now reinforced by a legal code. Law and God were henceforth inseparable; to transgress against one was to defy the other. The Decalogue was eclectic. It absorbed the best Law of the

day, but it added audacious insights. It did not emanate
from a ruler, like the Hammurabi Code. It was a sovereign
authority to which even rulers were subject. It embraced
all men, and extended its compassion even to the beast
who, like man himself, was to be granted respite on the
Sabbath. Possessing almost nothing, the Hebrew prized
human dignity as the greatest possession; depending on
his beasts for transportation and labor, he could only
treat them with tender care.

MUTINIES IN SINAI

Moses, leading his people in the desert (probably the last
quarter of the thirteenth century B.C.E.), and probing the
Canaanite frontier for porous defenses, was never quite
secure from Egyptian attack. The entire area was a chain
of vassal states under Pharaonic protection. The Exodus
had been a humiliating experience for the Pharaohs. It
probably paralyzed some of the major construction projects in the north, enlisted Egyptian malcontents of high
station, and set a melancholy example to all compulsory
labor. Furthermore, its law, proclaimed at Sinai, impeached the established order. The notorious Hebraic adventure had widely impugned the empire's prestige. A
late thirteenth century (B.C.E.) Egyptian record tried to restore the image of imperial impregnability by boasting of
a victory over the Hebrews: "Israel . . . laid waste, its seed
. . . naught."

A serious threat to Moses came from the Hebrew priesthood. It involved members of his immediate family, and
was the first assertion in Jewish history of tensions between church and state. Moses ruled the Hebrews through
law. But his brother Aaron, to assuage them, led the
people in worship of a golden calf. Their sister, Miriam,
who danced and sang before the people, sought to confine her brother's universal God to those directly descended from the patriarchs, and admonished Moses for
taking an Ethiopian wife. The Levites, the lesser clergy,
led by Korah, hoped to negotiate a place for themselves in
the ruling elite by accusing Moses and Aaron of exercising authoritarian power. There were, additionally, several
revolts instigated by a pro-Egyptian party, led by affluent

9

members of the Exodus who were dismayed by Moses' egalitarian law. The folk myth has identified the revolt of the lesser clergy with the rich, and has poured three thousand years of shrewd evaluation into a Yiddish idiom: Anyone who is wealthy, gross and selfish is "as rich as Korah."

REPOSSESSING CANAAN

In their wanderings, the Hebrews coalesced into a firm tribal federation. As they advanced into the Promised Land, their bonds weakened. Their first military triumphs were the result of a united effort by the entire people. However, the tribes already in possession of allotments as a result of earlier conquests were unwilling to continue the war for those still without lands. Those situated in the most secure regions were least ready to respond to the cry of the frontiersmen under frequent enemy attack. Geography contributed its mischief too. The Hebrews' territory comprised four regions, each separated from the other by distances that were sometimes long, and almost always hostile.

They were now no longer called Hebrews, but Israelites. The new name was apparently a sign of distinction. They were no longer an undifferentiated clan within the Semitic-Hebrew mass, nor merely a distinguished dynasty, the House of Jacob. They were a people called Israel, and as Israelites, they launched the most successful and peaceful phase of the Hebrew occupation of Canaan. The cistern system for storing rains had just come into use, and taking advantage of this, they fanned out across the sparsely inhabited interior which had been neglected by the Canaanites because of its inadequate water resources. It was soon dotted with hundreds of settlements which enlarged the tribal federation's contiguous frontier, placing it—in the eleventh century B.C.E.—on the main routes of Canaan.

TRIBES' ADJUSTMENT

All Israelite tribes governed their affairs similarly. Major decisions were made through general assembly. A shofet, or judge, the first among equals, arbitrated their differences and led them in war. His rank was not hereditary. His

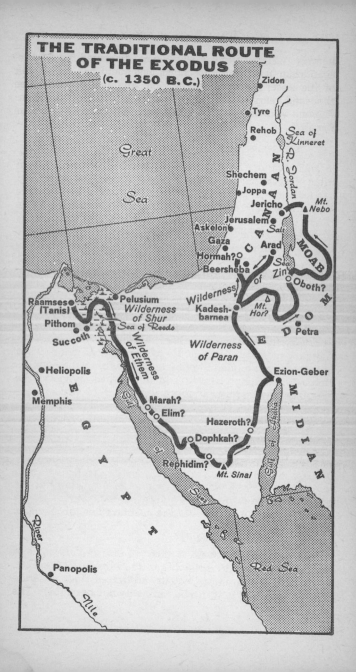

THE TRADITIONAL ROUTE OF THE EXODUS
(c. 1350 B.C.)

authority rested in his reputation for wisdom, equity, and valor. It sometimes extended to several tribes, and occasionally over the entire people. Their law, evolved during forty years in Sinai, was superior to all others, but their societal structure was simplistic compared with that of their neighbors.

This was partly the result of circumstance. The patriarchal system was well suited to herdsmen and farmers, which the Israelites now were. Remote from the seacoast and the primary land routes, the Israelites could engage in no other occupations. They had once probably been an urban people, however: in Mesopotamia, before Abraham started his wanderings, and in Egypt, too, before Pharaoh confined them to Goshen. But Abraham had deliberately left Ur, the metropolis, and chosen the bucolic life. And Moses, sated by the splendor of the Egyptian court, had no doubt a similar preference. The life of the Canaanites, conversely, was city-centered. The needs and perversities of a sliver of foreign nobility were serviced by a pyramid comprised of layers of partly free men—peasants, craftsmen and scribes, and a huge slave population.

The Israelites seemed content in their freedom.

"A KING UNTO US"

But there was the constant threat to their physical security and territorial integrity. There was no truly great power to maintain the peace in the region. The peril came virtually from the four winds. Everywhere there were greedy neighbors and rapacious foes: the Idumeans and the Schechemites; Moab, Ammon, and Midian, and from remote distances enemies who introduced totally new instruments of war.

In clouds of dust, out of the Syrian desert, came furious warriors riding camels—one of the early appearances of the camel as a carrier of burden over long distances. The riders were precursors of the Arab invasions of a later day. After several seasonal excursions, they were so effectively chastened by an Israelite force led by Gideon that they dared not return again for another four centuries.

The Philistines, fierce warriors from chariots, already well entrenched along the Phoenician coast, had probably

come from Crete, and were precursors of the Greeks. One of the reasons for a monarchist movement among the Israelites was Philistine harassment. The Monarchists argued that the tribal federation had relied too long on the fitful appearance of charismatic leaders to lead it in calamitous times. The federation needed stable government and a line of succession. Its multiple enemies and its diversified economy required better than improvised government. The tribes of Dan and Asher had become considerably urbanized and were engaged in shipping and commerce, having acquired these skills from the seafaring Phoenicians who were trading with all the habitable world. The demand for a monarchy became a unanimous cry as Samuel, the most celebrated in the long chain of judges, advanced in age. He sought instead to perpetuate the rank of judge and to establish its succession through his sons. But the people deemed them unworthy issue of a great father, and insisted that he "anoint a king unto us." Samuel did their will reluctantly, but shrewdly. He summoned to the throne a giant peasant from the fields, a man called Saul (1030-1010 B.C.), from the tribe of Benjamin, one of the lesser clans, thus circumventing strife among the larger tribes, each of whom aspired to have the distinction conferred on one of its own.

LOSS OF INNOCENCE

It was then that the Israelites lost their innocence. Samuel had miscalculated by assuming that he could exercise his powers through the king until forced by infirmity to retire. Although Saul, shy and reticent, had accepted the office with misgivings, he could not now, as a conscionable man, yield his authority to the revered old judge. Yet he was deeply depressed by his breach with Samuel. Valorous on the battlefield, but awkward among the elders, and uninformed of the intricacies of intertribal politics, he was now without counsel he could trust. He began to suspect melancholy plots in his own household and with good reason.

Samuel had already secretly anointed a royal successor, David, who was the king's protege and son-in-law and whose music dissipated the king's black moods. He was a

former herdsman from Bethlehem, richly endowed, a psalmist, with a stout heart in combat, and an easy grace with men. This latter quality served him well in achieving and retaining power. The remarkable affection of Saul's son, Jonathan, the heir-presumptive, for David is one of the most tender tales in all literature.

When the mob in the streets shouted David's praises above Saul's as the two returned from battle, the king comprehended suddenly who the claimant to his power might be. David fled for his life, and soon malcontents, probably dissidents from several or all tribes, began to gather around him, thus providing him with a small army. The Israelite federation had not yet achieved a standing national force. Each tribe marched under its own banners.

David's force lived off the land. Occasionally, it would establish its authority over a region, collect tribute from the farmers, and guarantee them security from raiders. But inevitably Saul's superior force would track them down. Finally, David's force obtained a haven in the territory of the Israelites' greatest enemy, the Philistines in return for a pledge to join them in their wars.

David was spared the embarrassment of chosing between his pledge and his people. When arranged for combat in a battle against the Israelites, the Davidic force was ordered back by a distrusting Philistine commander. In the catastrophic battle of Gilboa, the Philistines overran the Israelite territory, massacred its forces, and slew the king and all his sons, but one, the effete and irresolute Ish-Boshet. To sow dissension within his truncated little state, the Philistines named David king of a competitive sovereignty which embraced the southern territory they had seized from Israel.

DAVID AND SOLOMON

David's genius transformed this ignoble role into vindication and triumph. He reduced the nation's dependence on the tribal chieftains by establishing a standing army of mercenaries and a civil service of royal retainers who owed their loyalties directly to the king.

Centralized authority was a boon to security and commerce, but had distressing moral after-effects, because no

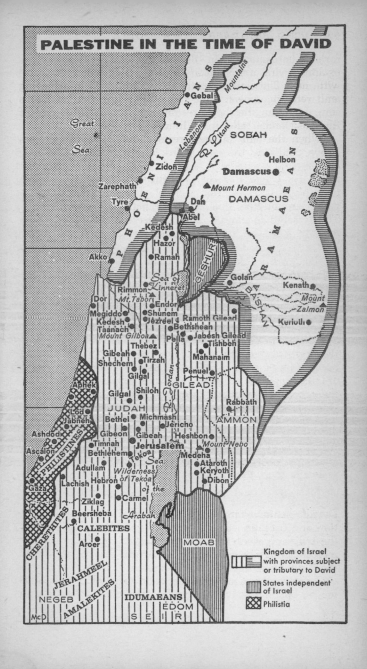

PALESTINE IN THE TIME OF DAVID

Great Sea

PHOENICIANS

Lebanon Mountains

R. Litani

SOBAH

Gebal

Zidon

Helbon

Damascus

DAMASCUS

Zarephath

Tyre

Mount Hermon

Dan

Abel

Kedesh

DAMASCUS

Hazor

ARAMAEANS

Akko

Ramah

Sea of Linneret

GESHUR

Golan

Kenath

Rimmon

BASHAN

Mount Zalmon

Dor

Mt. Tabor

Endor

Kerioth

Megiddo

Shunem

Kedesh

Jezreel

Ramoth Gilead

Taanach

Bethshean

Mount Gilboa

Pella

Jabesh Gilead

Thebez

Tishbeh

Gibeah

Mahanaim

Shechem

Tirzah

Gilgal

Penuel

GILEAD

Gilgal

Shiloh

Aphek

JUDAH

Rabbath

Lod

Bethel

Michmash

AMMON

Jabneh

Gibeon

Jericho

Ashdod

Gibeah

Heshbon

Timnah

Jerusalem

Mount Nebo

Ascalon

Bethlehem

Tekoa

Medeba

PHILISTINES

Adullam

Sea

Ataroth

Gaza

Lachish

Wilderness

Keryoth

Hebron

of Tekoa

Dibon

Ziklag

Carmel

of the

Beersheba

Arabah

CHERETHITES

CALEBITES

MOAB

Aroer

JERAHMEEL

AMALEKITES

NEGEB

IDUMAEANS

EDOM

SEIR

McD

Kingdom of Israel
with provinces subject
or tributary to David

States independent
of Israel

Philistia

spared little comprehension or compassion for the possessed and betrayed peasant-king Saul. It depicts him as pathetic, not tragic. David, his successor, who had been cherished in his people's memory for three thousand years, deserved well of them. He had moulded them into a nation, extended their territory, secured it from attack, and reputedly was the author of the Psalms, an enduring poetry of piety and penance. Solomon's alliances did not survive him. His kingdom split upon his death, and he left moral confusion behind. Yet he is cherished no less than his father; perhaps his very "vices" endeared him. From their very first appearance in history, the Jews often gravitated toward leaders who had returned to them from foreign courts. Joseph was their archetype. Then came Moses; David became their king after a sojourn with the Philistines. Solomon was the foreign potentate without ever having traveled beyond his country. All were men of cosmopolitan cast.

CAUSES OF DECLINE

Solomon's successors garnered that which had been sown before them. Canaan had been equitably divided among the Hebrew tribes and subdivided among their families, but sovereign events that affect history upset the symmetry conceived by man.

War and drought impoverished some of the tribes; other tribes, spared these misfortunes, flourished. And within the tribes, families, who for diverse reasons were unable to sustain themselves on their allotments, leased out their soil to others who had prospered. Thus, tribal society acquired its dispossessed.

Intratribal relations weakened as the tribes welded into a nation to survive the alliances shaping up against them. The dispossessed drifted into the capital, which evolved a sovereignty of its own, and became its urban proletariat. Its population was an admixture of many classes—royal retainers, absentee landlords, shopkeepers, craftsmen, foreign traders, and unskilled labor. None was certain of his fellow, and regardless of his wealth and station, each was a displaced person, evicted from the tribal tradition in which every man was his brother's keeper.

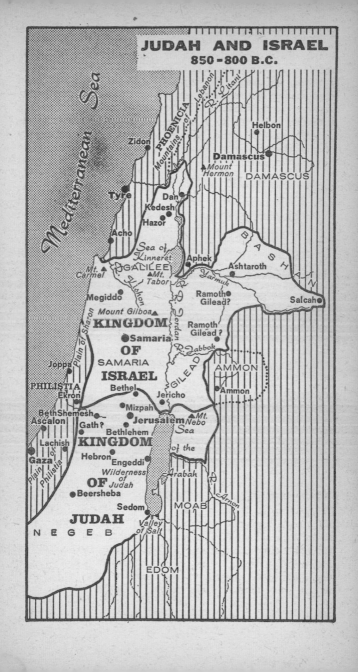

The Israelites, in their long sojourn in foreign lands, had been assimilating foreign cultures without forfeiting their authentic tradition. The Mosaic Decalogue, the Ten Commandments, provides a striking example of the mating of alien wisdom and Israelite culture. In their own land, however, they eventually lost some of their capacity to discriminate between wholesome and pernicious influence. Israel's urban society was beholden to no ancestors. Its affluent members welcomed seduction by outrageous Canaanite cultism and depraved Canaanite justice as a release from lingering tribal claims.

TWO KINGDOMS

When Solomon's heir, Rehoboam (930-914 B.C.E.), assumed his reign, a rebellion split the state into two kingdoms, Judah and Israel. He had refused to rescind his father's impositions, a circumstance exploited by tribal advocates of separatism who had chafed under centralization drives of David and Solomon, and were jealous of Judah's primacy. The loyalists were few, his own tribe and its allies, the small tribes of Benjamin and Simon. His kingdom, parenthesized between Mitzpah, north of Jerusalem, and Beersheba to the south, had few outside contacts. However, this did not affect the policy of permissiveness towards foreign cults. Rehoboam's mother had been an Ammonite princess. His wife, Maachah, a Jewess, who was to assume the regency during an interregnum several years after her husband's death, was a defiant worshiper of Asherah, the goddess of fertility.

However, conditions were infinitely worse in the kingdom of Israel whose monarch Jeroboam installed golden calves in two temples constructed in rivalry against the Jerusalem Temple.

Later renamed Samaria for its new capital, Israel embraced Galilee, central Palestine, and Transjordan, a circumstance which induced mercantile development and urbanization, but also impugned the ancient mores. The kingdom, founded in protest against the central government's tax policies and invasion of tribal autonomy, was perverted, as revolutions frequently are, into its antithesis —ruthless arbitrary rule, contemptuous of the people's

right. Its kings vacillated between heathen fashion and Jewish tradition. The heathen king was divine; the Jewish king was not. The heathen king was an absolute ruler; the Jewish king exercised absolute powers, but only by popular consent. His mandate became void if his performance fell short of the law. This was custom, not prescribed, but so valid that the Biblical account repeatedly presents "contrite" kings "seeking to find favor" with their God and their people. He consulted elders and prophets and sometimes a general people's assembly. When a Jewish king introduced alien images into his realm, it was certain evidence of his contumacious disposition, and of his frivolous disregard for that Jewish law which protected orphans and widows and the stranger in the gate.

LAW AND CHAOS

The first centuries of rule by monarchy (1030-586 B.C.E.) were marked by unusual cultural enterprise. It has been characteristic of Jewish genius ever since to respond most vigorously to crisis.

Among the dispossessed in the desert, the conceit that the Hebrews alone had the design for the perfect society went unrefuted. They were engaged in a monologue. Their confidence crumbled, however, amidst the advanced material society of Canaan. The crisis of faith was already evident in the days of the last of the judges, Samuel. It was accelerated under the kings, especially after the kingdom divided into two. This compelled the Hebrews to assemble their historical records to convince themselves of their worth, to collect their law to prove its enduring validity, and to establish that law as a standard by which the people could conduct themselves, judge their kings, and assay the foreign influences impinging upon them. Most of the law and historical narratives contained in the Bible were first committed to writing at this time.

Now, also, their great prophets began to address themselves to all the nations. The monologue became an interminable dialogue between Jewry and other cultures.

Prophecy was not an entirely new institution in Israel. Moses was called prophet, meaning seer. The first time the rank is used in the Bible in any institutional sense is in

reference to a woman, Deborah, who early in the twelfth century B.C.E. led the Israelites' triumphant defense against the Philistine-Canaanite alliance. The earliest prophets were soothsayers and mentors to their people. They had their counterpart in other nations. At the time of the kings, when the people were thrust into the maelstrom of world events, the function of the prophets changed altogether. They became an institution unique to Jewry alone. The Greek philosophers were perhaps their closest analogue. But the prophets were not philosophers. They were combined statesmen-poets-moralists. They held no office; their authority derived from their moral indignation. They were alternately consulted and hounded by the monarchs, and often rejected by their own people. But they were not martyrs. They were embattled men.

Christians sometimes distinguish between the law and the prophets. This is unjustified. Both institutions evolved simultaneously. The prophets, in fact, were the advocates of the law and its interpreters.

ELISHA, CROSSROADS PROPHET

Elijah, the last and most furious of the old line prophets anointed Elisha as his successor in the mid-ninth century B.C.E. Elisha epitomized the transmutation of the prophet's function. Not for him his master's loincloth, long hair, and association with frenzied ascetics. Not for him the sudden raids on the worshipers of Baal and exploiters of the people. Elijah's disciples may sometimes have wondered why the master had chosen as his successor a man so obviously at ease in the society they despised.

Elisha was a healer, a miracle-maker, a soothsayer in the old tradition, despite his urbane manner, but he was also a master of the coup d'état. His concern embraced not Israel alone, but also her neighbors. We may infer from his deeds, for little was left of his words, that he was the Jews' first universal prophet. But he was, like Elijah, a man of violence. The major prophets, after him, were indignant voices, but men of peace.

Elisha, like his predecessor, was determined to end the royal line of King Ahab (875-853 B.C.E.) who being a

uxorious husband, had permitted his wife, Jezebel, daughter of the King of Tyre, to install Canaanite conduct in Jewish territory. She resorted to perjured testimony, and imported hundreds of heathen priests to initiate Israelite youth into the homosexual and masochistic rituals of Baal and Ashera. In 842 B.C.E., eleven years after Ahab's death, when the queen mother was still pursuing her plots, Elisha engineered a coup d'état. Jezebel's kin and all Ahab's kin to the last were decimated. A similar fate befell Ahab's sister, Athalia, the queen mother, who had seized the reign in Judah (842-836 B.C.E.), where she duplicated Jezebel's performance.

Elisha's name is not mentioned in connection with what transpired in Judea. But he was apparently implicated in events in the Aram kingdom, in what is today Syria. He had predicted the succession to power of the regicide, Hazalel, before the ruling monarch's assassination. He also converted to Judaism the Aramaean viceroy, General Naaman. This was the first time a Jewish prophet was so involved.

ERA OF DOOM

The fortunes of the two kingdoms seesawed, but Samaria was the stronger, sometimes compelling Judah into vassalage. She was also wealthier, with more stone dwellings and prophets than Judah, two certain signs of wealth. The common people still lived in houses of clay and wood. Only the prosperous could afford stone. Yet the prevalence in Samaria of "bands of prophets," entire schools of vociferous critics of the established order, suggests that the Samarian kings dared not suspend altogether freedom of expression. The right to criticize government was inherent in an entrenched ancient tradition that the king must consult his people. Instead of forbidding criticism, the government spawned false prophets, who also cited the law and summoned god as witness, and sought to placate the people and justify the Kings. The effect was frequent public debate between the true and the false prophets, and untrammeled discussion of government policy, such as was unknown anywhere else at that time. Samaria's greater military strength did not prevent her

23

earlier downfall. She was conquered by Assyria in 720 B.C.E., which was 123 years before Judah was conquered by the Chaldeans, or Babylonians. Her greater prosperity, based on exploitation, sapped her morale. Her greater significance in world affairs plunged her irretrievably into international intrigue, which hastened invasion by Assyria, the dominant power at that time. She had been counseled against these traps by the major prophet, Isaiah, who began his prophecy in 755 B.C.E., in both kingdoms. He counseled, above all, against expediency. Samaria must neither join her neighbors in an alliance to check Assyria's advance, nor invite Assyrian protection. Assyria will sweep up the entire region, devour it, and die of imperial indigestion. Samaria must only be patient and endure in her law. Internal corruption has felled more regimes than invasion. The Samarian kings, shrugging off his counsel, alternated between the two expedient courses, and did anything but endure in the law. Perhaps they even suspended the ancient tradition of untrammeled criticism, which would explain why Isaiah addressed them from Judah, and not from Samaria. He was certainly outspoken for a reunion of the two kingdoms, and hopeful of the regenerative powers of Judah. After Samaria collapsed, and her population was dispersed and remembered only as the lost ten tribes, Isaiah counseled her sister state against a similar fate. Then he disappeared. He may have been assassinated. It is simpler to kill a prophet than to silence him.

THE REDISCOVERED LAW

Before her downfall in 586 B.C.E., Judah produced two significant documents of the Jewish genius, the Book of Deuteronomy and the prophecies of Jeremiah. In 622 B.C.E. the eighteenth year of his rule, the reform king Josiah was startled by the discovery of ancient manuscripts in the Temple. These included history, and ritual and civil law, probably a collection of old laws fallen into disuse, and constitutional reforms offered by the prophets and disregarded by previous governments. The manuscripts were unscrambled, and presented in solemn assembly by the king as a covenant between himself and his

people, the official constitution of the land, no less binding upon Josiah than on his subjects—the Book of Deuteronomy, all Hebrew social legislation in essence.

It assured the continued horizontalism of Israelite society. In all the neighboring lands, the law corresponded to the pyramidal structure; the higher the class, the greater its rights. But the most serious charge prophets could cite against a Jewish monarch was that his subjects were not treated alike under the law.

Deuteronomy formulated detailed legislation to perpetuate egalitarianism, in both the legal and economic spheres. It established the seven year cycle, which embodied a statute of limitations. Previously, the poor multitudes were reduced to slavery, because they were unable to discharge their debts. Now all debts were void on the seventh year. All Hebrew slaves were released after six years of servitude, which in fact replaced slavery with contract labor. And upon his release, the law read, the slave must be provided by his master with cattle, grain, and wine so that he might establish his own household. A fugitive slave must not be returned to his master, but permitted to settle wherever he chose "amidst you." "The wages of a laborer must not be withheld past sundown." Gleanings of the harvest must be left in the fields for the lesser clergy, the orphan, the widow, and the resident stranger. Egyptians must be accorded favorable treatment "because you were strangers in their midst." A female war captive must be permitted to mourn her kin, and only then may her captor take her as his wife, or else he must release her, but he may not retain her as his servant or sell her. He who is engaged to be married, or has built a house but has not dedicated it, or has planted a vineyard and not seen its first fruit, must not be drafted into the army, and the newly-wed is exempt from service for a full twelve months "that he might delight his wife."

FALL OF JUDAH

The death of King Josiah in battle with Egypt in 608 B.C.E. brought about a counter-reformation in Judah. The constitution was suspended, the underprivileged were scorned, public worship of heathen cults was resumed.

25

Assyria had now been replaced by the Chaldeans, come out of Babylonia, as the dominant world power.

Jeremiah counseled negotiated peace with Babylonia. The Judean royalist party denounced this as treachery, and indulged in luxurious living and blustering war talk, when the enemy forces were still remote, raising dust in distant lands. But when the enemy's banners lapped at the winds in the hills of Jerusalem, and the clang of his armor muted the speech of its residents, the royalists sued for peace (602 B.C.E.), even before a single battle had been mounted. It was an honorable and equitable peace, such as Jeremiah had previously advised. Judah agreed to pay an annual tribute. Babylonia pledged that she would not invade or otherwise molest her.

But three years later, taking heart from reports that the imperial forces had suffered military reverses, Jerusalem abrogated the treaty over the prophet's protests. In 597 B.C.E. when free of their other campagns, the Chaldeans sent a compact force across Judah's frontiers and lay siege to Jerusalem.

However, plots continued to simmer in the capital. Secret emissaries on hasty missions passed in and out of its gates. They carried messages from Egypt which forever plotted abortive military alliances against the Babylonian empire. Jeremiah, leading the peace party, warned against military alliances with Egypt, a frequent aggressor against Judah, and implied that a benevolent Babylonia trusteeship was perhaps better than reckless domestic tyranny. But the royalists easily aroused the multitudes against Jeremiah by charging that he was an agent for the Chaldeans, that the sugar of his words concealed the poison of treason. He fled the dungeons of the king, and the fury of the mob, but persecution could not stay the doom he predicted: Full and final destruction came in 586 B.C.E. in retribution for another abortive anti-Babylonian revolt by the royalist war party. The Temple itself was razed to the ground. The last remnants of Judah's elite were carried off into captivity. Jewish history reverted again to where it began, on the banks of the Euphrates.

Chapter TWO

DIASPORA
AND
RETURN

NOT ALL JUDEANS WERE DEPORTED. THE PEASANTRY WAS LEFT unmolested to collect the harvest. A Babylonian-appointed Jewish High Commissioner governed Judea's affairs. Jeremiah stayed on to comfort those remaining and refused a royal appointment. One day, Jewish guerrillas suddenly swooped down from the hills, assassinated the High Commissioner, and compelled the prophet to join them in armed retreat to the territory of their ally Egypt. Perhaps they feared that if the prophet were left behind, he might set up a satellite regime that would forever bar the restoration of their class to power, or that if they mounted another war he might rally the people against them.

They found small numbers of Jews in Egypt. These may have been carried off as captives in Egypt's frequent wars with the Jewish kingdoms, or may have been dispatched there in fulfillment of the no less frequent military mutual assistance pacts between the Pharaohs and the Jewish monarchs.

The exiles settled in Elephantine, a fortified city on the Nile near Aswan, populated by foreign legionnaires and their families, men of many nationalities organized into ethnic companies, each bearing its own distinctive banner. The Judeans supplied several such companies, intermarried with their neighbors, and although exalting Yahu, as they came to call their Hebrew God, also prudently placed little gifts at the altars of other deities. The Greeks constituted a majority of the fortress population, so this was the first meeting at close range between the two peoples who eventually were to become ambivalent partners in the

27

evolution of some of the richest occidental history. However, the Elephantine colony was irrelevant at this time. The stage of significant Jewish history was Babylonia, then the center of world culture and power. Unlike the Israelites, dispersed one hundred and twenty-five years earlier, whose identity had become blurred and whose customs had been suffused into those of the Canaanites long before their military debacle, the Judeans carried into exile the Book of Deuteronomy, their constitution, and the other books of Mosaic law. They also carried with them the fierce insularity of their region. This kept them intact, so that they eventually returned to Judah and gave their name to a people that has survived to this day.

The Babylonian deportees gravitated toward its capital city. It has been the pattern of Jewish history since Joseph's departure from Canaan to prefer the risk of residing near the center of world events to the safety of indolent provinces. The Judeans found favor at the court of Evil-Merodach, son and successor to the conqueror Nebuchadnezzar. He ordered at his feasts a special throne for the exiled Judean king, according him greater honor than all other captive monarchs.

There must have been more valid reasons for this than Evil-Merodach's benevolent disposition or the Judeans' inordinate grace. Perhaps it had to do with commerce. The exiles traded with their brethren in Judea, thus perhaps constituting an important intermediary channel for Babylonia's western trade.

Castration, forbidden by a Jewish law as a travesty on nature, sometimes seemed a requirement for high office at oriental courts. The numbers of Judeans in posts of trust at the Babylonian court suggests that there must have been eunuchs among them, but this apparently did not detract from their esteem among Jews, since their influence was essential to the welfare of the Jewish community.

The Jews demonstrated remarkable ingenuity in improvising means of surviving as a people on alien soil. The first need was to evolve symbols of authority to substitute for the government. It is probably at this time that the priesthood made its first bid for total power.

From earliest times, the temporal and religious func-

tionaries were separate. Moses was the lawgiver, Aaron the priest. Samuel anointed a king, not a high priest, to lead the people. Now conditions had changed. The king and his retinue were still evocative of past grandeur, but having worn captives' chains on their ankles, they also recalled humiliation and corrosion; furthermore, the Babylonian authorities might suspect subversion if princes were named to lead the Diaspora. The prophets, albeit admirable men, were too abrasive and erosive. The priests, however, were calm authority. The priesthood, at any rate, had sound arguments on its side. Out of this eventually evolved the church-and-state conflict which intermittently convulsed the second Jewish commonwealth.

There also evolved yet another elite that was to play a decisive role in the conflict. It was the sofer (scribe; plural: sofrim). Immigration always demotes, promotes, and reorders class relationships. The most elite and sheltered classes of the old order generally fare the worst under such circumstances. The sofer was a product of the social mobility induced by the dispersion. He was a scholar of the law, his rank neither hereditary nor conferred, but acquired on individual merit, very often a man from the lower clergy or even humbler strata; like the prophet, he held no office. The sofer was one of many institutions evolved by Babylonian Jewry for immediate purpose, and later served as a check on the ambitious priesthood when Judea was restored.

The Jerusalem Temple was distant and in ruins. The assimilated soldiery of Elephantine substituted a Temple on alien soil and offered sacrifices, which implied that Jerusalem was expendable. Babylonian Jewry improvised, instead of substituting. It founded houses of assembly, archetypes of today's synagogues. The Sabbath, which in Judah had been primarily a day of rest, was accorded new and solemn significance. Its celebration required no priestly intervention. Each man, even the least among Judeans, officiated at his own Sabbath. Thus, Babylonian Jewry accomplished two paradoxical purposes which it later bequeathed to the second Jewish commonwealth. It enhanced the priesthood and broadened its functions, but it also created several institutions, such as the sofer and the

29

Sabbath, which decentralized religious authority and made the people independent of the priesthood.

BABYLONIAN INFLUENCE

The environmental culture had enduring effects on the Judeans. The months of the Hebrew calendar bear names of obvious Babylonian origin; and their designative symbols are adaptations, divested of occult meaning, from the Chaldean astrological zodiac. That some of the Hebrew Psalms are similar in style to Babylonian Temple hymns does not mean that either borrowed from the other, but that they shared a common tradition. The convoluted metaphors and apocalyptic visions of the prophet Ezekiel, risen from among the Babylonian Diaspora, are an abrupt break from the precise imagery of all other Hebrew prophecy. His Weltanschauung also differs from the others in several respects. Jewish prophecy viewed sin as a societal malady, symptomatic of the suspension of God's law. Ezekiel gave the moral-legal relationship between God and man a mythological taint. Sin became personalized. He also insinuated for the first time in Hebrew thought, the motifs of life after death and resurrection, concepts preached by Zoroaster, founder of the Persian religion, who lived at the time of the Judean deportations or perhaps even earlier—in the seventh century B.C.E.

Judaism rejected Zoroaster's essential world view that the universe is divided between the forces of good and those of evil. The Jews could not countenance the proposition that evil was a sovereign power, and that, although good would triumph, man was somehow a satrapy of the two elemental forces struggling for his soul. Jewish culture has always insisted on the sovereignty of man. It regarded sin not as mythological, but as error remediable by man himself, who required no apocalyptic intervention to be restored in God's favor. Jewry's rejection of Dualism was the basis of its dialogue with Persian culture. It was to preoccupy Jewish polemicists increasingly in the following centuries, long after the destruction of the Temple. It has been resumed intermittently ever since. Yet some residual dualism has survived in Jewry side by side with its central tradition, but its focus has been ethical, not

theological. It first asserted itself vigorously in the Greco-Roman period as confirmed by the scrolls discovered in the Dead Sea region, with their concept of the forces of light and the forces of darkness. Christianity's concepts of Satan and the anti-Christ may thus be traced to Jewry's first exilic experience.

ANOTHER ISAIAH

Their dispersion to Babylonia placed the Jews near the seat of imperial power for the second time in their career as a people. The first time was during their sojourn in Egypt, before the Pharaohs enslaved them. The pre-exilic Jewish commonwealths, both united and disunited, were involved with lesser states, although some, like the Phoenicians, had a high culture. Solomon alone restlessly reached out beyond the region to savour the celebrated wisdom of the East. Now Babylonia was its center and, like all imperial capitals, more tolerant than her provinces. The Judean deportees, represented both at the court and in the market place, no doubt met many of the diplomats and traders who passed through her gates. They also became involved with the other political deportees, and their prophets further broadened their mission to other peoples, which Elisha had initiated when he intervened in the affairs of Aram.

None was more suited for this larger function than Isaiah, the second major prophet by that name. The first had lived in Judah some two hundred years before. He had witnessed the downfall of Samaria, and predicted the disintegration of Assyrian power when it was still in its ascendancy. The second Isaiah prophesied in exile when it was evident, to the politically perspicacious, that Persia would dislodge Babylonia.

In the penultimate period of her decline, Persia had probably reversed her laissez-faire policy toward the Judean deportees. Her high-handed manner of recruiting revenue, labor battalions, and soldiery for her defenses raised even the Chaldean priests against her. Indirect corroboration is provided by the commemorative columns erected for the Persian conqueror, Cyrus. He wished to be remembered as a liberator of subjugated states and op-

pressed nations. Surely this suggests that deprivation of freedom was the main issue of that day, and that the Persians, capitalizing on it, coined relief from tyranny as the slogan of their forces advancing on Babylonia.

CONSPIRACY FOR FREEDOM

Isaiah jubilantly anticipated Cyrus' triumphs. He may even have been the pivot of pro-Persian agitation. His prophecies are contained in the Book of Isaiah, chapters forty to sixty, inclusive. His style is a reversion from Ezekiel's hieratic incantations to the limpid brevity of classical Hebrew prophecy. He is a statesman, not a priest, a moralist, not a mystic. Yet one of his lean, virile addresses, chapter fifty-three, has peculiarly been seized upon by Christianity as foreseeing the coming of Christ. Christianity contends that his "man of sorrows" is Jesus. The Jews maintain that it is only a metaphor for their collective fate, that he was not inferring Christ's passion, but citing recorded Jewish history. Their suffering has not been predesigned martyrdom, like Christ's, and they are not mankind's Messianic absolvent. It has been a chastening experience, brought on by their human errors, and has endowed them with superior insights so they might lead all nations in the passion for justice, equity, and peace.

Isaiah differs in one respect from his predecessors in Hebrew prophecy. He accords to a heathen a complementary role in the redemptive process. Cyrus, even like the Jews, is an instrument of redemption; the Judeans will be restored through Cyrus and mankind through the Judeans, both discharging God's will and design.

Isaiah's agitation must have been of considerable importance to the approaching Persian forces. The Judeans were numerous in Babylonia. They still had a toehold in the Mediterranean hill country through their residual community in Judah, and there was Jewish soldiery in Elephantine, Egypt. The Hebrew prophet evidently also had an audience among the heathens. He frequently addressed them, preaching that God's law was universal law. There were, at the time, converts to Judaism in Babylonia, perhaps his disciples. It was perhaps as a reward for the prophet's pro-Persian agitation that in 538 B.C.E., within

a year after his triumph, Cyrus published a proclamation which permitted the exiles to return to Judah and restore their Temple.

The exiles were delighted with Cyrus' pledge, but did not hasten to emigrate. Their commerce in Babylonia flourished, their harvests were bounteous, and the emperor's proclamation obliquely confirmed to all the world their favored status at the court. Judah was desolate, remote from centers of civilization. Yet as listed in the Book of Ezra, those who returned included the most illustrious families in Jewry. Some hoped no doubt to retrieve in Judah the reverence due them which had been diminished by the exilic social mobility, and some were pretenders to the office of High Priest whose restoration was inferred in Cyrus' pledge, and to the crown of which there was not the remotest intimation.

But there were others who for three generations had borne Persian and Chaldean names. The assimilated aristocracy, they now laid down their robes of office as royal councilors and provincial governors. With people unlike them in custom and speech, yet whom they called brethren, they went forth into the wilderness that had been their ancestral land to found a more perfect society based on their ancient law. Perhaps, being closer than most to the sources of power, they had misgivings regarding the permanence of Babylonian Jewry's security.

The conditions they faced were analogous, in many respects, to what the Zionist pioneers of our own day found in Palestine. Judah, as it appeared on the Persian maps, was a precarious strip of land, twenty-five miles long, twenty miles wide, with a maximum population of twenty thousand, most of it crowded into the city of Jerusalem. It was not even a province, just a mere county attached to a larger administrative unit, then called "Across the River," today's Syria. They had anticipated the depressing material conditions and the outlawry, this being a backwaters region. They were stunned, however, by the political suspicions and intrigues that entrapped them.

Their sudden arrival with royal prescript gave rise to nervousness among all the inhabitants of the former Judean and Israelite territories. The innocent bystanders, the

common men of many nations, who were either deported here by Assyria, or had entered of their own volition during Babylonian rule, having heard that these lands were in public domain, now naturally feared dislodgement by the returning Jews. Their apprehensions were deliberately exacerbated by the neighboring states. Taking advantage of the change-overs in imperial power over the past two centuries, these neighbors had carved out and annexed generous and luscious sections of Hebrew territory. They now expected their acquisitions to be challenged.

The suspicions, rumors, and agitation thrived on the enthusiasm which the Return aroused among the residual Jewish congregations in Palestine, more numerous than the Babylonian Diaspora had estimated. North, in Galilee, and south in the Negev, on the country's central plain, and eastward in Transjordan were towns either wholly or substantially populated by the am haaretz, the Jewish agricultural proletariat whom the conquerors had spared. They had never ceased to regard themselves as the chosen of Jahweh, the Jewish God, and as obedient to his law, which they remembered only vaguely but fondly as poor man's law. They overwhelmed the Jewish nobility returned from Babylonia with gifts, affection, and petitions, which in turn probably suggested to all non-Jews incipient political conspiracy.

SAMARITAN FEUD

Most bitterly opposed to the Jews were those who had become most assimilated to them, the princes of the neighboring states who during the Judeans' exile had succeeded to their custom, even claiming Jahweh as their God. The enmity was reciprocal. Babylonian Jewry had perhaps been the first people on earth to offer its God as a gift to the world and not cherish it as a parochial possession. Ezekiel, and Isaiah after him, enlisted many proselytes. But these Palestinian half-converts were another matter, mixing Judaic custom with heathen ritual. The most tenacious of the Judeans' enemies were the Samaritans. The scriptures cryptically narrate that first they welcomed the Return, but became angry beyond reconciliation when their offer to jointly rebuild the Temple was rebuffed.

We can only guess at the deeper causes. The Samaritans had formally adopted both the Jewish God and the Jewish law books. But they were of mixed strain, descended from Israelites who had been frivolous with the law long before the Assyrian conquest, had frequently warred on Judah, and had intermarried with the heathen soldiery posted in Samaria after its downfall. Their astute and devious princes had long had designs on Jerusalem, which they now probably supplemented with designs on the generous gifts to Judea from Diaspora Jewry. Whatever the root of the feud, the Samaritans managed to prevent restoration of the Temple for eighteen years by obtaining restraining orders from Persian officials who probably gave as their reason the need to mediate the conflict. The Judean leaders, whose status derived from royal law, Cyrus' proclamation, could not conceive of violating the royal injunctions and obediently postponed construction.

But the delays turned younger men from Persian loyalists into Persia's enemies. And in 522 B.C.E., when a usurper tried to seize the Persian crown from emperor Darius, who had then been only two years on the throne, a prophet, Haggai, appeared in the market places of Jerusalem, stirring the crowds with his predictions of Persia's imminent collapse, and calling on the Judean leadership to begin work promptly on the Temple. Zerubbabel, scion of the Davidic royal line, and Joshua, heir to the office of high priest, reluctantly acceded to the popular pressure.

SATELLITE THEOCRACY

When Darius, having suppressed the rebellions elsewhere, turned to Jerusalem and found the Temple half-finished without his permission, he politically disarmed the rebels by contributing towards its completion, citing Cyrus' proclamation to justify the Jews' conduct. The Temple was dedicated in 515 B.C.E. However, Cyrus had pledged the Jews a Temple, not the crown, and Darius evidently made sure there was no head in Judah to fit it. He probably took advantage of an intramural Jewish feud. In Babylonia, the priesthood obtained supremacy. But among the returned to Judah a movement evidently started to re-establish the

old separation between secular and ecclesiastic authority. It must have had Haggai's support. He inferred that Zerubbabel was "God-anointed," i.e., the process by which the Jews installed monarchs into office.

Darius resolved the conflict by naming the high priest, Joshua, supreme authority over the Judeans, subordinate only to the Persian provincial governor. There is no further reference to Zerubbabel in Scriptures. Other ancient literature, the so-called Apocrypha, mentions that he had returned to Babylonia. Perhaps he had been deported by Darius, or exiled by Joshua. Thus, the Persians, not the Jews, laid the foundations for a Jewish theocracy ruled exclusively by priests.

The effects of Darius' decision may still be detected in some contemporary Jewish disputes. An extreme orthodox minority in Israel has been seeking to transform that state into a theocracy, based on rabbinical law, of course, not on priesthood. An extreme reform minority abroad, opposed to Jewish statehood altogether, had been pressing the view that the Jews are a religious denomination, and not a people at all. Both unwittingly echo an ancient Persian view.

DIASPORA INTERVENES

The fusion of secular and ecclesiastic powers was disastrous for the Judeans. It deprived their government of the check and balance system conceived and established by Moses. The prophets faded out. The institution of sofer, or scribe, of Babylonian origin, had not yet been transplanted to Judah. The High Priests esteemed men for the extravagance of their sacrifices at the Temple, even if they disregarded all Deuteronomic social law. Debtors in default were seized as slaves. The law that Hebrew slaves must be released in the seventh year was universally flaunted. The Judean elite intermarried with Samaritan and Ammonite princes, forming a transnational aristocracy of slaveholders, moneylenders and debauchees.

Gravitating traditionally toward the new center of power, the Diaspora now extended into Susa, the Persian capital. The Judean scandals must have reached the communities abroad whose gifts sustained the Temple. They

probably expected Judah, as American Jews today expect Israel, to make up in piety for the Diaspora's impiety. Two forceful exilic personalities appeared in Judah and took charge of its affairs (458-420 B.C.E.); Ezra, a scribe from Babylonia, and Nehemiah, from Persia, cupbearer to King Artaxerxes I.

Ezra was evidently an emissary from Babylonian Jewry. He brought priests with him, presumably to replace the corrupt clergy at the Temple. Nehemiah was Persia's new High Commissioner of Judah, through whom the High Priest was accountable to the Crown. The scriptural narratives relate that he had petitioned the king, who had high regard for his counsel, to appoint him to the Judean post because he was deeply distressed by reports of the low condition of the country. It is not unlikely, however, that in the pattern of a Joseph at foreign courts, Nehemiah's concern for his brethren did not precede but followed his royal appointment. The Scriptural account relates that at first he moved incognito through Jerusalem. He had perhaps been requested by the king to submit a confidential report on the rumored alliance of the Judean and Samaritan notables, and that their debauchery had reached the state of popular rebellion against the Crown. Or perhaps the emperor felt that the appointment of a Jew as supreme Persian official in Jerusalem would make the Jews proud and assure him the loyalty of the Jewish communities throughout the sensitive Mediterranean area.

Nehemiah's first action was to rebuild the fortified walls around Jerusalem and restore her gates, which delighted all Judeans. The fortifications, a privilege not ordinarily accorded a subject nation, secured their capital from marauders. It was also an action shrewdly disruptive of the alliance between Judean notables and Samaritan princes who now saw their design to eventually annex the city destroyed. The Samaritans instigated other princes of the area to join them in a petition to the emperor, which was absurd because Nehemiah was his trusted agent. Their assaults to prevent construction work only afforded this shrewd statesman a pretext to establish a Jewish defense force.

All Judeans, rich and poor alike, were pleased with

Nehemiah's reduction of the "governor's bread," a tax in grain and coin which was paid throughout the empire to sustain the provincial Persian governors or commissioners and their retinues. The wealthy were less pleased, however, with some of his other measures. He held open court periodically to hear complaints from the common man, and judged in accordance with Jewish custom. In the year of shemita, or remission, the cyclical seventh year, he publicly announced that, in accordance with Deuteronomic command, all his personal debtors were hereby released from their obligations. Many of the rich reluctantly emulated his example.

THE CONSTITUTION

Example was embarrassing. Official law was agony.

Ezra the Scribe obtained a royal prescript proclaiming the Torah as the law of the land; offenses against it were equivalent to offenses against the king. The people were convened in solemn assembly. After the law was read and interpreted to them, all the people took an oath to obey its commands. It was a dramatic re-enactment of their posture at Sinai. Ezra also carried with him authority from the emperor to appoint judges even beyond Judah's frontiers, "Across the River," in Syria, to judge Judeans in accordance with this law, and appoint officials to enforce it.

Ezra has sometimes been depicted as a Jewish Savonarola, particularly because of his edict ordering all Jews to turn out their heathen wives and their offspring. Intermarriage had previously been a common occurrence among Jews. The Bible lists intermarriages from earliest history, as though demonstrating that the Jews are all humanity in microcosm. Moses, the lawgiver, had taken Midianite and Ethiopian wives. Jewish monarchs married the daughters of royal kings.

Ezra was not one to break rudely with tradition, nor was he hostile to aliens. Indeed, he reaffirmed all the liberal Biblical law for the "stranger in thy gate," unmatched in most countries to this day. His edict, then, must have been a corrective for a circumstance peculiar to his day. It implies the high regard for women in public

affairs characteristic of Biblical and post-Biblical Hebrew literature. Miriam joined her brothers, Moses and Aaron, in leading the people. Deborah inspired them in war. Heathen women, too, were important influences in Jewry, both for good and evil. Jael brought relief to the Jews by slaying the heathen commander, Sisera; Delilah brought them defeat by shearing Samson's locks; and Jezebel's exercise of the royal prerogatives was catastrophic.

Ezra apparently feared another Jezebel denouement. He was aware of tremendous, although unuttered, opposition to the constitution among the wealthy classes who resented its egalitarianism. The heathen wives would feed this dissidence and encourage restoration of the Judean alliances with the Samaritan and Ammonite princes, their brothers and fathers.

It is customarily assumed that true theocratic and priestly statehood was installed by Ezra and Nehemiah. It is more likely that they only worked within the conventional terms of reference existent since Joshua, the High Priest invested by Darius. The Persians defined the Jews as a religious community. Ezra capitalized on it. A religious community should be ruled by religious law. Hence, the Bible is a valid constitution which mixes, fortunately, ritualistic and social law, restrains the rich, forbids the capture and return of fugitive slaves, and enforces the Sabbath as a rest day from labor for all, including slave and beast. But the Persians, wary of political leadership since the days of Zerubbabel, insisted that the Judeans be led by a priest. Ezra accepted and circumvented this premise. His law proclaimed the High Priest as the supreme authority, but he was selected by Ezra, and surrounded by representative institutions. The council of elders, a kind of senate, duplicated on the local level in most cities, had been composed exclusively of the clergy and the wealthy. It now also invited representatives from the lesser strata. Ezra and Nehemiah were apparently the founders of an additional agency, the great Assembly, a House of Representatives. But of greatest importance hereafter were the scribes, the interpreters of the law which the Jewish priesthood, copying the Pagans, had begun to regard as its own oracular possession. The scribes

returned the law to the people. Their power was grimly adumbrated in the tumultuous multitudes that surged through the streets of Jerusalem. They taught it in the market places and in the houses of worship and study which complemented the Temple. They interpreted it following patterns set by Ezra, who was the chief codifier and editor of the Bible, although the effort had begun before him, and was completed considerably later. Jewish law would soon confront Greek philosophy, and Christianity would be its by-product. Ezra's contribution to the evolution of western civilization was monumental. Had he not preserved Judah as a society governed by Jewish law, Greek culture would have poured into a vacuum. What that vacuum would have produced is beyond conjecture at this late stage in history.

READINGS: CHAPTERS ONE AND TWO

Albright, William Foxwell. *The Biblical Period from Abraham to Ezra.* New York: Harper and Row, 1963.

Heschel, Abraham Joshua. *The Prophets.* New York: Harper and Row, 1962.

Kaufman, Ezekiel. *The Biblical Account of the Conquest of Palestine.* Jerusalem: Magnes Press, 1953.

—— *The Religion of Israel from Its Beginnings to the Babylonian Exile.* Chicago: University of Chicago Press, 1960.

Orlinski, Harry M. *Ancient Israel.* Ithaca: Cornell University Press, 1954.

Chapter THREE

AMBIVALENT
ENCOUNTER

THE JUDEANS AND THE GREEKS WERE FROM THE VERY BE-ginning uncontrollably attracted to each other. The Greeks, alarmed by the disheveled mores of their own society, envied the serenity and symmetry of the Judean moral order. The Judeans, obsessed with law, moral motivation, and social responsibility, were entranced by the easy stride and wide arc of Greek culture, its philosophy, science, and unmatched talent for transcribing the dictates of the senses into voluptuous design. Both were universal people in a sense unrelated to territorial expansion. Both sought to impress their culture on all they met. Neither could dismiss the other from its thoughts. The Greeks passed on their fascination with the Jews to the Romans, and rabbinical literature, a millennium and one-half after the disappearance of Greece as a power, still pursued its polemics with "Greek wisdom." The term embraced secular culture generally, because to Jews Greece was its progenitor.

The first Greek-Hebrew encounter occurred very early in history, when the Philistines hurled their mighty chariots against the undersupplied Hebrew tribal forces. But those early Cretans were subsumed by Canaanite culture, as if they had never existed. There were several other encounters, brief and fitful. The Judean soldiery which retired to Egypt after one last abortive mutiny against the Chaldeans was domiciled with Greeks. In the fifth century B.C.E., Hebrew prophets told of the iniquitous "sons of Ion" who shared the flourishing slave trade with the Phoenicians, and had shipped Judean captives like chattel to the bazaars of Asian and African cities. Greek

41

traders and Judean exiles were then perhaps the most peripatetic peoples in the world. Hence, there were also encounters, no doubt, at the Babylonian court where Jews stood high.

Some Greeks were in the habit of claiming antecedents of their philosophers' insights in the wisdom of India, Babylonia, and the Hebrews. Clearchus claimed that Aristotle had obtained from a Jew proof of the soul's immortality. Hermippus erroneously claimed that Pythagoras' theory of metempsychosis had been acquired from the Hebrews.

The Greeks likened Judea to ancient Sparta, which was founded on courage, endurance, and discipline. Judea no doubt possessed some of these qualities, but had quite another order of virtues. The Greeks thought that she was governed by priests, and Theophratus called the Jews "a philosophical race." All these surmises were intelligent, yet inaccurate guesses. The Jews had never been at ease with their monarchs and High Priests; their primary concern was law not philosophy, society not government. This distinction is important.

The Greeks confounded government and society, believing that the former spawned the latter, and both could be initiated from a concept blueprinted by philosophers. They experimented with different forms of government, beginning with the absolute monarch whose title was hereditary, who claimed divine descent, and combined in his person the functions and powers of priest, warrior, political leader, and judge. Next came the tyrants, and then the oligarchies which were succeeded by the democracies which excluded entire classes from suffrage. The Greek territories were politically in a state of constant construction like our modern cities, a new type of government always replacing its predecessor, and the pattern varying from region to region.

The Jews had even then spent much of their history under foreign rule, and most of it in foreign lands. They had survived without formal government. Hence, they were convinced that the key to sovereignty was not government, but society; the former required territory, but the latter, ruled by law, could function even in transit.

Even if you dismantled a state and exiled its people, you could not suspend the law they carried in their hearts, habits, and customs. Judean law was not conceived by philosophers. It was given in public assembly to all the people. Both the Greeks and the Jews had an organic law and an oral law. In Greek society, the latter often abrogated the former. Thus, law itself was as unpredictable as fashion—in mode today, out of mode tomorrow. To the Jews written or revealed law was their permanent constitution, by which all oral or custom law had to abide.

THE PSEUDO-HELLENES

The true historical relationship between Jewry and the Greeks began only after Alexander the Macedonian had added Judea to his list of conquests. Jerusalem welcomed him warmly, according to Talmudic legend. He is immortalized in Jewish folklore as, next to Solomon, the wisest and most handsome of monarchs. It is almost as if Judea courted subjugation to Alexander.

This attitude is not odd at all, however, considering the nature of Alexander's rule and Judea's checkered, earlier experience. Isaiah and Jeremiah had advised long before, in respect to the Assyrians and Chaldeans, that it was safer to be a docile satellite of a powerful empire than to enter into anti-imperialist alliances with pugnacious, treacherous neighbors. Had the Judeans then acted on that advice, they might have been spared dispersion. Chastened by their exilic experience, they now were determined never again to repeat their error. Furthermore, the presence of a vigilant imperial power in the region was salutary. It kept the peace, and since it embraced both Judea and the Diaspora communities, it sustained Jerusalem's status as the spiritual center of Judeans wherever they might be.

The Judeans had been loyal to their Persian rulers. But there came a time of disenchantment, and the last of the Persian monarchs, unnerved to the point of madness because he was presiding over his empire's liquidation, compelled a break between Judea and Persia. He rescinded some of the privileges granted them by his predecessors. He penalized the protesting inhabitants of Jericho by banishing them to the most remote exile, on the Caspian

coast. This was one reason why Judea welcomed Alexander, who restored the ancient Persian policy of religious freedom. He sacrificed to the national gods of the countries he overwhelmed. He also brought traders, merchandise, and coin, and a retinue of wise men, artists, and craftsmen —another reason why Judea embraced him. For nearly a century, Judea had been a civilizational backwater, the remote province of a declining, obsolete empire. Judean culture needed greater scope for its growth. Greece was the shock it required. For its affluent classes, Alexander's entry linked Jerusalem once again to the cosmopolitan manner; for its intellectuals, it meant an exciting contest between Jewish law and Alexander's widely reputed alien wisdom. The Judeans anticipated a stimulating encounter, not a drag-out conflict.

It is likely that the hostile tensions which developed later between Greek and Hebrew had their beginnings not in Judea, but in the Diaspora. And not with the real Hellenes, but with the hybrid pseudo-Hellenes of the Levant. These were offspring of Greeks who had been migrating eastward since the Persian conquests and of peoples who had been moving westward from regions east of the Euphrates. Their culture was the admixed sediment of Greek and Oriental mores, beliefs, and superstitions. They were settled in Palestine, Syria, and Egypt, and had intermarried. The Diaspora Jew in their midst repelled them. He was subject directly to the emperor, not to the local authorities. He abstained from public worship to the local deities, claimed a superior faith, and did not intermarry. He was also enviably adaptable to new circumstances, able successively to be meticulously loyal to the Pharaohs, impeccably devoted to the Persians, and irreproachfully faithful to the Greeks. This no doubt was a talent acquired from his several dispersions. Although he was engaged in a wide range of occupations, those of his kind that were traders could hold their own against the sophisticated Egyptian and Syrian Greeks, their neighbors. Their Diaspora contacts in many lands no doubt provided them with intelligence useful to merchants on trends and events in the empire.

The power struggle among Alexander's adjutants after

his death delayed the skirmishes between Judea and the imperial powers—in fact, a conflict between the only two supranational cultures of that day, Greek and Hebrew. Judea was for a full century in the nervous grip of the Ptolemies who ruled from Alexandria, the Greco-Egyptian capital. The Seleucids, ruling from Antioch, the Greco-Syrian capital, also kept a greedy eye on her. Both contestants occasionally clashed on Judean soil, which was the crossroads between them.

Of the two contestants, the Judeans favored the Ptolemies who ruled them and the important Alexandrian Diaspora. It was in Alexandria that the Greek translation, the first in any language, of the Pentateuch, the five books of Moses, was produced in the third and second centuries B.C.E. Legend has it that Ptolemy the Second, or Philadelphus, had requested it. He was a lover of books and, like Alexander, an eclectic who sought to absorb and adapt the cultures of the diverse peoples of his empire.

More likely, the incentive for the translation came from Alexandrian Jewry itself. The community was an admixture of old settlers, involuntary exiles, and subsequent voluntary expatriates. The number of the latter was large after Alexander incorporated Judea into the empire's chain of satellites. The Jews behaved differently from other conquered peoples. The Egyptian priests, for example, withheld their sacred texts, concerned with the occult, even from their own people, and offered no more than summaries in Greek. The Pentateuch was public domain, restored to the people by Josiah, the reform king, and subsequently by Ezra and Nehemiah. There was no inhibition against giving this law wider circulation through translation. Alexandrian Jewry may have had several good reasons, besides a desire to please the king, for publishing the Septuagint. The first was to remove the "mystery" concerning the Jewish faith Alexandrian Jewry was as obsessed as contemporary American Jewry with interfaith relations, with sponsoring a favorable image of the Jew in Gentile society. Secondly, it hoped by means of the Septuagint to sustain Judaism among a younger generation of Jews, "Greek to the soul," who knew no Hebrew and contemned Aramaic, the Babylonian exiles'

"Yiddish" that had been a previous generation's mercantile tongue. A third reason was a desire to missionize the Jewish faith in the Hellenistic world at a time when its intellectuals were seeking improved law, pondering the fate of the slave, and groping toward monotheism.

However, in trying to make the Pentateuch comprehensible to the Gentile reader, the translators here and there substituted Greek for Hebrew concepts. The effect was ambiguities which later served the purpose of the Church Fathers who were culling the Bible for proof that the supercession of Judaism by Christianity had been preordained. In their search, they also turned to another Alexandrian Jewish literary source, the works of the philosopher Philo (20 B.C.E.-50). He was a Pharisee, but also an Alexandrian, a citizen of the Hellenistic world. He labored to interpret Pharisee Judaism, and stumbled over Greek concepts. He introduced into Hellenistic Jewish thought the element of intermediary factors between the supreme divinity and man. When Christianity broke upon the world, its trinitarian concepts were uncomfortably reminiscent of Philo's logos.

DIFFERENT KINDS OF JEWS

In no respect were the Judean and Alexandrian Jews more dissimilar than in their attitudes toward Greek culture. The latter comported themselves like embarrassed guests, either too diffident or too forward, although they had probably lived in Egypt uninterruptedly for two hundred and fifty years before Alexander's conquest. The Judeans, conversely, were hosts, sometimes relaxed, sometimes sullen about Greek intrusion. At the beginning, both groups were indiscriminately hospitable to the new cosmopolitanism. It pleased their eyes, suffused their senses, altogether overwhelmed them. Along the coast and in the interior of the former Hebrew territories, almost within the sound of the Levites' chant in The Temple, Greek cities were springing up with their compact squares and columned architecture, and wondrous rhetorical speech was forever ringing through their streets. A Judean traveler stopping for shade at mid-day near the forum would carry home a striking phrase or a snatch of a closely

reasoned argument, no less haunting than a melody. Wealthy Judeans sought respite from Jerusalem puritanism by spending a night or weekend in Hellenistic pleasure houses across the border. But this involved more than a deviation from Judean sex mores. The Hedonist life was expensive, restricted to a small upper-class segment which was reordering Jewish society from a horizontal to a pyramidal structure, and for this reason waiving Jewish social law. Thus, what has sometimes been presented as a movement toward religious reform and cosmopolitanism was really a trend toward socioeconomic parochialism, government by the few at the expense of the many.

CONSPIRING HIGH PRIESTS

Grecized Judeans cited the High Priests' Hellenic affectations as sanctioning their own conduct. Since Persian days, the High Priests had been recognized by foreign rulers as the supreme authority over Judean affairs. Constancy had never been among the Priests' virtues. Even Aaron yielded and constructed a golden calf when the multitudes cried for an idol. Nehemiah was summoned back from Babylonia because the High Priest violated the Hebrew constitution from which his own powers derived. The ancient records cannot spare a single charitable word for all the High Priests who officiated in Judea under Greek rule, except Simon who held office in the first quarter of the third century, and was called The Just because "he cared for his people." Married into wealth, they conspired with it and defended its prerogatives. Sharing in the excises, they became ruthless tax commissioners for the foreign kings. They even meddled needlessly, with frightful results, in international affairs.

The Seleucids of Antioch, in their contest for Judea, courted the High Priests. The Jews had no reason for discontent with the Ptolemies, who granted them home rule and treated benevolently the Alexandrian community, which was responsible for a substantial portion of the gifts to the Temple. But the High Priests, or rivals for the post, evidently had other considerations. From time to time, they became involved in plots with the Seleucids who coveted Judea. In the decisive war for Jerusalem in 200

B.C.E., which ended a century of Ptolemaic rule over the city, they backed the victorious Antiochus III, who rewarded them by covering from the royal treasury the costs of repairing the war-damaged Temple and city walls, exempting the priesthood from all tax levies, and declaring Hebrew law the law of the land, as interpreted and applied by the priests. Antiochus III probably did no more than reaffirm a de facto situation which had prevailed in Judea since Persian days. It was now accorded the Greco-Syrian imprimatur. Thus, for the second time since the days of Ezra and Nehemiah, sacerdotal government was installed in Judea not by Jewish decision, but by imperial imposition.

Ezra and Nehemiah capitalized on their franchise to establish a priestly government in which the people nonetheless prevailed, and the Torah, the five books of Moses, was the official constitution. The High Priests under Greco-Syrian rule managed things differently. They preferred to be the law themselves, and abetted by a "council of elders" drawn from their own class, the wealthy Hellenized elite, they moved to alter Jerusalem into an Antioch. They moved gradually, cautiously.

Their audacity only came into full bloom under Antiochus IV, or Epiphanes, "the Mad Man," who "had the Greek disposition for debauchery and the Roman disposition for war." Both were expensive dispositions. The Temple's supreme post became lucrative for him. The High Priest Jason (175-72 B.C.E.) dislodged his brother Onias by pledging to raise Judea's already unbearable annual tribute to Syria. Menelaus (172-163 B.C.E.), who was not even remotely in the line of succession, replaced him by delivering to Antiochus IV the public and private funds on deposit in the Temple, pledging to construct sports stadia in the capital. The first was an economic blow, the second struck at the people's faith. All sports contests involved ritualistic devotions to the pagan gods. The priests under Menelaus abbreviated the sacred service and rushed off to the stadia to enter the athletic competitions. Contestants appeared in the nude. The priests may have been among those Jews who submitted to surgery to remove the mark of circumcision.

Twice when the Syrian forces were campaigning in Egypt, the people rose against Menelaus. Each time he appealed to Antiochus, who rushed reinforcements which quelled the rebellion.

The first appeal reached Antiochus in 169 B.C.E. when he was inebriated with triumph. His armies, which had just ground the Ptolemaic forces to dust, entered Jerusalem and plundered the Temple.

The second summons reached him in 168 B.C.E., at the hour of his greatest debacle. When he had been about to tighten the noose around Egypt, the newly emergent arbiter, Rome, compelled him to retreat and made him her vassal, even as Judah was his. Imperial structures in that day were pyramidal. He continued to rule his satellites, but henceforth had to share his excises with Rome. This put him in a bitter mood. He granted his soldiers several days to betake themselves as they wished with lives and property in Jerusalem. He also built a citadel on one of the hills overlooking Jerusalem. The Hellenized Jewish elite moved into the compound for greater security.

In 167 B.C.E., relations between the Judean people and Antiochus Epiphanes had reached the breaking point. He published a series of decrees which seemingly gave effect to a new principle in the Greek imperial policy. The Judeans were told that "all people under the Syrian empire must be one people and each must abandon its separate ways." This was not duplicated in any other country in his domain, and was in sharp contrast to Greek tradition handed down from Alexander which provided religious freedom. In fact, Alexandrian Jews were favored above all other peoples in the city, except the Greeks. His troops desecrated the Temple. A pig, forbidden to the Jews, was henceforth sacrificed daily on its altar. The Mosaic constitution was abrogated. Circumcision, the dietary laws, and observance of the Sabbath were interdicted, and across the country outdoor altars were constructed to which Jews were dragged from their homes by armed sentries to at least witness, if they would not join, the hog sacrifices.

Elias Bickerman, a foremost expert on this period, has found it incredible that Syria should, without reason, have

devised for Judea a policy so different from that which applied to other countries under its rule, and which transformed a Hebrew civil war into a war against the empire. He has advanced the convincing thesis that Antiochus was the promulgator, but not the initiator of these decrees. He published them at the High Priests' request. The Mosaic Constitution had long been an annoying reminder to him and all Hellenized Jews of their obligation to the people. Now there would be no law except Menelaus'. This was not inconsistent with imperial policy, which everywhere recognized the local ruler's law as binding upon his people. All the coercive measures were a ruthless attempt by the Hellenized, rich Judeans to forcibly and quickly Hellenize their entire people.

Revolt had long been brewing. It fed on several sources: the rural population, mulcted by the urban aristocracy; the intellectual Hassidim (not to be confused with the contemporary movement of the same name) who were probably Scribes, and constituted themselves defenders of the Constitution; and finally the disenfranchised urban lower classes—the blacksmiths, tanners, cobblers, tailors, the mob at the Temple gates. The revolt was sprung from rural Modin, a village near Lydda. Its leaders were Mattathias, the Hasmonean, an obscure village priest, and his five sons. There had always been a sharp cleavage between the upper clergy, aligned with wealth, and the lesser clergy fanned out across the country among the depressed classes. The early scribes, who made the law accessible to the people, probably derived from the latter.

The hills beyond Modin were infested with fugitives, essentially decent men whom an arbitrary government had coerced into lawlessness: small farmers, tired of sowing and harvesting for the tax collector, who brought their flocks and families into the hills. A traveler found with his neck slit was more likely the victim of professional bandits. Conversely, a royal tax agent in similar condition, had no doubt been waylaid by tax delinquent farmers.

Mattathias, who launched a revolt in 166 B.C.E. gave this bitterness tongue, purpose, organization, and the legitimacy of a cause. When he passed away in less than a year, his third son, Judah the Maccabean, succeeded him. He

formulated his cause succinctly when he cried, "We fight for our laws." To the Modin farmers, the Hebrew Scriptures were poor man's law which put need above greed. Judah Maccabeus accordingly applied the Deuteronomic draft exemptions in the territory under his guerrilla control. Late in 165 B.C.E. his lightning raids began to make their impression, and by the spring of 164 B.C.E. he was in control of the road between Jaffa and Jerusalem. The circumstance became embarrassing all around. Menelaus had pledged Antiochus larger revenue, but his receipts dwindled instead. The Pilgrimages, a major source of income, had almost ceased. Few dared travel the roads to the capital, and the Temple, in its desecrated state, could not entice visitors from afar. Tax revenue also had diminished. Collectors refused to penetrate the interior.

Morale in Judah's ranks, his victories notwithstanding, probably was also uncertain. The farmers among his soldiery had a habit of defecting when the planting and harvesting seasons approached. The rural population, compelled to feed the Maccabean forces, may have begun to mutter that, whatever the cause, the army is never the farmer's friend.

The war had also become a terrible annoyance to Antiochus. Embroiled in a campaign against the Parthians in the East, he could not spare his main forces to rout the Maccabeans, and his auxiliary soldiery was evidently inadequate. Yet he had no desire that Rome believe him unable to liquidate a local mutiny.

Thus, all parties to the conflict—The High Priest, the Maccabeans, Antiochus—required respite from war. A Roman diplomatic mission on its way to Antioch sought out the rebels and offered them its good offices. Soon thereafter Antiochus published a general amnesty and rescinded his ban on the Jews' religious practices. However, he did not restore Hebrew law as the law of the land.

The rebels returned to their villages. They planted, and harvested, and late in the fall, when their crops had been garnered, hugged their wives and children and again vanished into the hills. In December 164 B.C.E. they besieged Jerusalem. Menelaus fled. The Temple was cleansed

and rededicated. That occasion is celebrated as Chanuk-kah, the Feast of Lights.*

Judean law was restored as in the days of Ezra and Nehemiah. Judah took no rank, no title, no office. He apparently patterned himself on the ancient warrior judges of the Israelite tribal federation. Oppressed Jewish minorities in Palestine territories under heathen rule appealed to him for relief. His commandos struck north as far as Galilee, and east into Transjordan, where they assembled the imperiled Jews and rapidly retreated with them to Judea. It forcefully and perhaps unwisely demonstrated to Syria the Maccabeans' capacity to range far beyond their frontiers, and eventually press their irredentist aims. In 163 B.C.E. a mighty force roared down from Antioch and laid siege to Jerusalem, then suddenly turned back. Antiochus had died and the force's commander rushed home to assume the regency. He promptly acted to pacify Judea by having the young king publish an apology revoking "our father's project of bringing them over to Hellenism," and ordering the execution of Menelaus "because he was the cause of all evil in that he persuaded Epiphanes to abolish the ancestral constitution of the Jews." That constitution, as in Persian days, now received royal endorsement.

It was the greatest triumph of the Maccabeans, the peak of their glory. Hereafter, their revolution would become blurred, their name tarnished, their purpose ambiguous.

One, Alcimus, was named High Priest by the Greco-Syrian King. Even the Hassidim approved him. But Judah Maccabeus did not. He was the advocate of so-called permanent revolution, of war until every last objective was obtained. No High Priest should be named to the purple by a foreign ruler. Anyone so named, must go. Major motivation was perhaps a conviction that Judea must not commit herself injudiciously. The country's mood was pro-Syrian. The new rising power was Rome, which had expelled Epiphanes from Egypt, and probably extracted

* This chronology advanced by Bickerman differs from the conventional by dating the Maccabean victory after, not before, the amnesty.

his amnesty for the Judeans. Judah Maccabeus perhaps recalled the counsel of Isaiah and Jeremiah that small states should ride with the tides of Empire. He rode them prematurely. A special Hasmonean mission was dispatched to Rome. Some of its members bore Greek names.

The rebels were not fanatic opponents of everything Greek or Roman. They were typical, traditional synthesizers. The Judean mission achieved its purpose. "The nation of the Jews" was the first in the east to obtain a military mutual assistance pact from the Roman Senate.

In the spring of 161 B.C.E. less than a year later, to challenge the pact major Syrian forces were hurled against the Judeans and routed them. Judah Maccabeus perished in battle. Marching boldly against him this time were Judean volunteers, perhaps former supporters of Menelaus. The people had turned against the Hasmonean hero. They wanted peace, not a cause, and Rome evidently was not prepared at that state of her imperial career to commit herself beyond paper to a small and remote ally.

Nonetheless, the treaty was not a complete loss. It placed Judea in Rome's line of vision, which accounts in part for the favored treatment Jews everywhere received from the conquering Roman forces, and perhaps also for the immediate serious attention of Romans to Judean utterances whether from the Talmudic academies, the courts, or the Wilderness sects.

When Alcimus died in 159 B.C.E., the king appointed none to succeed him, perhaps to assuage the Maccabeans still hiding out in the desert and in the hills. In 157 B.C.E., the last guerrillas, now led by Jonathan, another of Mattathias' sons, surrendered, were confined to a special district, and forever barred from Jerusalem.

In 153 B.C.E., this state of quiescence ended. Alexander Balas, a pretender backed by Rome, arrived with a fleet to make his bid for the Syrian crown. Both sides solicited Jonathan's help, and the king authorized him to raise a force. Jonathan did, marching it off to aid Balas, however; and Balas, even before the issue had been decided in his favor, invested the Hasmonean as High Priest, vassal prince, and commander, and conferred on him the Greek symbols of his office, a red mantilla and a crown.

In accepting the High Priesthood from a heathen monarch, Jonathan turned on an essential principle of the Hasmonean Revolution. Simply by accepting the office, he flouted Jewish tradition. None other but the High Priest was permitted into the Holy of Holies. No man who had shed human blood, whatever the reason, was allowed in its precincts. But nothing evidently deterred Jonathan from assuming the post. He was the antipode of Judah, his brother, who ruled without office or rank.

The Syrian contest for power weaved violently from one royal successor to another, from incumbent to pretender. Jonathan and his brother Simon—whom Balas had appointed commander of Jaffa, the Syrian-populated port—maneuvered cunningly among the disputatious Syrians. They fought the wars with mixed Judean-Syrian troops, seized control of tremendous territory in the former Hebrew domain, and held it "in trust" for the crown. The Syrians became suspicious when they learned that Jonathan had secretly obtained Senate reconfirmation of his deceased brother's military assistance pact. They invited him to a conference from which he never returned.

He was succeeded by his brother, Simon, the last survivor of Mattathias' five sons. Simon pursued Jonathan's policy of acquiring former Hebrew territories "in trust." Judea, at his death, was twice the size it had been when the revolt began in Modin. The various Syrian contenders for the crown petitioned for his help and paid his price. In 142 B.C.E., the price was release of Judea from all further tax payments to Syria, and in 139 B.C.E., the price was permission for Judea to mint her own coin. These concessions were virtual independence.

The most significant date for Jewish history was 140 B.C.E., when Simon assumed his brother's three titles—High Priest, Prince, and Commander. However, he did not request them from a heathen king. Instead, he convened a people's assembly which conferred the titles upon him, declared them to be hereditary, and announced that absolute power of decision in all matters, impeachable only by a prophet that might arise, would henceforth be his.

No Judean had ever before been invested with such authority. Simon now held both secular and religious

power, which the Judeans had always carefully separated. He was a tyrant, in the old Greek sense, not necessarily opposed to the people, but an absolute ruler nonetheless. Thus, the last of the first generation of Maccabeans had become possessed by the spirit the Maccabeans had sworn to exorcize. Very soon, under the rule of Simon's son, a struggle ensued between the people and its tyrants. A minority turned away in revulsion from all mundane preoccupations to preach otherworldliness, and eventually produced Christianity. The majority opposed arbitrary government with firm law, and perpetuated Jewish culture.

Chapter FOUR

THE FATEFUL
CONTEST

THE JUDEANS WERE NEVER NETTLED BY FOREIGN IDEAS, IF ALlowed to assimilate them judiciously to their own culture. But they would not countenance imposition, and were always wary of power.

The Maccabean dynasty revealed early a disposition to exercise power arbitrarily and copy Greek ways, thus duplicating the conditions which caused its founder to launch a revolution. The break between the ruling Hebrew princes and the people was from the first violent and irreparable. Eventually Judean delegations appealed to Rome to remove the Maccabean descendants. But when Rome's procurators and governors substituted force for law, Judea ignited a revolution that spread across the eastern empire.

CRISIS OVER THE COURTS

A decisive role in these Judean struggles fell to the sanhedrin. The origins of this institution are obscure. Historians cannot agree on its precise functions. But none dispute that it was patently an agency of formidable prestige.

Sanhedrin is derived from synedrion, the Greek word for assembly, and was probably a generic name for all Judean tribunals of justice. Yet there was only one sanhedrin whose authority derived from popular consent and whose opinions have been handed down in Hebrew jurisprudence. It was a combined high court, legislature, and academy of higher learning. Its members served without compensation, Jewish tradition proscribing all material benefit from teaching or dispensing the law. It was not until late in the Middle Ages that the rabbis, successors to the earlier judges, began to accept remuneration.

Because of its frequent clashes with the executive, the sanhedrin's judiciary powers were confined through most of its existence to religious matters only. Yet it spoke its mind on all matters affecting the commonweal, including foreign policy. It acted as a vigorous brake on the Maccabean ruling house, which responded by packing the court with members of the landed and mercantile aristocracy, and when this stratagem failed, transferred the court's function to royal ad hoc tribunals which were also called sanhedrin. These were composed of the Grecized wealthy and presided over by the High Priest, who under Maccabean rule, was the prince himself, or his appointee. Under Roman rule, the High Priest was named by the procurator.

EMERGENCE OF POLITICAL PARTIES

The schism between the judiciary and the executive eventually led to the formation of two major parties which endured for more than two centuries, until the destruction of the Temple in the year 70 of the Christian era. The Pharisees defended the law, the Sadducees defended privilege.

The Sadducees, like all true Hellenists, were martial-spirited hence constantly embroiled in wars against the neighboring Hellenist states. The Pharisees, who opposed assimilation to Greek habits, also opposed all irredentist wars.

The Sadducees, the ruling class, rejected the oral law and recognized only the revealed law, the Bible. Since much of the latter law was formulated for a patriarchal tribal society, it needed reinterpretation in the complex latter-day Judea. Hence, in the absence of supplementary oral law, the priest-prince would be the country's sole arbiter, his rulings not subject to any objective legal gauge. Conversely, the Pharisees, representing the independent judiciary, argued that there was a consistent and firm legal tradition dating from Sinai, that the Rabbinical enactments and custom law were components of that tradition and hence part of revealed law.

The Sadducees and Pharisees also disagreed on metaphysical issues. For example, although the combined doc-

trines of reward and retribution hereafter and of resurrection were imbedded in Greco-Oriental culture, the Hellenized Sadducees denied them. The Pharisees, on the other hand, propounded these doctrines after placing them in a Hebrew conceptual framework. By extending divine judgment past the here and now, they were able to sustain the faith of the people in the invincibility of justice and the universality and perpetuity of moral order. However, they did not deal with the resurrection of a mythical deity that had descended on earth and perished, but with the good men of all nations who would be rewarded in the hereafter and resurrected on the universal judgment day. Unlike the Greco-Oriental doctrine, Pharisee doctrine provided firm gauges by which the good might be judged. The rewards were linked to obedience of God's law, to collective responsibility, to the redemption of Israel as a people, and to the establishment of a new order for all mankind. The Sadducees opposed it because it was uncomfortably linked to objective standards by which the conduct of the ruling class might be judged. It was altogether too egalitarian.

ORIGIN OF CONFLICT

The tensions between the judges and the Maccabeans' line, between the Pharisees and the Sadducees, came into sharper focus, sometime during the thirty year reign of John Hyrcanus (134-104 B.C.E.). He seemed fated for nothing but the briefest tenure when he succeeded to the dual office of ruling prince and High Priest after Simon, his father, was poisoned by the governor of Jericho, an ambitious son-in-law. The assassin marched on Jerusalem to challenge the succession, and Judea spent all her energies routing him. Before she could enjoy her respite, the Syrians appeared in force, compelling the surrender of all the Hasmonean territorial acquisitions except for the capital and a sliver surrounding it.

John Hyrcanus was able to endure these crises and defeats, and ultimately recoup his losses to Syria, only because the Pharisees mobilized popular support behind him. Not that the Pharisees were completely pleased with their ruler. This first Maccabean of the second generation to

rule their country was considerably Hellenized. Like his father, he insisted on exercising both secular and ecclesiastic powers, and entered the Holy of Holies even though, as a military man, he had shed human blood.

When he compelled the conquered Idumeans to choose between expulsion from their lands and conversion to Judaism, they cried shame and blasphemy, and argued that none may intrude by force between a people and its faith.

He apparently took Pharisee criticism into account, however, in providing for his succession. He separated the ecclesiastic and executive powers by the simple device of naming his widow chief of state, which was not the first time one had served in that capacity. Females, however, were automatically debarred from ecclesiastic positions, and he bequeathed the High Priesthood to Judah Aristobulus, one of his sons, whose ambitions were larger, however. Judah had his mother thrown into a dungeon and starved to death, assassinated one brother, imprisoned three others, and then proclaimed himself King of Judea, a title that the Jews reserved for the day when compassionate Providence would restore the Davidic dynasty. This was as good a pretext as any for withholding from their rulers a rank that implied unlimited powers by Divine sanction.

FRATRICIDE AND MATRICIDE

Nature provided for Judah Aristobulus no better than had his father. Having discharged all his evil capacity, he died of natural causes after less than a year on the throne, and was succeeded by Alexander Jannaeus (103-76 B.C.E.), one of his brothers, under whom the struggle between the Pharisees and Sadducees achieved full and violent bloom.

Alexander Jannaeus, a third generation Maccabean, was even more Hellenized than his father. Retaining the title of king, and enlisting mercenaries from all the east, he extended his southern domains down to the Arab desert, and his shoreline from Acre—excepting the city itself— through Gaza. He was by all standards a king to delight a conventional people, which the Jews were not, however.

The Pharisees were a swarm of gadflies. They protested that their king held two offices, entered the Holy of

Holies, which was forbidden to a man of war, and forcibly converted conquered peoples to Judaism.

There was generally a great deal of social unrest under his rule which none but the Pharisees could check. But the Pharisees would do nothing to defend him from the consequences of his conduct. In 94 B.C.E. a social revolt erupted which lasted six years. There is no evidence, however, that the Pharisees engineered it. The rebels were assisted by Syrian troops. The king was forced to flee. When the Syrian allies refused to depart from Judean soil, the rebels crossed en masse to the king they had deposed. He conveniently forgot this event when he was returned to his throne, and lashed out relentlessly against all suspected "enemies of the state." He convened special tribunals which suspended the rules of evidence of the Judaic legal tradition, and handed down death sentences by the thousands. The Pharisees, whatever their stand in the six years war, feared for their lives. Many fled to Egypt. This flight had a decided and enduring effect on Diaspora Judean relations.

ÉMIGRÉ INFLUENCE

Torn between the culture of his environment and the custom of his ancestors, the Diaspora Jew probably nursed both an idealized and condescending image of Judea. They regarded her as both innocent and obsolescent. The exiled scholars' contention that Judea, not unlike other states, was ruled by a tyrant, may have met with great resistance. But it also destroyed the myth of Israel's obsolescence. The fugitive scholars offered an alternative to Hellenist fatalism. They were a living demonstration of their conviction that man was a free agent, that he must choose because he can choose, and must hold himself responsible for both deed and utterance, without invoking the myth of blind destiny to justify himself.

Egyptian Jews had until then been presumed to be the natural ally of Judea's Hellenists. They had many external habits in common. But the presence of the Pharisee émigrés seems to have altered this, a circumstance beneficial to both Jewries. Alexandrian Jewry thereafter pro-

duced several scholars of such caliber that they were named to the presidency of the Jerusalem sanhedrin.

The émigrés were shrewd students, with a great capacity for synthesis. The Jewish Hellenists were bartenders; they mixed cultures. The Pharisees were chemists, who created new substances. Judea's universal educational system, introduced after Alexander Jannaeus' death (76 B.C.E.) was clearly patterned after the Greek gymnasia, although it differed in its emphases, of course. It was devised by two Pharisee scholars, Simon ben Shetach and Judah Tabai, both repatriated from Egypt, named by Queen Salome-Alexandra (76-67 B.C.E.) to chair the sanhedrin. Succeeding to her husband's throne, she purged the Sadducees from all but the military posts, claiming that this had been her husband's last instruction.

The Restoration, which did not survive the Queen's passing, re-established Pharisee legal procedures, and instructed all judges punctiliously on the rules of evidence, although miscarriages of justice were inevitable in the change-over. A world-wide Temple tax was introduced which few could afford. Its effect was to bind the Diaspora closer to Judea, and to reduce the supreme institution's dependence on contributions and gifts from the very rich, among whom the Sadducees were impressively numerous.

ROMAN INTRUSION

After the queen's death, her sons Aristobulus II and Hyrcanus II plunged the country into civil war over the succession. This was additional proof, if any was needed, of the unfitness of the Maccabean line. Behind Aristobulus were the Sadduccees. Behind Hyrcanus was a grey eminence, Antipater, father of Herod and descended from Idumeans whom an earlier Hasmonean monarch had forcibly converted to Judaism. He was using Hyrcanus to advance his own family into fortune. The Pharisees had none to chose from. Nonetheless, some aligned themselves with Hyrcanus, who had been favored by the late queen.

The struggle for power between the two Judean princelings continued inconclusively until Pompey appeared in Damascus in 63 B.C.E. to solidify Rome's eastern empire.

Regional princelings queued up to negotiate dignified vassalage. The two Judeans also appeared, each seeking to be confirmed king of Judea. They were followed by a delegation of two hundred notables, evidently Pharisees, who branded both princelings as usurpers and petitioned "for a high priest, not a king." A high priest meant full religio-cultural autonomy, which was better than a so-called sovereign king who would be Rome's puppet anyhow, with the power to intrude into all internal affairs and to transform Judea's culture.

Pleased by the Judean cleavage, Pompey set off on another of his campaigns, meanwhile deferring his decision. But Aristobulus, fearing a negative denouement, fortified Jerusalem against the Romans.

Then Pompey's legionnaires returned and approached the capital; they were welcomed into the lower city by Hyrcanus, but were compelled to fight doggedly, with heavy cost in lives, for the Temple area held by his brother. They retaliated by slaughtering the priests at their altar, and removing the Temple's treasury.

Pompey promptly ordered the plunder returned and the Temple restored to a decent condition so that the Jews might resume their services. He also confirmed Hyrcanus as ruling prince, not king, and the Jews' right to live in accordance with their laws. He stripped them, however, of considerable territory, cutting them off completely from the sea. It was generous treatment nonetheless, hardly worse than would have been obtained had they not resisted at all.

The mood was thus set for Judean-Roman accommodation. It was prevented however by three abrasive elements: the frequent guerrilla raids organized by Hasmonean pretenders, which conveyed a false impression of widespread popular contumacy; the imperial agents and their tax farmers, who mulcted the people ruthlessly; and Antipater who instead of using his cunning to protect his people, collaborated in fleecing them.

CAESAR GOES COURTING

Then, briefly, hope flared up in Judea. Its past experience with great conquerors—Cyrus and Alexander—had been

exhilarating, and now Julius Caesar streaked across her skies, making her privy to Rome's agony.

Judea appeared important in Caesar's bid against Pompey, because of her influence as the spiritual center of an unusually able and remarkable dispersed people. Jews constituted twelve per cent of the Egyptian population, were prominent in her shipping, influential in her letters. In Athens, they had lived for more than a century, and in Rome were of sufficient number to give rise to myths. There were Jewish communities along the African coast, and even in the Crimea on the Black Sea. Jewish-populated regions were virtually autonomous states in the Parthian domains which still held out firmly against Rome.

They were well worth courting everywhere. Caesar summoned Aristobulus II, then on restricted liberty in Rome, and pledged him the Judean throne for leading two Roman legions against Pompey. The latter's agents thwarted the plot, however, by poisoning the Hasmonean. Julius Caesar was warmly welcomed by Jewry, nonetheless.

Antipater, who had earlier declared himself for Pompey, now interposed a Judean column between Pompey's reinforcements and the front lines. Alexandrian Jewry contributed to Caesar's triumph by keeping his forces well supplied. Caesar thought this was the result of Hyrcanus' proclamation summoning Jews everywhere to his banner. Actually it was an automatic Jewish response. Pompey's legionnaires had violated the Temple, and the Jews could never forget it.

The victorious Caesar treated the Jews magnanimously by any standards. He returned to Judea some of her dissevered territories, including the Galilee, and exempted her from all vassalage obligations, such as paying an annual tribute, and supplying auxiliary forces for Rome's military expeditions and winter quarters for her legions. However, he reconfirmed Hyrcanus as prince and also appointed Antipater imperial officer for Judea, which in the eyes of Judeans negated his magnanimity. Some very significant history might have developed differently had Caesar dealt with the Pharisees instead.

He was even more generous to the Diaspora communi-

ties, conferring upon them a wide range of rights and privileges that constituted virtual home rule beyond their ancestral soil, so that forever after in their petitions to Rome they cited Caesar's pledges and rulings as sacred canon. At his death (44 B.C.E.), Roman Jews lay for days prostrate at his coffin. Judea mourned him more moderately.

Antipater, as if he had no time to spare, promptly committed Judea to the chairman of the assassins, Cassius.

Poisoned by Judean patriots (43 B.C.E.), Antipater left his two sons with titles, estates and a painful dilemma. He had named Herod governor of Galilee, and Phasael governor of Samaria and Judea, but both required confirmation from Marc Antony and Augustus Octavian, whom their father had opposed. Herod undertook the mission to Egypt to explain to Antony.

Traveling in the same direction was an official Judean embassy which offered to place their country under the direct protection of Rome, in return for religio-cultural autonomy, preferring the burden of Roman imposts to a Hebrew tyrant's intrusion into Jewry's internal affairs. The embassy was well received. Antony reconfirmed the rights and privileges Caesar had conferred upon the Diaspora. Like Caesar, he extended Judea's territory, and like Caesar and Pompey, he missed the central issue, the cause of the Roman-Judean agony, when he named Antipater's sons joint ruling princes of Judea. Perhaps he decided, as the delegation addressed him, that such conscionable men can have no imperial uses.

ENTER HEROD

One year later, the Parthians sprang from the East, forced the Romans out of Syria, and placed a Hasmonean pretender on the Judean throne. Phasael took his life rather than be captured. Herod fled to the Nabateans who turned him out, then to Egypt where he was offered and refused an appointment to command Cleopatra's garrisons, and finally sailed for Rome where the Senate named him King of Judea, investing him into office with solemn ceremonies at the Temple of Jupiter. Intended to dissuade the Judeans from the Hasmonean pretender, the ceremonies only

demonstrated the ineptness of Rome and Herod's igno-rance of the people he was to rule.

The Judeans required no dissuasion. They had had their fill of Hebrew tyrants and pretenders. The most effective dissuasion would have been a disavowal of Herod by the Senate. His investiture, in pagan manner, seemed a de-liberate mockery of "our laws."

After a three year war with the Hasmonean pretender and his Parthian allies, Herod entered Jerusalem, took office in 37 B.C.E., and promptly confirmed his reputation for cruelty and contempt for Jewish law.

His long reign (37-5 B.C.E.) was in the extravagant fashion of Roman emperors. He taxed mercilessly, built prodigiously—cities, stadia, and monuments to his ephem-eral glory—played hard and fast with appointments to office, especially the coveted post of the High Priest, and continually hacked away at conspiracies incubated by his diseased imagination.

One of his first acts was the execution, almost to a man, of the Pharisee sanhedrin. Then he eliminated, one for one, almost all the members of his household; his victims over the years included: his wife, Mariamne, a Hasmonean princess; their two sons; her grandparents, brother and uncle; and Herod's two sons by another wife.

Of these, only three were in any way guilty. One of his non-Hasmonean sons was implicated in a plot on Herod's life; Mariamne's uncle, Antigonus, was the pretender who for three years ruled Jerusalem under the Parthians; her mother, Alexandra, had been overtly scheming to acquire the diadem for one of her sons or grandsons, a true Hasmonean. Because Cleopatra was her friend, she was spared the penalty which her conspiracies merited. But in 29 B.C.E., after Cleopatra's death, she too joined Herod's list of victims.

The ubiquity of Herod's informers and the intensity of his terror were only two reasons for the country's political apathy under his rule. Another reason was the prosperity which the urban upper classes enjoyed and which trickled down also to the middle bourgeoisie. This was a direct result of his ambitious construction projects. Like the Roman emperors, he hoped to immortalize his name in

stone. The Temple he constructed in Jerusalem, which was still unfinished at the time of his demise in 5 B.C.E., was reputedly more beautiful and sumptuous than Solomon's. Thousands of masons, carpenters, gold- and silversmiths, architects, and foremen were employed in its construction. They in turn dispensed their earnings among the city's shopkeepers, innkeepers, physicians, cobblers, tailors, perfumers, and entertainers. They also introduced the high life of alien cities. Herod taxed brutally to finance his undertakings, but except for one year of famine due to poor harvests, Judea's cities enjoyed unprecedented prosperity under him.

The true sufferers were the peasants. Tax collectors sequestered their harvests, soldiery trampled their fields, and their sons were seized for army service and forced labor on Herod's construction projects. Hence, the rural areas erupted in frequent revolt. This was especially true of the Galilee. Another class of sufferers were the Pharisee teachers of the law, cowed by Herod, despondent at the quick Hellenization of the cities, unable to communicate, let alone associate with the brigand rabble, the am haaretz, of Galilee. Some of them retired to the desert where they formed an ascetic community called the Essenes. Its members renounced all worldly possessions, wore robes of rough cloth, and spent their days in menial chores, ablutions, and prayers.

Jewish tradition had always treated ascetics gingerly. The Essenes were a radical departure from all previous kinds. The hirsute men who threatened the worshipers of Baal some eight hundred years before were fiercely committed to society and sworn to reform it, albeit by swift and violent retribution. The Essenes, conversely, had abstracted themselves from society. They regarded man as a contaminated vessel, and allowed no margin for regret, no catwalk for escape. They converted the prophetic concept of Jewry as a Chosen People guiding all mankind to salvation into a vision of themselves as Chosen brethren who would alone survive when all mankind perished. The Pharisee vision embraced the pure-hearted heathen; the Essene debarred even fellow-Jews. The Pharisee End of Days anticipated universal harmony. The Essene consum-

mation was horrible battles between forces of light and darkness.

The Pharisees had to act quickly to contain Essene pessimism, restrain rebel recklessness, and rebut the Sadducees. They also had to devise a means of communicating the law to the people in counterpoint to Herodian caprice. They managed superbly, perhaps because their leader at this time was a cosmopolitan such as the Jews have always esteemed above others.

CIRCUMVENTING TYRANNY

The sanhedrin had been intermittently headed by men who had lived in Alexandria and were conversant with Greco-Roman culture. Simon ben Shetach and Judah ben Tabai were the first repatriates to chair the sanhedrin. Shemayah and Abtalion (60-35 B.C.E.) were both either native Alexandrians or had at some time lived there. They assumed joint chairmanship of the sanhedrin in bad days when legislation and verdicts were handed down by improvised Sadducee sanhedrin which Herod appointed and convened at will. The Pharisee body by that name, once revered by the people, was confined to religious matters and hypothetical discussions. The people looked to it for leadership and comfort and received counsels of caution. But when the great Hillel (75 B.C.E-5 C.E.) assumed chairmanship, he managed both to deflect Herod's suspicion and restore the Pharisees' authority with the people.

Hillel, it is generally assumed, was from Babylonia. Some opinion inclines to list him as another Alexandrian. He was in a most difficult position when he assumed the chairmanship. The very existence of the Pharisee sanhedrin may have inadvertently conveyed the impression of an independent judiciary and a free forum. This could repair Herod's unfavorable image abroad. The sanhedrin's great accomplishment under Hillel was its ability to state hypotheses so lucidly that the people had no difficulty applying them to specific situations. Hence, two legal systems functioned side by side—the governmental, composed of capricious edicts, and the inferred law handed down by the sanhedrin under Hillel.

Herod even contenanced the court's occasional audacious

sallies against him. Hillel postulated that "he who does not seek the law for its own ends, shall perish." Speaking for the conservatives, rigorists in rituals and reputedly skirting subversion politically, Shammai demanded new and severe tests of faith for those wishing to convert to Judaism. His proposals were formally within his competence as a religious judge, but the implication was audaciously political—Herod was descended from proselytes.

Hillel, heading the liberal majority, opposed these measures, and reduced the test of faith to an apothegm: "Do not do unto others which thou wouldst not done unto yourself, this is the entire law, all else is exegesis." This was spoken one-half century before the Sermon on the Mount, and rested on a still older Leviticus dictum.

More than 500 years before Justinian published the first substantial code of Roman law, Hillel began to codify Hebrew law, the chaotic state of which was a threat to Jewish unity. The dispersed communities each had their own peculiar customs and practices, and even inside Judea the Sadducees were governed by one code, the Pharisees by another; some ignored everything post-Biblical, and others revered the most perverse ancestral superstition as if it were revelation from Sinai. To provide a single resilient and enduring law, Hillel devised a simple formula. He ruled that the written law, the Bible, was supreme, and only laws and customs based on scriptures were its legitimate issue. This fused the written and oral law into a single code, and established a constitutional test for all future legislation. This method was adopted by Christian and Islamic jurists who also tested their oral law by their respective written canons. Hillel's principle is applied by the U.S. Supreme Court each time it passes on the constitutionality of a law.

AGE OF THE PROCURATORS

Herod died leaving a sardonic will. He divided his domains among three of his sons, and imperiled their legacy by disinheriting their three brothers.

The heirs traveled to Rome to obtain confirmation from the Emperor. An embassy of Judean notables interposed its objection against them "because the anguish (Herod)

inflicted on the Jews exceeded anything they had suffered since Babylonia," and presented its customary offer that Judea be declared a Roman protectorate and guaranteed noninterference with its laws. The emperor compounded the classic blunder that was the root cause of the Judean agony. He confirmed Herod's will.

Revolt spread across the land when Archelaus, one of the sons, arrived to assume rule over the essential Judean territory which included Jerusalem. He had been confirmed ruling prince, not king like his father. The people would have him under no conditions. However, he endured with the support of Roman legionnaires, until his removal in the year 6, for malfeasance in office. Rome finally acted perversely on Judea's past request. The country was placed under Roman procurators ruling from Caesarea.

A procurator's tenure was brief. Each new Roman regime named its own; a procurator furiously used his time in office to enrich himself.

A tax on agricultural landholdings compelled the peasants to surrender a specified portion of their harvested crop, and a tax on herds compelled them to surrender a specified portion of their livestock. There were also income and per capita taxes. Yet Rome treated Judea no worse than other protectorates.

Judea, however, was different from all the others. Elsewhere, a Roman procurator claiming a bride's first night was only succeeding to the privileges of the indigenous rulers. The Judeans knew no such abominable custom. Its men took up sentry duty. Its brides would not be treated like slave girls.

Rome announced a population census, and Judean males swelled the rebel bands roaming the hills. The census might presage a draft, or an increase in the per capita tax. Above all, it strained a tradition against population counts dating back to a census by King David which was followed by an epidemic. (For the same reason, the Israel government several years ago still met vigorous census opposition from some of its ultraorthodox citizens.)

Judea's woes were further compounded by her neighbors, the tale-bearing, heathen states which kept carrying to the procurator and the imperial court itself charges of

Judean plots, both true and fictitious. This was typical of the irascible and feuding people of that region who continually intrigued one against the other. What made this case exceptional was the strange circumstance that, however divided on other issues, these states were always vociferously unanimous against Judea. She was the egregious, lone dissident from their common heathen culture. It has its modern parallel in disunited Arabdom's unity against Israel.

The religio-cultural peculiarism and universal dispersion of the Jews—the Diaspora population even then outnumbered the Judean—invested the little state with an inordinately high, and often disadvantageous visibility.

Rome had reached that adult state when a civilization's pristine purpose becomes a blurred and irretrievable memory. The contemplative section of the Roman elite yearned for some value beyond power and lust. They pondered Judaism, which was the only Eastern religion permitted in Rome. It offered a discipline through life: Its moral incentives seemed a redeeming substitute for all other frustrating drives of man.

Rome buzzed with rumors about metuentes sabbata, Sabbath observers in the emperor's own household. Whenever a dismissed public servant appealed for public sympathy, especially a procurator recalled from Caesarea for malfeasance, he imputed his contretemps to these men and women who had assumed some of the Jewish disciplines, although they were not real converts. The sanhedrin, which ruled overtly on religious matters, and guided covertly the nation through its crises with imperial policy, was too preoccupied to missionize Rome. Yet heathen intellectuals were alarmed by the encroachment of Judaic cultural influence. Horace and Ovid, Plutarch and Tacitus committed to posterity their bitter, uninformed remarks about the Jews. "The habits of this felon nation have been widely accepted, it has followers in every land, so that peculiarly the conquered had imposed his law on the conqueror," charged Seneca, Stoic philosopher and statesman. And one hundred years before him, when the Jews were less numerous in Rome, Cicero (106-43 B.C.E.), another Stoic, while exulting that it is evident "how much the

immortal gods abhor this nation . . . from the fact that it had been conquered, heavily taxed, and beaten to the ground," warned bitterly against its penetration. The bitterness of Cicero and Seneca is perhaps explained by the fact that Stoicism, which counseled moderation in conduct, was Rome's closest parallel to Judaism. The Stoics may, therefore, have regarded Judaism as a rival philosophy.

THE DIASPORA

There was a third ambiguous factor—the Jewries outside Israel. The Diaspora's influence at the imperial court undoubtedly benefited Judea, but Judea was too often an inadvertent victim of the Diaspora's feuds with the heathens abroad.

Since Julius Caesar's day, the Jews had enjoyed high and exceptional status in the Roman territories. Alexandria, Egypt was the most important of these communities, a "subcapital" for Jewry, its influence second only to Jerusalem.

Augustus Octavianus, first Roman emperor (27 B.C.E.-14) was especially munificent, appointing a high official of the Jewish community to the post of superintendent of harbors, then a more important office than Biblical Joseph had held. Not even a Roman senator could sail into the Alexandrian harbor without imperial permission, yet a Jew was its chief custodian, and by virtue of his post, boss of all Egyptian trade by sea and by the Nile.

This only exacerbated the enmity of the Greeks and the Egyptians, the Jews' commercial rivals who hired a stable of orators and pamphleteers to incite public opinion of all strata by circulating malicious myths about the Jews. Apion, the most prominent of these, alleged that the Jews slaughtered heathens and drew their blood for ritualistic purposes; Christian anti-Semitism, adapting this myth in the twelfth century, nursed it into the twentieth century. These indiscriminate allegations, far from alienating the Emperor's affection for the Jews, only met with his disfavor. The pamphleteers then devised a new strategy. They raised the cry of dual allegiance. Calling Egyptian Jewry disloyal to the crown, they accused it of complicity in Judean rebellions. The effect was sufficient to constrain

71

the philosopher Philo, the most august Jewish figure in Hellenistic letters, to draft a statement of clarification, which read today has poignant familiarity, as though from the mimeograph of an American Jewish community relations agency.

"The Jews, dispersed in the Diaspora," he wrote, "see the Holy City in which the Temple is located as their metropolis, but the countries in which they have been bequeathed the right of residence by ancestors and great-ancestors they regard as their native lands."

Philo may have been addressing both the heathens and the Jews, among whom some perhaps had hoped to still anti-Semitism by disavowing their bonds to Judea, not realizing that the agitation was far more concerned with extirpating their vigorous presence in Egypt than removing the Jerusalem mote from the procurator's eye.

AMERICAN JEWRY'S PREDECESSOR

Alexandrian Jewry of more than two thousand years ago presents the closest analogue to contemporary American Jewry in every respect, but the juridical. The individual Jew ranked with the Greek citizen, a distinction denied Egyptians. It was conferred on him by a collective charter, a pyramid of privileges, rights, and obligations, expanded by the Romans, but dating back to the Ptolemaic rulers, which designated Jewry as a favored nation, self-governed, a state within a state. This substantially was the status of all Jewish communities in the Greco-Roman territories, an arrangement peculiar to pre-Christian history.

The legacy that Egyptian and American Jewries share across the space of two millennia is religio-cultural dualism and their responses to it. Few Alexandrian Jews understood Hebrew. They read their Bible and recited their prayers in Greek. They mixed Greek and ancestral custom, and tried to bridge the essential religious difference between Jew and Greek by claiming common roots for the two cultures. The Judeans, a majority in their own land, and illiterate about a minority's compulsions, may have treated these efforts with disdain. Alexandrian Jews in turn may sometimes have wondered whether their brethren were not indeed stiff-necked as the heathen claimed, and

whether Judea should not consider, before taking precipitous action, its effect on the Diaspora communities which so generously supported the Temple.

The Judeans cried blasphemy when Herod sponsored gladiatorial matches in Palestine's Grecized cities, because to them the contests were savage, and opened with pagan prayer. In Egypt, the philosopher Philo, a punctiliously ritualistic Jew, had no objection to these relaxations, proscribing them only for women because the male contestants were naked. When Herod unveiled the completed sections of the new Jerusalem Temple to delight the Judeans, they rioted instead against the Roman Eagle mounted on its gates. The Jewish houses of worship in Egypt, conversely, were embellished, walls and gate, with golden garlands and wreaths dedicated to the emperor.

Like American Jewry, the Egyptian Jews had a penchant for sumptuous synagogues. The Greco-Roman impact on them went beyond the architectural. The Jerusalem Temple preserved the egalitarian tradition. Its congregation stood humbly before God, a compact multitudinous mass, rank and station intermixed, for all alike were His servants. In Alexandria, the council of elders, comprising seventy-one members, the same number as the sanhedrin, was seated on golden chairs, and the congregation in sections, graded by trade and occupation.

Hellenist Jewry's split personality is revealed in its reading habits. From the Hebrew it translated proverbs demonstrating the essential affinity between Judaism and Stoicism, apocalyptic scrolls conveying Pythagorean flavor and Pharisee texts boldly counterpoising Judaism to Greek philosophy.

Original Greco-Jewish writing in all genres—philosophical dialogue, epic poem, and drama—mixed polemics and apologia, stressed the common root of both cultures, imputed Judaic inspiration to the Greeks, and then claimed the Greek manner for Judaism. It presented Greece as Jewry's debtor, then measured the Jew by her gauges.

This compulsion towards self-justification, analogous to the public statements by spokesmen for American Jewish organizations, only parochialized the genius of an essentially cosmopolitan community, while the "parochial"

Judean Pharisees, hobbled by no such inhibitions, produced during this time law that is universal and timeless.

To win Greek favor, Greco-Jewish writers even bent sacred texts and tampered with history. They allegorized the Bible to give it philosophic cast. Judean writers defined the Maccabean revolt as a war for national independence, boldly implying its parallel in the Roman-Judean conflict. Greco-Jewish writers, apparently fearing the charge of retroactive complicity, defined it as a war for religious principle. Today, American-Jewish agencies, but no serious writers or scholars, pursue a similar policy of de-emphasizing anything in the Jew that might offend current popular prejudice, thus completing the parallel between two great Diaspora communities across the gulf of two millennia.

Suddenly one day, calamity engulfed Alexandrian Jewry. The emperor had withdrawn its immunity. It occurred in the third year of the mad Caligula's reign (37-41). All Roman emperors were divine, yet obligingly deferred their full deification until after death. But Caligula was a man of precipitous nature. In 40, he proclaimed himself the Living God, and among other things, ordered his statue installed and worshiped in the Jerusalem Temple. It was a demand beyond Jewry's accommodation. The order to worship man struck at the Jewish moral order. Judea balked. Anti-Jewish feeling swept the empire.

Alexandrian Jewry was now able to assay the merits of its affluence and apologia. The entire charter of its imperial rights and privileges was abrogated at one stroke by the city council. The officers of the Jewish self-government were jailed as hostages. Troops searched Jewish homes ostensibly for arms and carried away plunder. Mobs invaded the synagogues, defiled the Holy scrolls, and replaced them in the Holy Ark with the emperor's bust.

The humbled community sent a delegation to Rome to petition the youthful emperor who sniffed his flowers as he listened with only half-cocked ear; then he abruptly interrupted to ask point blank why the Jews would not worship him, and turned his back before their spokesman, the aging Philo, could reply.

The philosopher, immersed in both Hebrew and Greek culture, now learned the high cost of living in two cultures, although he would probably not have wished, even if reborn, to alter the circumstance.

AGRIPPA I

The Judeans, situated on their own terrain, prepared to meet the emperor's threat in quite another manner. They sent no delegations to Rome. Instead, their smithies worked around the clock to equip with arms the volunteers who poured into Jerusalem to defend the Temple from any attempt to enter it with the emperor's images. Only the emperor's assassination in Rome in 41 prevented a catastrophe.

The Roman senate, considering successors, was persuaded to name Claudius by an astute lobbyist, Agrippa I (10 B.C.E.-44), a Jew and down-at-the-heels monarch of some of the former Hebrew territories. The grateful Claudius added Samaria and Jerusalem to Agrippa's domains, conferred on him the coveted title of King of Judea, and ordered that "the Jewish people should in no way be restricted in its rights" and that "in no Greek city should they be deprived of the rights accorded them in the reign of the Divine Augustus, and . . . that throughout the imperial territory the Jews be permitted, uninterfered, to observe the customs of their ancestors."

None would have surmised, from his beginnings, that Agrippa would some day emerge a Joseph at court in the classic pattern. The grandson of Herod and the Hasmonean princess Mariamne, he was still in his late forties, an impoverished, untitled bon vivant, brought up at the Roman court where his friends included Emperor Tiberius' son Drusus, who died young, and Caius Caligula. He was disentangled from gambling debts by the generous purse of the head of the Alexandrian Jewish community, Philo's brother, and from other troubles by his mother's intercession with her friend, the emperor's sister. Nothing could keep him out of jail after he had been overheard saying that he could not wait for Caligula to become emperor, but, when that indeed came about six months later, he was conferred several territories and the title, king, by his

friend Caligula. But not even he could later persuade the mad emperor not to force his statue on the Temple.

Agrippa, as King of Judea, quickly won the affections of his people. A Pharisee in Jerusalem, an urbane Roman in Caesarea, he participated in athletic contests in the Grecized coastal cities, walked humbly with the common people in the seasonal processions in the capital, and, restoring an ancient rite, periodically convened assemblies in the Temple courtyard; he read to them the Book of Deuteronomy, the essential constitution which solemnized the union between Judean monarchs and their people. One of the great events of his reign was the state visit in 43 of King Izates and the Queen Mother Helen of Adiabene, an Asian enclave between the Parthian and Roman domains. The king and his mother were proselytes, and they rode with Agrippa in royal procession through the streets of Jerusalem. The multitudes hailed this return of Judean glory after years of rule by the procurators and forgot their traditional indisposition to all monarchy.

But the Greco-Egyptian conspiracy set to work again. It carried word to Rome that Agrippa was fortifying the Judean cities. Claudius ordered the work suspended. Later, the Governor of Syria, supreme Roman official in the region, descended on a feast tendered by Agrippa and dispersed his guests, who were local ruling princes. The Governor had been informed that they had assembled to plot disseverance from the empire.

Agrippa suffered a fatal seizure (44) at a gladiators' spectacle shortly thereafter. This was probably Rome's gracious way of disposing of an ally who could no longer be trusted. Claudius suspended Judea's independence. She was again a subjugated colony. The Sadducees were returned to their posts in Jewry's intramural institutions. They had been the war party when the enemy was neighboring heathen states. They were collaborators now that the enemy was imperial Rome. They disported themselves in Caesarea, sought admittance for their sons and daughters into Roman society, and advocated accommodation at any price. It is of them, that the people cried: "They are High Priests, their sons—assessors, their sons-in-law—supervisors, and their servants lash the people with canes."

PALESTINE ON THE EVE OF AND DURING THE EARLY CHRISTIAN ERA

The Pharisee sanhedrin, conversely, came under the rule of the Shammaites, also representing wealth and conservative in all respects. They advocated ritualistic rigor, complete isolation from the heathen, and war on Rome. The latter goal was the only basis for their alliance with the Kanaim, a new activist party of veteran rebels who, having lived for years beyond the pale of the law, could hardly revere possessions, and were disposed to economic radicalism. There also was a small but ferocious association of patriots of bandit disposition called Sicarii because they carried a sica, a small Roman dagger, under their garments. Mixing with crowds, they pinned down their victim, Roman official or Judean collaborator, before he could cry out or anyone noticed. Yet even if the assassin were caught, he was released by the procurator for a bribe. The Sicarii obtained the monies to pay him by periodically seizing wealthy Judeans for ransom. Thus, whenever a wealthy Judean was seized, the people knew that a terrorist would soon be released.

This condition of cynical lawlessness brought economic activity to a standstill. Just before the rebellion erupted in 66, the situation was further aggravated by the completion of Herod's Temple which released tens of thousands of workers, further swelling the ranks of the unemployed. A stupid Roman procurator, Florus, with a special reputation for venality, precipitated the crisis. The Kanaim had appeared in the streets one day mockingly soliciting contributions for "poor Florus." When Jerusalem refused to identify and surrender his detractors, Florus retaliated by crucifying scores of Judeans, including men of rank. When he entered the capital with an armed guard on a later occasion to seize the Temple funds, the Kanaim seized his soldiery as hostages.

However, the situation was still remediable. Hillelites requested that Agrippa II lead a delegation to Rome to petition Florus' removal. Like his father, Agrippa had been brought up in the imperial household, and was neither fully Judean nor Roman. The father made a triumph of this odd circumstance. The son reduced it to bathos. Not wishing to appear to favor the contumacious Judeans over an imperial agent, he turned down the Hillelite request. It

was one of those moments when the thoughtless decision of a little man turns the tide of history. The extreme elements now shunted the Hillelite moderates aside, and proclaimed a tax strike throughout Judea. Agrippa II, who had no tongue before the Romans, had cheek before the Jews. He convened them in public assembly, and almost persuaded them to capitulate. A tax strike, he warned the multitudes, was synonymous with rebellion, and Judea was like a fly in the emperor's fist. Even noble Athens yielded, and who was Judea to resist? And who would her allies be against invincible Rome? Not even the Jews would come to her side. Parthia would debar involvement by Babylonian Jewry; Adiabene, the proselyte kingdom, was barely more than a fiction. The Greco-Roman Diasporas "will be devastated by the enemy if you rebel."

The people cried that their quarrel was not with Rome, that they would resume paying the emperor's tax and lay down their arms if only Florus would go. Agrippa II might then have proposed to intercede on this issue if they would suspend the rebellion. Instead, he replied that Rome must be obeyed, and until replaced, Florus was Rome. At this, the assemblage petered out as if through a sieve. The rebellion was on by popular consent. When Cassius Gallus, Roman governor of Syria, descended on Jerusalem with thirty thousand mercenaries and was beaten back, Rome's humiliation was compounded by a case of nerves.

Allies were entering Jerusalem. The Samaritans, who also were embroiled with Rome, suspended their ancient feud with the Jews and offered assistance. The Idumeans entered in full force. From Adiabene, on the banks of the Tigris, came the son and brother of King Monobaz. Rumor reaching the imperial capital magnified these numbers and depicted Judea as the heart of a world alliance. There was a heady air of triumph in Jerusalem.

THE WAR FOR JERUSALEM

However, as Agrippa II had predicted, anti-Jewish riots swept the Diaspora. In Antioch, the mob was led by the apostate son of the head of the Jewish community, and in Alexandria by another apostate, its governor Alexander Tiberius, former procurator of Judea. In Caesarea, twenty

thousand Jews perished, and the rest, to a man, were transported to the slave markets. In Damascus, the women of the nobility, menuentes sabbata, foiled one plot, but another succeeded. In most places, the assailants resorted to ruses, not daring to face the Jews in fair and open combat. Jewish irregulars who had not yet joined the main forces of the rebellion rushed to the defense of besieged communities in former Jewish territory. In Jerusalem, a sanhedrin under extreme Pharisee control voted eighteen rigid enactments forbidding all social and commercial contact with the heathen.

The revolution had become so popular that the taciturn, hard-bitten Kanaim leaders, only recently emerged from their redoubts in the hills, could not even preserve their stake in it. Men who had been undecided and had even opposed it now joined the revolutionary coalition government. The major commands were filled by the Jerusalem aristocracy.

The most crucial command went to an unstable young dilettante only recently arrived from Rome, Joseph ben Matthias, later known as the historian Josephus Flavius, descended from the Hasmoneans. He had studied under Pharisee teachers; and when asceticism became the passing mode, he retired to the desert where he briefly lived close to the Essenes. Then, apparently without sensing the paradox, he set off for Rome, with a letter to the Jewish actor Altirus who introduced him to Empress Poppaea, known to be fond of half-tamed exotic youths. He had hitherto moved among provincial pretenses. Now he faced the stage of great events and longed to become enshrouded, like the celebrated among the Romans, in a nimbus of elegance and myth.

The occasion presented itself immediately upon his return to Jerusalem. Everyone spoke rebellion, and Joseph was a zealot for fashions. He was named commander of the Galilee, a region of heathen cities, and the gateway for Roman forces descending from Syria. Instead of solidifying the guerrilla forces (no other kind of warfare was possible there), he pompously established, in grandiose Roman manner, a formal chain of command and a complex administrative apparatus of local senates. He forcibly

detained a commission sent by the Jerusalem sanhedrin to investigate charges filed against him by the commander of the leading Galilean guerrilla forces, John of Gischala, and unconscionably proceeded to dispose of the more rabid partisan commanders.

When Vespasian, who had routed the Britons, appeared (67) in Acre at the head of a force of 60,000 men, and was welcomed by the heathen cities, the unprepared Galilee crumbled. Joseph, reneging on a collective suicide pledge, surrendered to the Romans.

However, small bands of irregulars continued to hold out and harass the main Roman force, and it was only when further resistance seemed hopeless that John of Gischala retired with a detachment into Jerusalem. His arrival signaled a reign of terror. He accused the moderates of the Galilean debacle, because they had endorsed Joseph's appointment. The Sadducees faded away. Even the Hillelites began to flee. Summary court martials handed down death sentences quickly and dispassionately.

The Sicarii, under Simon ben Giora, now entered the city and demanded even more thorough purges. John of Gischala opposed them, and tried to oust them. The city was finally divided between them, by agreement, with frequent skirmishes between their men.

Vespasian, taking delight in Jerusalem's violent infighting, meanwhile proceeded in calm and orderly fashion to garrison mixed cities and to plant the Roman standard in areas in which the rebel forces were sparse. Instead of descending on Jerusalem like a deluge, he trickled slowly, almost surreptitiously in its direction, hoping that the dissension among the rebels would eventually bring him an effortless victory. He also had private ambitions. Nero was dead (68), and Vespasian had no wish to jeopardize his own selection by wasting forces he might need to press his claim in Rome.

In 69, Vespasian was summoned to the capital and proclaimed emperor. He then ordered his son Titus to mount an all-out campaign in Judea. In the spring of 70, Titus besieged Jerusalem, but it was not until August of that year that he captured the city. The rebels, now reunited, held out fiercely. However, because previously, during the

war between them, the city's grain stores had been destroyed, Titus' great ally now was famine. His forces fought for Jerusalem, district by district, street by street, house by house, from the lower city to the upper city, from the Temple's outer courtyard to its inner courtyard, and, when the Temple fell, the last Kanaim held out in the Herodian palace, and then the fighting continued in the subterranean cistern network, the rebels' last escape.

All this time, four "Jews from foreign courts," distortions of the classical image, were at Titus' side: The apostate, Tiberius Alexander, served as his chief of staff; King Agrippa II commanded a large auxiliary army; Berenice, his sister, was Titus' mistress and hopeful of becoming Empress of Rome when Vespasian would be succeeded by his son; Joseph ben Matthias, once the revolutionary governor of Rome, now served as the historian of Titus' campaign.

Guilt-ridden, Josephus Flavius, as he was now called, extolled in his works both the rebels and their conqueror, Judaism and Roman culture. The times were inopportune for paradoxes. The valor of Jerusalem's defenders only increased the interest of the Roman aristocrats in a faith that inspired such fortitude. Rumor that his own family had been infested by sabbath observers alarmed Emperor Domitian (81-96), who established heresy tribunals and ordered violent purges of all crypto Jews and Judaizers. Josephus Flavius is believed to have perished at this time, his works indicting him as a Judaizer.

CONTINUAL REBELLION

Even when the Temple collapsed on the ninth day of the Jewish month of Ab in 70, a date still annually commemorated in Jewry with fasting and prayer, Jewish resistance continued for several years from three Dead Sea fortresses, the last of which, Massada, was taken by the Romans only in 73. That same year an abortive rebellion in Libya by a fugitive Sicarii force of two thousand men, set the entire empire on guard.

An Israeli historian, M. Avi-Yonah, assessing the factors favorable and adverse to Judean success, offers this explanation of the revolt's failure. Although large Roman

forces were tied down by police duty in Gaul and elsewhere on the Continent, more than half of her forces
were in the East to prevent possible revolts and to prepare
for further conquests. Roman invasion of the Sudan was
called off when the Judean uprising erupted. The Roman
presence, albeit small in numbers, discouraged potential
Judean allies and probably prevented Alexandrian Jewry
from decisive action, such as sabotaging the harbor and
preventing the delivery of provisions to the Roman forces.
This is the reason also that a Jewish people of seven
million in the Roman empire, and nearly two million of
this number in the East, could only marshal 25,000 warriors to defend Jerusalem. Hostile Romanized cities located
between Judea and other Jewish population centers cut off
Jewish reinforcements and prevented co-ordinated Judean
action. Above all, under Herod the Judeans had turned to
quietism and, with the revolt erupting suddenly, they had
no time for adequate training.

However, the Jews learned from their errors.

Nearly fifty years later, another Jewish revolt erupted,
spreading across all of Rome's Asian and African possessions. It was triggered by Emperor Trajan's (98-117) decision to consummate a triumphant life by a great push
eastward against the Parthian empire. He seized Armenia
and portions of Mesopotamia in 114, the tiny Jewish
enclave Adiabene in 115, and after penetrating Babylonia,
he believed he had achieved what all Romans since Julius
Caesar had attempted unsuccessfully.

Unfortunately for Trajan, the Babylonian Jews con-
trolled crucial defenses in the line of his further advance.
They had home rule under Parthia and fought ferociously,
as no other people in the domain, to defend her. Their
troops clashed head on with Trajan's legions; their irregulars fanned out into the pacified regions to harass his
auxiliaries.

The emperor pulled out of Parthia, but even his retreat
was enveloped in catastrophe. Rebellion flared wherever
there were Jewish communities. It spread to Cyprus and
to Africa. It was an astonishing eruption by a stateless
people. Rome's leading commanders rushed to douse the
conflagration. Had there been a Judean state, with a central

military command, the Jews might have brought the empire down.

Jewish statehood was briefly restored by the residual Judean Jewish population in a revolt in 132 during the reign of Emperor Hadrian (117-138), who had succeeded Trajan. The revolt's ideologian was Rabbi Akiba, one of the great teachers of the law. He had traveled indefatigably through the Diaspora, including Babylonia, for several years preceding the event, apparently to enlist support. The military genius of the rebellion was Bar Kosiba, whom the people affectionately and hopefully named Bar Kochba, the Morning Star. Before his revolt was put down three years later, he had re-established the authority of Jewish government over several hundred Judean towns and fortresses.

The rebellion crushed, Hadrian cracked down on all Jewry. He was determined to dispose of the Jews for all time. He forbade instruction in Jewish law and custom and ordered a mass slaughter of all teachers. A group of ten teachers of the law, including Rabbi Akiba, was put to death publicly by particularly exquisite torture. Jewish history calls them The Ten Killed by Government, which suggests that it preferred to remember them as victims of political tyranny, not as martyrs, a Christian concept.

Indeed, a tribunal of jurists which met secretly in Lydda considered and prescribed martyrdom only when the alternative to death was compulsory idolatry, adultery, or murder. It implied furthermore that where no disavowal of cardinal principle is involved, one may dissimulate his faith to save his life.

Having rejected the doctrine of the Pauline Christ, who bears mankind's penance in his wounds, they could not emulate him. Affirmation of life, here on earth, as God's supreme gift to man, has always been a cornerstone of Jewish tradition.

Chapter FIVE

AGE OF
THE
APOCALYPSE

JESUS EXPIRED ON THE CROSS FOUR DECADES BEFORE THE DE-struction of the Temple. He had made no special impact on his times. His passing went almost unnoticed beyond the circles of his close devotees. His only mention in contemporary Jewish records is a brief paragraph in Josephus Flavius, probably interpolated by a latter-day Christian editor. Other Jewish mention of him dates no earlier than the end of the first century. Herod and the procurators had conditioned Jerusalem to the horrible wails of Jewish patriots expiring in Golgotha. Jesus was only another Jew on the cross.

Speaking the Aramaic vernacular, he had been one of many baptists and healers that addressed themselves to the am haaretz, the unlettered peasants and fishermen, who comprehended nothing of the ideological debate among the Jerusalem factions, brooded sullenly about the diverse mishaps that befall man during his brief tenure on earth, bore an abiding hostility for the city, and felt imposed upon by foreign soldiery and patriot alike.

Like the Essenes, Jesus offered otherworldly salvation, and unlike them he welcomed everyone into the redemptive fraternity, even the publicans who used the rod against tax delinquents. He wore on his garments the fringes of the pious, and avowed that he had not come to alter the law; his Sermon on the Mount reaffirmed Hillel and the Book of Leviticus.

Some of his maxims, however, were peculiar to no previous tradition. Hillel had warned against demanding from man more than his nature would yield. Jesus, conversely,

85

counseling "turn the other cheek," when Jewry was being goaded by Pilate, proposed that man transcend his nature.

He taught, "Submit yourself to every ordinance of man for the Lord's sake as supreme." Hillel had subjected all law to the constitutional test; Jesus would treat even the procurator's caprice as divine-ordered fate. Hillel eased the admittance of heathen into Jewry by summarizing the law in a single maxim. Jesus, closer to the Shammaite view, taught, "Give not that which is holy unto the dogs, neither cast ye your pearls before swine, lest they trample under their feet and turn again and rend you."

The record shows that the Pharisees' sanhedrin had no competence in capital offenses, that it was deeply divided, that Jesus' own views ran the full scale of these differences, that he shared their contempt for the Sadducees, and that the leading Pharisee Gamliel twice defended the Christians from criminal indictment by the Sadducees.

The sanhedrin that tried Jesus was headed by the High Priest. Any tribunal so chaired was composed of Sadducees and functioned as a mere rubber stamp for the procurator who named the High Priest. Tacitus, an impartial witness in this circumstance, puts the blame for the crucifixion squarely on Pilate.

The clue lies in a sign which the Roman soldiery had placed at the foot of the cross with the derisive epithet "King of the Jews," a claim or legend which would indeed disturb a Roman official on guard against pretenders to the throne. Any gaunt figure followed by a mob sufficed to arouse Pilate's suspicion. He had already been three years in Judea. Rome's dossier no doubt was filled with malicious rumors by contenders for his post. He had not quite abided by the emperor's shrewd advice, "Shear them (the satellite peoples), but do not skin them." Pilate skinned them mercilessly. Like Eichmann, he was a cautious and precise man. Never knowing when and for what actions he might be summoned home, he prepared a detailed alibi. Hence, he washed his hands in public of the blood he had spilt. He was indeed recalled several years later, in 36, for having ordered an unwarranted massacre of the Samarians. By that time the case of Jesus had probably been forgotten in Rome.

PAUL'S ACCOMMODATIONS

Except for the belief in Jesus as the Messiah, there was little that was radically contrary to Judaism in the teachings and practices of the Christ sectarians until the appearance of Paul (died approximately 67), who reordered their relations with Jew and heathen.

Jewish tradition divided universal history into three eras: The era of chaos which preceded Genesis, was followed by the era of law, which would ultimately be succeeded by the Messianic era when law itself would wither. But the Jews had no desire to precipitate that era. Jochanan ben Zakkai, a Hillelite teacher and Paul's contemporary, offered this counsel: "If you are planting, and are suddenly told that the Messiah had arrived, continue with your labors and finish them, and only then go out to welcome him."

Paul preached that the Messiah already having come, law and deeds had become null, and henceforth man was measured by his faith alone and governed by God's grace. In the Jews' view, grace was man's reward for his obedience to God's law, and deeds were the measure of that obedience. The Pauline doctrine removed the factor of reciprocity from the God-man relationship, and threw man back into the Greek limbo where he was tossed around by capricious gods. The first consequence of Paul's teachings was a doctrinal split among the followers of the Nazarene. The Judean followers, like their master Jesus himself, upheld the Hebrew law and abided by its commandments. Paul courted the Diaspora Jews, who were finding the commandments burdensome, and the heathens among whom conversions multiplied when he abolished the rite of circumcision. So he toured the Diaspora to gather proselytes, Judean Nazarenes followed him, like a "lie brigade" in modern elections, to challenge his version of Jesus' teachings. James, brother of Jesus, was among them. "What does it profit my brethren," James asked, "though a man say he has faith, and has not works? Can faith save him? By works man is justified, not by faith alone." This did not deter Paul. He transformed a small Hebrew cult of Populist origin into a mystery faith attractive to sophis-

ticated urbanites. A Diaspora Jew, he was familiar with the Diaspora habit of accommodating Judaism to heathen comprehension, and of absorbing Hellenistic elements into Judaism. This knowledge served him well. His doctrine of resurrection offered personal salvation, and was entirely unrelated to the Hebrew concept. It was an outright adoption of the pagan myth of the Godhead come unto earth, who dies only to return, and by means of the sacrament transmits the gift of eternal life to elect mortals.

Paul's missionary efforts no doubt benefited from events in Judea. The Jews' heroic defense of Jerusalem against formidable imperial forces exicted Romans' interest in the Torah from Zion. This was particularly true of the Roman aristocracy. It also aroused similar interest among God-seekers in other cities of the imperial realm. The Judeans were too preoccupied with their struggle for survival to solicit proselytes. Paul and his disciples, however, presented their doctrine as a Judean doctrine. To the uninitiated heathen, this was the real Torah from Zion.

Not even Paul's doctrine managed to agitate the Judea of that day. The country and its people were preoccupied with graver matters, issues of survival. The Nazarenes were a peripheral sect. Their intramural schisms were of no interest. It is for this reason that we have no eyewitness account of the Crucifixion, and are not even certain of the authenticity of all that is attributed to Paul. The first record of the movement is of Christian origin, the Gospel of St. John, which was written some fifty years after the Crucifixion. The first mention in the Talmud dates back to the second century. If the movement had made any impact, there would have been contemporary mention in Jewish record. The contention that the record was deliberately censored is contradicted on two scores. First, if it were, all mention would have been deleted; second, the Bible demonstrates how meticulously the Jews had always recorded the presence in their midst of heretics and heresies. It was in the second century that Christianity first compelled the attention of the Jews. It distressed them as a gnostic faith, and because some of its practitioners allegedly took to informing against the Jews to the Roman authorities.

THE TALMUD

Jewry had suffered several traumatic shocks: the Fall of Jerusalem (70), an abortive revolt of the Diaspora Jewries (115), the collapse of Bar Kochba's revolt (132), and the Hadrian persecutions. It had to hammer out the instruments for survival without a central territory. Previous experience offered no instruction. Babylonia transplanted the Jews en masse from Judea, and preserved them as a compact, territorially concentrated people. The second dispersion, most of it voluntary, was far-flung, and began before the fall of Jerusalem. Judea, although stripped of administrative self-governance, was still the Jews' spiritual center. The Temple in its midst seemed to endow Judea's pronouncements with supreme authority. Now the Temple was in ruins.

The initiative in dealing with the crisis was taken by a Hillelite teacher of law, Jochanan ben Zakkai. According to legend, he escaped from the besieged capital in a coffin, to obtain from Titus permission to establish an academy (yeshiva) for the teaching of law at Jabne, a town between the seaports of Jaffa and Ashdod. It is possible, conversely, that Jabne was merely an internment camp for politically harmless Judean scholars. Whatever the circumstance, Rabbi Jochanan ben Zakkai's plea was granted. He was a known advocate of peace with Rome, and to permit the Jews to live "in accordance with our laws" was an ancient tradition dating to Julius Caesar. His academy also functioned as sanhedrin (court).

History credits the Jabne academy with launching the compilation of the Talmud, one of the most extraordinary undertakings in intellectual history. The work was probably initiated a century earlier by Hillel, just before the Common Era. It was completed only in the sixth century.

The written law had been Jewry's counterpoint to Hellenism. The Talmud had been its counterpoise to Christianity. That is why it was frequently interdicted by the Popes and burned before jeering multitudes in the public squares of Europe many centuries before Hitler's book-burnings. It consists of two essential sections: the Mishnah and the Gemara.

The Mishnah is the Jewish oral law. Its editors are called tanaim. Its formulations are so succinct that even before the last generation of tanaim had passed away, some of it had become obscure. Trusting the jurists' erudition, it does not cite the constitutional, Biblical basis for each law, and although presenting conflicting juridical opinions, does not present the line of argument advanced to defend them.

The amoraim, who succeeded the tanaim, undertook the task of explicating, elucidating, and amending the Mishnah which lasted into the sixth century. This portion of the Talmud is called Gemara. It is not all law, however. It digresses into politics, science, history, and religion by artfully constructing on a single Biblical phrase a pyramid of myth, fact, and speculation pointing toward a lesson in ethics or faith. Inseparably interwoven into the Gemara, this last homiletic element is called aggada or midrash, and its primary source was not the academy and sanhedrin, but the synagogue, where it was presented as sermons. The method of midrashic interpretation was adopted by the Church fathers for their polemics with Jew and heathen, and is to this day the basis of all homiletics in church and synagogue.

The Talmud legislated over a wide range of human preoccupation and endeavor. It was, first of all, civil law governing the affairs of an economically diversified society. From Babylonia to Palestine, the Jews were engaged in agriculture, crafts, and commerce. They were farmers, date and wine growers, producers of sesame and olive oil, and traders between east and west. However, they held some occupations in low esteem: They were neither camel drivers, nor shepherds, perhaps because the latter was the pursuit of predatory Arab nomads; they deprecated the jeweler, cosmetician, and beautician for engaging in frivolous, wasteful labor, but the construction worker, shoemaker, blacksmith, and carpenter were in high regard as indispensable to society.

Accordingly, the tanaim and amoraim were men from all walks of life, including, among the earlier tanaim, Jochanan, a cobbler by occupation, and among the amoraim, Abba Areeka, a philanthropist and landowner, Isaac,

a blacksmith, and Simon Resh-Lakish who was posted outside the ring in a circus to restrain animals that broke loose. They provided that the day wage must compensate for a worker's time from the moment he leaves home for his labor; that he must not, without consent, be transferred from the work for which he had been hired to other labor that might be injurious to his health. They listed as "grave transgressions—stealing, or even withholding wages overnight, imposing one's chores on others, and treating (subordinates or the poor) superciliously." They stressed the dignity of labor: "as craftsmen need not rise before teachers of the law . . . he who subsists on his own labor, precedes the pious . . . skin animals in the market place to earn your wage, but do not boast I am a priest, an aristocrat."

Compelled by economic realities to lift the ban on interest loans, they adopted vigorous measures against usury which "is like a snakebite, the swelling appears later," and admonished the courts to be wary of the testimony of loan brokers. The church, faced later with the same conflict, preserved Christian virtue by compelling the Jews to perform as society's moneylenders.

THE CONTINUAL PROCESSION

Calamity could not abate the spontaneity of the Jewish people's response to life. The Talmud records some of their richness and diversity.

As Jewish society evolved from rural to urban, woman lost some of her equality, but nonetheless retained sufficient dominion to puzzle the amoraim, some of whom spoke in her praise, fewer in her disparagement, although the consensus seemed to be that "women are a separate race." The Talmud reveals that cosmetics and opulent dress were the fashion, and that women resorted to birth-control pills to preserve their figures.

To "avoid sin," marriages were contracted early; the usual age was eighteen, and engagements were earlier still, prearranged by parents, sometimes assisted by marriage brokers. The amoraim warned, however, against forcing a marriage before the young couple had become acquainted and without their consent. Social status was a major con-

sideration, but the gauge was learning, not wealth. "Sell all your possessions to marry the daughter of a scholar, or to marry your daughter to a scholar."

Spinsterhood was a blight: "When your daughter has reached the age of consent, release your slave and have him marry her." Although a European rabbi was to legislate against polygamy much later, it had virtually ceased by this time, for it was too expensive and too disturbing to household relations.

St. Jerome (Hieronymus) reports that all Jewish homes had bulging bookcases. The Jewish elite knew Greek, Latin, and Persian, in addition to Hebrew and the Aramaic vernacular. Elementary education was universal, all children were taught the Bible, ten per cent of the elementary school population went on to high school where they studied Mishnah, and one per cent went on to the yeshiva (academy) and studied Gemara. Twice a year in Babylonia assemblies were convened for adults seeking to refresh their learning.

SYNTHESIS

The Talmud's overriding concern was not to merely legislate and govern Jewry in its mundane concerns, but to preserve it as a living witness to the validity of the Jewish ethic in a turbulent world.

The Mishnah is a record of the extremes in Jewish reaction to the calamities that befell them in the century and a half beginning with the Fall of Jerusalem. During its residence at Jabne, the sanhedrin tended toward introversion, the natural response of a vigorous people to its defeat. Hadrian dispersed the Jabne sanhedrin; diminished in numbers by the persecutions, it later reassembled at Usha, a resigned body, some of its members confused by the doctrines they had opposed at such great peril, and plagued by doubts.

Had the earlier introversionist attitude prevailed, the Jews might have become mere sectarians, have steadily diminished in number, and eventually have faced oblivion. Had the later confusion prevailed, the Jews might have dissipated through self-doubt. The proponents of both extreme views were fortunately in the minority. The middle

of the road majority, opposed to assimilation and segregation alike, favored resumption of the dialogue with Rome, this being in an ancient tradition.

The xenophobic period produced laws forbidding Jews to be attended by heathen barbers and physicians, and to purchase oil from the heathen. The first had its precedent in Roman legislation, and was probably dictated by concern for the safety of the Jews in heathen cities in which mob violence had become frequent since mad Caligula's day. The second law—perhaps economic-protectionist, to sustain the price level of Jewish oil—was passed in the later stages of the Judean rebellion when Vespasian was welcomed by the heathen population in mixed cities.

Yet even extremist Jewish legislation was not devoid of the traditional ethic. Wild beasts were not to be sold to the heathen, who pitted them against war captives, and no Jew was to work on the construction of stadia in which such performances were staged.

None of this discriminatory legislation outlived its impulse; a second generation of tanaim, and amoraim after them, rescinded it. The church, one and one-half centuries later, adopted similar laws against Jewry, which endured, however, into modern times. The Jewish law had been the excessive defensive response of an alarmed minority; church law served the coercive purpose of a majority endowed with police power.

Even when feeling ran high against Rome, a majority of the sanhedrin voted to include in the sacred canon two works patently in the Greco-Roman literary tradition: *The Song of Songs,* perhaps the first direct erotic statement in Hebrew literature, and *Ecclesiastes,* a work in bland Epicurean style. The rabbis allegorized *The Song of Songs* as the passion between God and the Jewish people, and presented *Ecclesiastes* as Solomon's mature comprehension of God. Even as allegories, the two works are good examples of the synthesis of Greek form and Jewish purpose, and their canonization may be judged as an almost demonstrative vote for continued Greco-Roman dialogue. Divested of rabbinical exegeses, *The Song of Songs* celebrates passion, but it also celebrates constancy, thus rejecting Greek unbridled pleasure and

Pauline mortification of the flesh. Although "full of contradictions," *Ecclesiastes* impugns two essential Greek ideals. It is an Epicurean's admission that pleasure falls short of its promise, and that knowledge, explored to its extreme frontiers, is found equally wanting. Several brief passages in which *Ecclesiastes* reaffirms his Jewish faith are probably posthumous interpolations. It remains essentially a work of skepticism, but its inclusion is triumph for Jewish synthesis, and for Jewry's tolerance at a time when the ashes of defeat were bitter on the people's tongue.

NEW LIBERALISM

The third century amoraim in Palestine revived dialogue with other cultures and freewheeling debate inside Jewry. The lead was taken by two brothers-in-law, Jochanan bar Nafchah and Simon Resh Lakish, chairman and vice-chairman, respectively, of the academy in Tiberias. Both defied the taboos of predecessors.

Jochanan formally sanctioned the universal study of Greek; men required it for political and commercial reasons, he explained; women, because it somehow enhanced their charm. He boldly opposed Roman rule, and just as boldly coupled Greek philosophy and Jewish faith as twin gifts from God. Resh Lakish went beyond him. He challenged the historicity of the Book of Job, and called it only a parable. He scorned the belief in angels and evil spirits as superstition of Persian origin, which had by then won over even some of the amoraim. He challenged the inviolability of legal precedent, contending that his own generation, tested by persecutions, was more meritorious than its predecessors.

One or two generations earlier such suppositions would have been refuted as rank heresy, but Jewry had now returned to its tradition that ideas are to be contested, not banished, and that debate must precede rejection. There was amicable association and calm discourse with Christian writers. The theologian Origen (185-254?) whose polemics had none of the bitterness of earlier Christian argument, had moved from Alexandria to Caesarea, and visited the amoraim who instructed him in Hebrew.

The relaxed dialogue was terminated by Christianity one century later; since the Roman emperor, Constantine I (280?-337), had become a Christian, it could rest its case on force. Hieronymus, later St. James (340-420?), also took instruction from the amoraim, but in secret, apparently because association with Jews had by then become suspect. He became sufficiently proficient to translate the Bible into Latin. This did not deter him, however, from castigating the Jews as "this unhappy people, deserving no compassion." That the amoraim taught him, although they could anticipate his purpose, is a measure of their passion for dialogue and confrontation.

The tanaim established the circumstances for the liberalism of the amoraim. Haunted by calamity, and amidst a dispirited Jewry, they labored to re-establish morality and law, which seemed a hopeless task. Theirs was not a time for laissez-faire. The amoraim were removed from the traumatic experiences in which the compilation of the Talmud began. Jewry was again a people ruled by law because of the stern labors of the tanaim.

RABBIS AND REBELS

Their predecessors, the tanaim, were entrapped in a maze of moral dilemmas. One of these was how to deal with the Judean rebel bands, an admixture of professional outlaws and professional rebels, who erupted periodically without consulting responsible opinion, and imperiled each time Palestinian Jewry's considerable home rule which included an independent judiciary and executive, the latter headed by a patriarch, or Nassi.

It was the rebel custom to strike when Rome was occupied elsewhere. But there was a sufficient Roman police force on hand to retaliate by shutting down all the Jewish institutions. One such occasion occurred in 161 when Rome was embroiled in another war with Parthia. The rebels struck; the Romans promptly dispersed the sanhedrin. The Jews were divided. Some favored formal and vigorous denunciation of the rebels; others argued that Jewry retain the state of mind of a captive nation until its right of access to Jerusalem was restored. Three tanaim, discussing the issue in an inner circle, touched on the

95

merits of Roman rule. Rabbi Judah ben Ilai cited Rome's beneficences in Judea—the bridges, the city squares, and the public baths—to which Rabbi Simon bar Yocha angrily replied that the Romans had done all these for their own gain, that they took pleasure in their baths, collected tolls for the use of their bridges, and enjoyed watching the harlots promenade in the public squares. Rabbi Jose ben Chalafta held his tongue. But the conversation leaked out. Rabbi Jose, called the Prudent, was banished; Rabbi Judah rewarded for his loyalty to Rome; and Rabbi Simon, sentenced to death in absentia, hid in a cave for thirteen years. In commemoration of Rabbi Simon's death, orthodox Jews to this day maintain an all-night vigil once a year at his tomb in Tiberias.

In the year 200, Rome was involved in another inconclusive war with the Parthians. Jewish guerrillas, as was their custom under such circumstance, swung into action. Two sanhedrin members accepted the Roman warrant to ferret out the outlaws. The collaborators were by coincidence sons of men involved in the earlier episode—Rabbi Ishmael, son of Jose the Prudent, and Rabbi Eleazar, son of imprudent Simon bar Yocha. Rabbi Eleazar later claimed that he had rendered a public service; he had cleared "the vineyard of thorns," because the men were common outlaws; and Rabbi Ishmael whimpered that refusal to collaborate with Rome would have cost his life. The first was reminded that he should have "left it to the Lord of the vineyard to extirpate the thorns himself," and the second was told that he could have fled as his father had fled in Hadrian's days.

ESTABLISHING AUTHORITY

One of the marvels of Jewish history is how the post-Hadrian sanhedrin, founded at Usha in 138, established its universal writ. A self-constituted body, without enforcement powers, a high court and legislature composed of amnestied repatriates, it was largely a state of mind. It was supreme authority only because Jewry chose to regard it as such.

It survived numerous crises: periodic intrusions by Roman authority, judiciary-executive tensions; and a

threat of separatism from Babylonian Jewry. The executive powers were in the hands of the Patriarch who tried to impose his will on the court. He alone had definite status and function, as Jewry's intercessor before Rome and the latter's liaison with Jewry.

The Usha jurists resolved the conflict between the judiciary and executive by naming the patriarch Simon ben Gamliel, chairman of the tribunal's three-man praesidium. Conflict was not completely avoided, as he insisted on absolute precedence for the chairman, which the proposed compromise had not intended. His son, Judah I, who succeeded him in 165, was a man of austere habit. A liberal legislator and an authoritarian executive, he converted the sanhedrin into an instrument of his will. He also was the ranking jurist of his day, dedicated to a monumental task: He revised, reordered, and supplemented the numerous earlier and incomplete compilations of oral law, and produced one unified Mishnah, thus completing the work of codification begun, at the latest, when the Jabne sanhedrin was established.

He was succeeded by men of lesser intellectual and moral caliber, but equally authoritarian. They comported themselves in grand manner, were supported by a voluntary universal tax, and continually sought to impose themselves upon the sanhedrin. When they had their state, the Jews bristled against their rulers, and put law above government. Now all world Jewry supported a patriarchate that comported itself with regal pomp, and sometimes behaved as if it were the embodiment of the law. Greco-Roman grandeur had apparently had its effect on the Diaspora.

The challenge from Babylonia was not unanticipated. Its Jews were the third largest nationality group in their land, concentrated in a region 68 miles long, on the Eastern Euphrates, which was virtually a Jewish state, and in command of key waterways and fortresses.

When the sanhedrin dispersed during the Hadrian persecutions, an ambitious former Palestinian, Rabbi Chanania, saw his chance and established a sanhedrin in Babylonia. He refused to dissolve it even after the Palestinian institution was re-established at Usha, and was vigorously

endorsed by his exilarch, who perhaps hoped to become the prince of all Jewry. For a while the two tribunals published conflicting religious instructions, which had all the elements of an East-West schism, the kind that later split the Christian church. The results might have been disastrous, with scores of sanhedrin springing up, each publishing its enactments and spawning its sect. Rabbi Simon ben Gamliel who served as Palestinian patriarch for a quarter of a century (140-165) carried the issue directly to Babylonian Jewry which overwhelmingly endorsed Usha as the supreme authority. Thus, it was a struggle not alone between the sanhedrin and the usurper tribunal, but also between the patriarch and the exilarch as to who would be prince of all Jewry. The struggle between the latter was sometimes so bitter that two tanaim bitterly remarked, "The Messiah will not come until the two princely houses in Israel, the House of the Patriarch and the House of the Exilarch, will have passed away."

THE "PRINCES"

The arrogance of the exilarchs in Babylonia eclipsed the haughtiness of the Palestinian patriarchs. Sometimes gross and unlettered men, empowered to tax Jews, they struck the costly posture of oriental potentates. Their retinue, from councilor to menial servant, bore the exilarch's crest on its garments. They were carried through the streets on litters, and surrounded by an ostentatiously uniformed armed guard; they traveled in stately carriages, were awakened in the morning and retired at night to string music, and mercilessly ordered lashes for anyone who seemed insufficiently reverential toward them. The post was hereditary. The imperial court confirmed but did not appoint the exilarch, and intruded only when the succession was contested.

The exilarch alone appointed the Jewish judiciary, which nonetheless was remarkably independent. The judiciary's sovereign conduct led to frequent conflicts with the exilarch, thus re-enacting the historical tensions between priest and prophet, ruler and scribe. The law came from the academies, besides which functioned the courts which dispensed it. The Palestinian sanhedrin, however, retained

the exclusive right to determine the calendar of religious festivals, a major factor in unifying Jewry.

The first two great Babylonian academies were founded in 219, others were established in quick succession almost immediately thereafter. The founders and deans were Babylonians who studied in Palestine under Judah I. The Babylonian academies became vigorous collaborators in expounding and elucidating the Mishnah through Gemara. Thus, Babylonian Jewry, through the amoraim, gradually and easily succeeded to the rank of Jewry's spiritual center when Palestinian Jewry faded away in the fourth century, under Christian persecution. Produced under less adverse conditions, the Babylonian Talmud is more voluminous and complete than the Palestinian, which is called the Jerusalem Talmud.

Babylonia became embroiled in religious civil wars between the Parthians and the neo-Persians, between the syncretists who absorbed Christian and other foreign elements into their faith, and the Magi, who were Parsi purists. Jewry discovered, as governments alternated, that the exilarch, far from being an effective pleader for his people, was sometimes a highly compromised figure himself; as a ranking government official, he was inevitably a party to the larger conflict.

A new type of Joseph at Pharaoh's court, or interfaith good-will ambassador, was required. The role fell to the learned amoraim, the teacher of the law, and rabbis have ever since everywhere, including contemporary America, performed in similar fashion. This type came to be called shtadlan, a Hebrew word which suggests a compassionate volunteer lobbyist. A Babylonian shtadlan had considerable bargaining power at his disposal. The government solicited the good will of Babylonian Jewry, strategically located and important in commerce and defense, and of the Jewish populated Greco-Roman cities from which the Romans staged their invasions, and which were also the first to be invaded by the Parthians and neo-Persians.

"DUAL ALLEGIANCE"

The strategic role of shtadlanim in the governmental change-overs in the mid-third century fell to the founders

of the first two great academies or yeshivot, Abba Areecha (175-247), called plain Rav or Master, and Samuel (180-257), whose name was often prefixed by Mar, the Aramaic for Master. Rav was the shtadlan at the court of Artabenus IV, (211-226), the last Parthian monarch; Samuel was the confidante of Shabur I (241-272), second in the neo-Persian Assanide line.

The Magi who helped the neo-Persians take power in 226 engaged in unceasing persecution of all nonbelievers —Greco-Roman heathens, Christians, and Jews.

When Shabur ascended the throne, he sternly restrained their excesses. Samuel was an authority on Jewish civil law, Rav on religious law. The latter was rigorously opposed to all contact with the fire-worshipers and advocated self-segregation. "Even a single thing learned from the Magi merits death," was his dictum in the stern tradition of the school of Shammai.

Samuel, a physician, astronomer, and student of Persian culture, established the principle that "the law of the land is binding law." The brevity of Samuel's principle and time have blurred its precise meaning. Did he advise that the Jews defer to the law of the land, even if it conflicts with the principles of their faith? Whatever Samuel's intent, his formula became indispensable to the Diaspora which cited it repeatedly through the centuries in defense from allegations of disloyalty leveled against the Jews by heathen, Christian, and Muslim.

Because of his role as apologist for neo-Persian culture, Samuel was nicknamed Arioch, the Aryan. Like some contemporary American Jewish spokesmen, he was anxious about interfaith relations and the public image of the Jew. He was an egregious abstainer when all Babylonian Jewry went into mourning on learning that Shabur's soldiery, sweeping through the Roman-ruled lands, had massacred 12,000 Jews in Asia Minor on the unlikely pretext that they had taken up arms to defend detested Rome. Samuel, accepting at face value the government's version, argued that the Jews "should not have resisted" the neo-Persian forces.

Samuel was thus the initiator of a policy of extreme accommodation to the ruling powers. Rabbi Huna (219-

299), his junior, maintained that "being in Babylonia is the same as being in the Holy Land," although he later implied a distinction by having his remains interred in Palestine. And Huna's contemporary, Judah ben Ezekiel (220-299) went even further, contending that the Return to Palestine under Ezra had been a grievous error.

The Babylonian Jewry in the third century opened the floodgates of a debate that has never ceased. Their third century origin is transparent in the issues so frequently debated between the Prime Minister of Israel and American Jewish spokesmen—whether there is a difference in the degree of their Jewish fulfillment between an Israeli and an American Jew?

The Jews have taken a middle course throughout the centuries. They have never forfeited their devotion to Palestine, and hope for an eventual Return, but they have sought their spiritual guidance from whichever center, at the given moment, was supreme in scholarship. They no more assumed Samuel's posture of acquiescence in governmental policy toward Jews than Rav's of closing his mind to other cultures. They sustained their dialogue with others and enriched their own. It was not the rabbi, but the church that eventually terminated the dialogue between the Jews and Christianity.

Constantine the Great (280?-337), the first Christian Emperor of Rome, vacillated before yielding to the bishops' demands for legislation against nonbelievers. His Greco-Roman conditioning had disposed him toward religious tolerance. He published in 315 his first anti-Jewish legislation. After that, for the next two centuries, a stream of synod rulings and royal edicts raised the walls against the Jews progressively higher. Intermarriage with the Jews, even feasting at their tables, was forbidden. Compelled to surrender their slaves, the basis of the agricultural economy in those days, the Jews had no choice but to also sell their lands. The inadmissibility of Jewish testimony against a Christian barred the courts to them. These prohibitions were at first perhaps more often breached than observed, but their purpose was clear. A total war, the strategy of which was to segregate a people historically accustomed to deal with many nations and cultures. The

intent was to besiege the Jews and drive them stir-crazy until they surrendered their faith.

The finest Christian minds were committed to this purpose. St. Augustine (354-430) proclaimed the purpose, and provided the motivation for all future persecution, in his pronouncement, "Let them bear the mark of Cain till they turn to Christ." Christian conquest of Rome was hollow without Christian conquest of Jewry. The empire soon divided into an Eastern Empire, its residence Byzantium (Constantinople) and a Western Empire, its residence Rome. The majority of Greco-Roman Jewry lived under Byzantium, and was beset by its ancient Greco-Egyptian foes. In Rome, still warmed by the religious tolerance of its heathen days, Pope Gregory I proclaimed, "I forbid you to molest the Jews or to place upon them restrictions not imposed by the established law," which was sufficiently restrictive, however.

The "Aryan" heresy in Christianity was bitterly persecuted by the Church, because it refused to equate God and Jesus. This experience made its lands more tolerant to the Jews. They were still relatively safe also in the territories of the unconverted pagans. The Goths, the Huns, and the Vandals, albeit rapacious conquerors, bore down no more heavily on the Jews than on others. It is to these islands of sovereignty from church domination that the Jews turned for respite.

The Jews were not passive martyrs. They struck back whenever occasion presented itself. In 351, when Palestine was the stage of a Roman assault on Persia, a surprise midnight raid on the Roman garrison in Sepphoris provided the initial arms for a Jewish rebellion, which Rome took more than a year to subdue.

The Jews, fighting for their lives, were the best soldiers among the forces under Clovis, King of the Franks, who held back the Catholic advance at Arles in 508. In 537, they held Naples against the Catholics when everyone else was prepared to surrender the city. In North Africa, they joined the Vandals against the Christian forces. In the autumn of 608, they erupted violently in Antioch, and a large Roman force was required to subdue them.

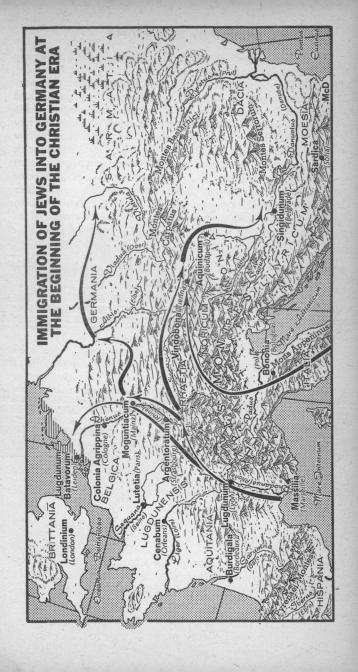

IMMIGRATION OF JEWS INTO GERMANY AT THE BEGINNING OF THE CHRISTIAN ERA

In 614, a Persian division which broke through Lebanon to Palestine's frontiers was welcomed, by prearrangement, by Jewish guerrillas who escorted it to Jerusalem. The Persians held the country for fourteen years. They reneged on their pledge to re-establish the Jewish state, and treated the Jews as a conquered people, not as an ally. The embittered Jews succumbed to specious Byzantine promises, and when Emperor Heraclius' troops advanced toward Palestine's borders, Jewish guerrillas welcomed them, by prearrangement, and entered Jerusalem with them. The priests, the bishops, and the monks raised loud protest. Heraclius, who had given his pledge to the Jews, readily accepted the clergy's assurance that there was nothing absolution could not repair.

Religious fanaticism in the Christian world was matched by religious fanaticism in Persian-ruled lands. The Christian world had its Catholic clergy; the Persians had their Magi priests. There were frequent persecutions, closure of academies, and dispersal of Jewish children to the Magi faith. Yet there was, however, a great and essential difference between the Christian and Persian lands. The Jews suffered from Persian relapses; but the Magi were not always at the helm, not always unrestrained, and their persecution was directed not primarily at the Jews but at all non-Magis. It was a cold war in which the Jews were caught up with all humanity in that part of the world.

EASTWARD MIGRATION

Diverse religio-social reform movements tried to impose themselves on the Persian empire from the mid-fifth century through much of the sixth century. The Jews were often compelled to take up arms to defend themselves from the general licentiousness. Late in the fifth or early in the sixth century, a Jewish force, led by an exuberant young exilarch, Mar-Zutra II, seized the district of Mechuza in Babylonia, and for seven years ruled it as a sovereign Jewish territory. It became Jewry's citadel against the religio-Communist revolution of Mazdak whose doctrines on sex relations struck at Jewish law and family custom.

In the first half of the fifth century, many Palestinian

Jews fled to Babylonia; in its second half, Jews, like all others, began fleeing Babylonia for more stable lands. The Christians, primary target of the Magi attack, naturally turned westward. The Jews' only alternative was eastward migration. In 490, the ruler of Cranganor, India assigned a district in his domains to Babylonian Jewish refugees, and granted them self-government there. The B'nai Israel Jews of Cochin, who in recent years have resettled in Israel, are believed to be descended from them. Many Jews, of course, fled to the closer Arabian territories where the next important unfolding of history was to occur more than a century later.

READINGS: CHAPTERS THREE, FOUR AND FIVE

Bickermann, Elias J. "The Historical Foundations of Postbiblical Judaism," *The Jews: Their History, Culture and Religion*, edited by Louis Finkelstein (see p. viii).
—— *The Maccabees*. New York: Schocken Books, 1947.
Cohen, Gerson D. "The Talmudic Age," *Great Ages and Ideas of the Jewish People*, ed. by Leo Schwartz (see p. viii).
Epstein, Louis M. *Marriage Laws in the Bible and the Talmud*. Cambridge: Harvard University Press, 1942.
—— *Sex Laws and Customs in Judaism*. New York: Bloch Publishing Co., 1948.
Feuchtwanger, Lion. *Josephus, A Historical Novel*. London: Secker and Warburg, 1932.
Finkelstein, Louis. *The Pharisees*. 2 vols. Philadelphia: Jewish Publication Society, 1938.
Goldin, Judah. "The Period of the Talmud," *The Jews: Their History, Culture and Religion*, edited by Louis Finkelstein (see p. viii).
Josephus. *The Works of Josephus Flavius*. Translated by William Whiston. Edinburgh and New York: T. Nelson and Sons, 1873.
Marcus, Ralph. "The Hellenistic Age," *Great Ages and Ideas of the Jewish People*, ed. by Leo Schwartz (see p. viii).
Montefiore, C. G. and Loewe, H. *A Rabbinic Anthology*. London: Macmillan and Co., 1938.
Moore, George Foot. *Judaism in the First Centuries of the Christian Era*. 3 vols. Cambridge: Harvard, 1927-1931.
Tcherikover, Avigdor. *Hellenistic Civilization and the Jews*. Philadelphia: Jewish Publication Society, 1961.

Chapter SIX

ISHMAEL,
MY
KINSMAN

FROM ARABIA, IN THE SEVENTH CENTURY, A NEW RELIGIOUS doctrine, Islam, broke upon the world, and Jewry found itself again on the crossroads of imperial collision.

The Arabs and Jews were not strangers to each other. In their wanderings between the Euphrates and the Nile, the patriarchs had frequent contact with the tribes that later formed the Arab nation. The Midianites who sold Joseph into Egyptian slavery were among its progenitors. Although the myth that the two peoples are "cousins" has no support, Arab and Jew had indeed intermarried. Moses' wife, Tziporah, and her father and uncle, who counseled the Hebrews during their forty year desert trek, were from a tribe that later coalesced into the Arab nation. The various tribes and nations that ingressed from the desert into the Hebrews' territories after the conquest of Canaan by Joshua were also among its progenitors, as were even more directly the Nabateans, Judea's neighbors across the Jordan from Hasmonean days, her allies and her foes, and frequent intruders, by invitation, in her civil wars.

Even as the Arabs moved westward, the Judeans moved eastward. Legend has it that the first Jews to settle in Arabia were political fugitives from King Saul's wrath, that they subsequently were joined by sailors of King David's and King Solomon's fleet, whose international trade embraced Africa and India, and later still by multitudes of Judeans who fled to the winds after the Destruction of the First Temple. A burial chamber dating to the year 200, excavated near Haifa, contained the remains of Arab Jews that had been carried fifteen hundred miles

across perilous territory to be deposited in the soil of the sacred land. The same cemetery also contains the burial chambers of Jews from other lands. This custom of the Jewish rich (none else could afford it), to be invested in old Canaan after death, constitutes mute evidence of this people's indivisible bond to its ancestral estate.

The Arabs, before Mohammed (570-632), were at approximately the same stage of societal development as the Jews had been under the judges, just before the monarchy. Like the early Hebrews, they lived in a tribal society, close to the natural austerities of the desert. Among such peoples, it is not walls but the common fate imposed by natural catastrophes such as drought, sandstorms, and locusts, that makes good neighbors, and stern privacy is treated as a reprehensible evasion of responsibility. Like the Hebrews, the Arabs were conditioned to reciprocity in human relations, to treat hospitality and charity as an inalienable element of their religious doctrine. Because the initiative of even the least in such a society is indispensable to the total scheme, the Arabs, like the Hebrews, walked with easy stride in the presence of their elders, treated their slaves as members of the household, refused to regard human authority as God-conferred, and chose their chieftains, as the Hebrews their judges, not from a reigning line but as circumstance required.

The Arabs were still largely pastoral and nomadic, but they had also acquired an urban merchant class. Arabia had long been a crossroads between East and West, and traders and conquerors of many races had left on it the thumbprint of their cultures. Hellenic influences, dating perhaps to Alexander the Great, are still traceable in Israel today in the work of Jewish gold- and silversmiths from Yemen. It is safe to assay that the torrents of humanity that poured into the western territories in the days of Mohammed's successors were, at the least, no less civilized than the Christian Crusaders who poured eastward some five centuries later.

The Jews of Arabia were devout, pious, and jealous of their antecedents. Yet it was evident from their culture that Jewish history had passed them by. They were remote from its central stage, from the educational centers in

Babylonia and Palestine. Like their Arab neighbors, they were still in an earlier stage of societal evolution. Their tribes fell into two general categories. The northerners, closer to Babylonia, and hence of a greater Jewish culture, engaged in agriculture, were celebrated as planters of dates, and lived in fortified towns and villages. The southerners probably possessed a greater secular culture, and belonging to the merchant class, which catered to the trade caravans, they must have spoken many tongues and perhaps even journeyed deep into Asia. Both alike were Arabized in habit and produced warrior-poets whose names have endured in Arab legend.

Having no contiguous territory, their security was based on mutual defense pacts with their pagan neighbors, which sometimes compelled one Jewish tribe to war against another—thrice within one hundred years, in the sixth and again in the seventh century. The Jews of Arabia missed occasions to convert the Arabs to Judaism, perhaps mount with Arab assistance an offensive against Christianity, and finally to subvert Islam itself to Jewish purpose. The Jewish tribes of Arabia, were incapable even of comprehending such opportunity, let alone acting upon it.

JEWISH RULERS OF YEMEN

The first opportunity occurred when Abu-Kariba, the ruler of the Himyarite kingdom, the territory that is today Yemen, embraced Judaism. He was persuaded in this by Hebrew teachers of the law. He had met them in Yahtrib, later Medina, which he had passed during one of his military campaigns, and brought them home to proselytize his people. Probably trained in the Babylonian yeshivot (academies), they must have advised him that Jewish tradition opposed coercion. Contrary to his arbitrary impulse in other matters, he permitted his subjects full religious freedom. Many remained pagans and worshiped nature gods. Yet the fact of their king's conversion had a deep impact, and princes of several related tribes also embraced Judaism.

This is treated by some, not all, historians as a freak episode. It was appreciably more. The Himyarites were powerful rulers, situated on the trade routes between the

east and the Byzantine empire. Most other Arab tribes were their vassals, paying them tribute and committed to assist them in war. Byzantium courted Abu-Kariba's friendship even while encircling him by converting some of his satellites to Christianity.

A showdown was precipitated by his son and successor, Zorah-Yussuf, also called Du-Nowahs, Curly Locks, who was passionately concerned over the persecution of Jews under Christian rule. In retaliation, he seized and executed a caravan of Byzantine merchants passing his territory. One of the independent Arab princes feared its economic consequences. All Arabia would lose a major source of revenue if the Christian caravans were frightened away by Himyarite terror. He declared war on Zorah-Yussuf and defeated him, but the latter was still sufficiently strong to coerce one of his refractory satellites, a Christian tribe, to embrace Judaism.

This was a direct and violent challenge to Christianity's advance in the Arab peninsula. The Near Eastern bishops, outraged and alarmed, circulated impassioned appeals to the Christian monarchs to intervene. Byzantium offered material aid but not manpower. Ethiopia sent her fleet, and assisted by Arab Christian tribes, pinned the Jewish fleet down. Zorah-Yussuf had perhaps counted on the assistance of the Jewish tribes; none came to his rescue, however (530). Perhaps they did not regard the Himyarite as a real Jew, or were appalled by his compulsory conversions, more fitting of a Christian or pagan chieftain. But, more obviously, they lacked that sense of unity that could commit them beyond their separate fortresses. They were unable to read the tides of history. An all-Jewish tribal alliance might have released him from Ethiopian entrapment; and a greater alliance, embracing the pagan tribes committed to help them in war, might have begun—one century before Islam—to thrust Christianity back across the Mediterranean.

MOHAMMED

The second opportunity presented itself when Mohammed (570-632) announced himself as prophet, and solicited

Arabian Jewry. He esteemed its power and sought in its history antecedents for his mission.

Judaic doctrines had circulated in Arabia even before the Himyarite conversion. Judaism preached not morbid asceticism, but manly austerity, the kind that appealed to a nomad people; it also advocated law, which appealed to a mercantile society harassed by raids on its caravans and imperiled by the discord that attends all commercial rivalry. Furthermore, although thoroughly Arabized, the Jews were still distinct and distinguished among the Arabs. The historian, Baron, credits the Jew with introducing progressive agriculture into Arabia, and significantly states that most of the farm implements used in Arabia at the time bear names taken from Jewish Aramaic speech. Their relative immunity from illness, a result of Mosaic dietary and hygienic regulations, seemed to endow the Jews with special powers against disease. They were also an inordinately literate people. The small number of Arabs who could read and write learned Hebrew script from the Jews.

That is probably why Mohammed so completely accommodated himself to the Jewish texts in the early stages of his mission. He was surrounded himself by Jews. Waraka-ibn-Naufal, his wife's cousin, was a convert to Judaism; his scribe (the prophet could not write) was a Jew. Rejected by Mecca in 622, he went to Jathrib, or Medina, and upon arrival immediately set out with fierce determination to court the Jews. The younger Jews responded with great enthusiasm to his summons, perhaps even hoping that he would be their instrument of retribution against Christianity, and while following him, continued to observe Jewish commandment and custom. Mohammed expediently encouraged their belief that there was no discrepancy between his preachments and Judaism by instructing Muslims to face toward Jerusalem when praying, and to fast on the Jews' Yom Kippur. He simultaneously sought to entice Arab Christians by mixing their myths into his compound.

Seasoned men among Arab Jewish leadership, alarmed by this syncretism, denounced him as an impostor, not a prophet; prophecy was confined to the Jews and ceased after their return from Babylonia. They refuted his claim

that the Bible confirmed his succession by proving his ignorance of the Book, to which he replied that they had distorted and perverted the original texts.

The complete and irreparable rupture was precipitated by Mohammed's first savage triumph in war over the heathen at Bedr, after which he assumed a more combative attitude toward the Jews and all dissenters, reflected in the second half of the Koran. His irritation was exacerbated by two celebrated Arab poets, both Jews, the sage Abu Afak and the female Asma, whose laments for the Bedr victims rallied his foes. He ordered obliteration of patently Jewish symbols, substituted the thirty day Ramadhan for Yom Kippur, replaced Jerusalem with Mecca, the ancient sanctuary of the Arabs' pagan gods, and proceeded from violent rhetoric to physical violence.

Here was an occasion for an all-Jewish tribal alliance against him. Assisted by heathen tribes, they might have beaten him. But even as they had not come to the rescue of the Himyarite kin, each now guarded its own ramparts as Mohammed picked them off, tribe after tribe. Their valor was to no purpose, but their force had already been spent when they formed an all-Jewish alliance (628).

In the two decades after his death, his successors, the Khalifs, swept up the Persian territories, and Palestine, Syria, Egypt, and the North African territories that had been under Byzantium.

JEWRY CHOOSES SIDES

The Jews had no obligation of loyalty to the Christian and the last Persian kings who persecuted them without bounds. But the reports of Mohammed's atrocities against Arabian Jewry, carried westward by refugees, gave them no cause to enthuse over the advance of the Arab forces. These invaders were not liberators, like the Persians under Cyrus, or the Romans under Julius Caesar.

Yet after a while, under Mohammed's successors, Jewry's attitude began to alter from passivity to active collaboration, a change not unrelated to the early khalifs' political expedience.

The Visigothic rulers of Spain virtually forced the Jews into an alliance with the Arabs by debarring them from

111

all livelihood and inflicting on them all other manner of persecution. In 694, the Visigoths uncovered a seditious Jewish conspiracy that was to have been synchronized with an Arab invasion from North Africa. Another plot was launched in 711, and succeeded. The Jews rose in arms and delivered Spanish city after city to the Arab invaders whose vanguard included a full division of indigenous North African Jews under Jewish command. Having entered a city, the invaders turned it over to their Jewish allies, and raced on to further victory.

The Jews, everywhere, began discovering affinities with the Muslims. Even without persecution, life would have been dismal for them in class-stratified, sin-obsessed Christian society, which vacillated between the extremes of self-indulgence and renunciation. The Jews' rule was to be moderate in all things, to enjoy but not indulge, to take pleasure but not pursue it. The Koran made a virtue of pleasure, and even pledged dividends-in-kind in the hereafter. The Jews were more comfortable with Arab excess than with Christian.

The Christian world was church-governed. Islam, like Judaism, separated administrative and religious functions, stressed law, not theology, took its counsel from legalists, not priests, was stimulated by untrammeled debate, countenanced so-called heresy, and did not possess a supreme religious authority. Like the Christians, it drew a sharp distinction between the chosen true believers and all others, but its toleration, albeit qualified, was more in the early Persian and Greco-Roman tradition. Its culture was so close to the Hebraic root that the Jews could partake of it without guilty conscience or appearing as intruders. The essential reason was that Christianity predicated its redemption on the Jew, and saw him as the ubiquitous and relentless frustrater of its purpose. The Muslim faith had fulfilled itself at birth, and did not require the Jew as "witness."

On its books Islam matched, probably law for law, Christianity's legislation against the Jews. It adopted, indeed, many of the laws that preceded it in the conquered Byzantine territory. Yet in practice, it waived them. Christian and Jew were formally barred from holding public

office, yet they were vigorously solicited for these posts, perhaps because, like Jewry in its statehood days, the Arabs had a distaste for government.

The yellow Jew badge was first decreed by Haroun-al-Rashid in 807 and reconfirmed by several later fanatics, but never really enforced. In Christian Europe, the badge was introduced by the Fourth Lateran Council in 1215, and endured into the modern era.

LAW AND PHILOSOPHY

Jewish history under the Arabs may be divided into two overlapping periods, the Bagdad and the Spanish. Although historical evolution defies precise or even approximate chronology, the Bagdad period may nonetheless be said to have begun with the Arab invasion of Babylonia and to have been succeeded in the mid-tenth century by the Spanish period which terminated approximately in the twelfth century.

When Omar I, the second Khalif, occupied Babylonia, he rewarded Jewish collaboration by restoring the post of exilarch. When Ali, the fourth Khalif and son-in-law of Mohammed took power (656-661) with half of Islam against him, the Jews supported his succession.

The institution of the gaonate, reputedly dates back to his reign. The rank of gaon was normally shared by the deans of the two major yeshivot which, like the antecedent Palestine sanhedrin, were a combined legislature and high court. (The opinions of the U.S. Supreme Court are also sometimes pseudolegislative in nature.) The gaon, then, was both chief justice and chairman of the senate. His writ was law for all Jews in the Muslim lands, and respected also beyond. His broad powers were resented by the exilarch; in the style of earlier Jewish history, there was frequent friction between the judiciary and the executive.

The yeshivot under Arab rule created a new type of judicial literature, called Responsa, or sha'alot u'teshuvot, which literally means questions and answers. The Mishnah had updated the written law. The Gemara had updated the Mishnah, and now that the Talmud was a closed and sanctified code, the need arose to supplement it with additional

113

opinion, tailored to new circumstance. It is for this purpose that the Responsa were devised. The academies' actual competence was confined to the Khalifate, but their legal opinion was sought even by communities under Christian domain. The questions or issues thus submitted were considered by large assemblies of scholars. Whichever decision was favored by consensus was then communicated, under the gaon's signature, as his definitive opinion. The Jews, like the Arabs, were never governed by the equivalent of the Papal encyclical. When the two academies disagreed on a point of law, its determination, by default, was left to that most efficient of all referenda, public compliance, producing a diversity that provided the dynamics which sustained Jewish law as living law.

The free-wheeling debate that spread in Islam from the start suited Jewish habit and proclivities, but it also strained Jewish faith and discipline. A peculiar historical metempsychosis was taking place, especially in the eighth and ninth centuries. The Arabs had acquired through Greco-Christian sources all the heresies and dissent that had afflicted Judea during the era of the Second Temple. These were now re-enacted within Islam. The Jews, caught the infection a second time from their Muslim hosts.

Sufism, advocating redemption through personal saintliness, was in the pattern of the Essenes. The Mutazilites, who opposed anthropomorphism, the attribution to God of human features and qualities, and interpreted such passages in the Koran allegorically, were successors to a Jewish tradition dating back at least to the third century, to Amora Simon Resh Lakish, and before him, to Philo, the Alexandrian Jewish philosopher. There was also a strong disposition within Islam toward comparative religion. This too was duplicated in Jewry. Even so great a figure of conventional Judaism as Abraham Maimuni (1185-1254), son of Maimonides, praised the Muslim mystics, the Sufi, for abiding in some respects more truly than the Jews by the authentic manner of the prophets. He even proposed introducing certain Muslim practices into Jewish worship on the ground that they were of Jewish origin.

114

KARAISM

The true challenge to Jewish tradition came in the second half of the eighth century from a doctrine called Karaism. The first to advance it was Anan, son of David, an unsuccessful contestant for the post of exilarch. It was a paradoxical movement. Like the Sadducees, nearly one thousand years before, it opposed the oral law, advocated fundamentalism, and proscribed mysticism. But unlike the Sadducees, who were the wealthy Grecized upper class, Karaism seems to have been a populist movement. It apparently was led by those among the elite that chafed under the discipline of the law handed down by the academies, and was supported by the underprivileged, who perhaps felt that the law no longer served the common man.

It was also a strongly Zion-centered movement, a further indication of its lower-class support. The affluent had no reason to seek repatriation from Babylonia and Persia. They could accommodate themselves to changing regimes. But the poor, who were the first victims of violence that erupted repeatedly as the Muslim dynasties fought for power, advocated the Return as each man's immediate and personal obligation; they indeed returned to Palestine in considerable numbers. They rejected all Talmudic law as invalid for repatriates, contending that its sole function had been to sustain the Jews in the Diaspora.

The Karaite heresy persisted for several centuries. Its sectarians have survived into our own day, and have been admitted into Israel under the terms of the Law of Return, which regards each Jew entering the land not as an immigrant, but as a repatriate. Thus, the Karaites, after twelve centuries, are being reintegrated into Jewry.

Anan ben David, who went down in Jewish history as a disrupter, advanced the spirit of free inquiry in Jewry. He admonished his disciples to defer to no authority, "build not on my opinions," and to pursue independent investigation of the Biblical texts. This, in turn, compelled the rabbis, as Luther later compelled the Catholic church, to refute Karaism by independently pursuing the study of Biblical syntax and sentence structure. This laid the basis

for Hebrew linguistics, and gave rise to a Hebrew literary renaissance.

RENAISSANCE MEN

The era of Arab-Jewish symbiosis was Jewry's second confrontation with Greek culture. The first occurred in Judea under adverse circumstances. Hellenism was introduced by Greco-Roman force to a subjugated people. It was cosmopolitan, and the Jew was still largely rural. It was polytheistic, and the Jew was a monotheist. Under Arab circumstance the confrontation was infinitely more favorable. The Jew was urban. He was in the Diaspora through no fault of Islam. The dominant culture, like his own, was monotheistic. It is nonetheless a distortion to suggest that it was through the Arabs that the Jews made their first acquaintance with Greek philosophy and science. It is true that the Jews until then had shown no disposition for philosophy and speculative thinking. It is also true, however, that they were later no less active than the Arabs themselves in translating Greek philosophy and science into Arabic.

Their interest in medicine predates even the Greco-Roman era. The Bible bears that out. This interest was no doubt accelerated through their intercourse with Greco-Roman civilization. The execrated Judeo-Hellenists and Alexandrian Jewry must have served as transmitters of science from the Greco-Syrians and later from the Romans. The Talmud is a veritable treasury of botanical and medical information, some of it no doubt predating the first Jewish-Greek encounter. The sages were students of anatomy. The Talmudic schools of the third century, considerably before the Arab era, included astronomers of some competence. *Mishnat Midot*, attributed to Rabbi Nehemiah, which contains the rudiments of geometry, dates back to 150. It was subsequently incorporated into the work of the Arab mathematician Mohammed ibn Musa (880). The Indian mathematician KanKah, who influenced Arab mathematics at its beginning, was reputedly assisted by a Jew, who knew Sanskrit, in translating his works into Arabic (771-778).

There were Jews among the ranking early Arab writers

on mathematics. Figures of inordinate stature were Masha'-alla (770-820), Latinized into Messahala, and his younger contemporary Sahl ben Bishr, the astrologer. Mathematics, astronomy, and astrology were intermixed until well into the Middle Ages. Masha'alla, precursor of the European Renaissance man was also an engineer, an architect, and a city planner, who helped design the Khalifate's first capital, Bagdad.

There were other Jewish scientists, of the Renaissance type, at that time. Some of these were also Jewish scholars. Equally at home in Arabic, and Hebrew, they were simultaneously Talmudic interpreters, physicians, mathematicians, and translators of philosophical and scientific works from Greek into Arabic. Sahal Albatri, from Tabaristan, on the Caspian Sea, was among the first of this astonishing intellectual breed. A rabbi, an authority on Hebrew law, eminent as both physician and mathematician, he was the first to note the refraction of light, and the translator into Arabic of Ptolemy's texts, which were the standard work on astronomy until impeached, as was all other work in this field, by Copernicus' new evidence. Another Talmudic authority Yitzhak Israeli (845-940), known to later generations in Christian Europe as Israel Judeus, was the author of numerous medical textbooks translated into Latin by the monk Constantinus Africanus, reputedly born a Jew.

Saadia ben Joseph (882-942), better known as Saadia Gaon, Egyptian-born dean of one of the two major Babylonian academies, was the first ranking philosopher to arise among the rabbis.

In Saadia's day, infected by Muslim heterodoxy, the Jewish elite vacillated between agnosticism and mysticism; the first dismissed Revelation and the miracles as myth, and demanded evidence for everything; the mystics relied on faith alone, and inclined toward the irrational and superstitious. Saadia Gaon, trying to reconcile both extremes, was mocked by one, denounced by the other. The orthodox attacked his mating of faith and philosophy as miscegenation; the rationalists argued that his reasoning was predicated on faith. Yet if Judaism may be said to possess a theology, he was its founder. A similar attempt

117

to formulate a rationalist theology of Judaism was later undertaken by Maimonides.

Saadia also undertook a study of comparative religion. Debating Christianity and Islam, he revealed an erudition in these faiths which extremely pious Jews must have found suspicious in a rabbi.

He wrote voluminously on linguistics, compiled a Hebrew dictionary, translated the Bible into Arabic, and composed prayers. With all these scholarly and literary preoccupations, however, he was also a busy man of affairs, a contentious figure, who debated scathingly with the Karaites; he challenged, at great cost to himself, the competence of the exilarch who sought to dictate to the judiciary, and sided with Babylonia in its conflict with the residual Palestinian academies over which was empowered to determine the religious calendar. It was another stage in the struggle, going back some five hundred years, between Palestine and Babylonia for hegemony over Jewry. It is re-enacted today in nonreligious terms, whenever American Jews challenge the Israelis' right to speak for Jewry beyond Israel.

SPAIN RISES

Soon after Saadia's death, Jewish hegemony began to pass from Babylonia to Spain, with a brief interlude in North Africa. Its instigator was Chasdai ibn Shaprut (915-970), the first in a long line of Jewish statesmen whose linguistic proficiency made them indispensable to the Arabs in dealing with minorities inside Arabdom and with foreign governments. He was court physician, custodian of the treasury, and adviser on foreign affairs to the Spanish Khalifs, Abdur-Rahman (912-961) and Hakim II (961-976), whose ambition was to dislodge Bagdad as the center of Muslim scholarship and Arabic literature. Chasdai had complementary ambitions in Jewry. He persuaded one of Iraq's leading scholars to settle in Cordova, establish an academy, and ordain rabbis there, a rite which had by consensus hitherto been confined to the Palestine and Iraqi yeshivot. His Khalifs probably approved his plans, for as a Jewish center Cordova would deflect some of Jewry's international trade from Bagdad.

Chasdai, the prototype of the Christian Maecenas of Renaissance Europe, was a man of many accomplishments. He knew Hebrew, Arabic, and Latin, in which only the highest clergy was instructed, and collaborated with a Byzantine monk, Nicholas, on an Arabic translation of Dioscorides' medical works. His greatest dedication was probably to his diplomatic assignments as negotiator for the contentious Abdur-Rahman, with the Muslim rulers of Bagdad and Egypt, and the Christian kings of Northern Spain. No foreign diplomatic missions to the Khalifate could bypass him. It was probably his greatest hour when Christian embassies traveled to Cordova to negotiate alliances with the Khalifate against other Christian states. It may have seemed to him irrefutable proof of Christianity's collapse. Another great experience, no doubt, was his communication with the Khazar Jewish kingdom.

KHAZAR INTERLUDE

The Khazars were probably descended from Turcoman tribes in the peripheral regions of the Persian Empire. Sometime in the late sixth or early seventh century, they must have undertaken a long trek in search of permanent domicile and finally settled between Derbent, in Daghestan, on the Caspian Sea, and Astrakhan, on the Volga River. Like the early Hebrew tribes, they were ruled by judges. Their central government was headed by "a judge of judges" who was also their leader in war.

In the eighth century, they emerged as a formidable regional force which harassed its neighbors, expelled the Greeks from Crimea, exacted tribute from the Byzantine kings and the Slavs, and occasionally united with the latter in joint action against the Christians. Some of the Khazars converted to Christianity, some to Islam, and in the mid-eighth century, the khan or chief justice and his retinue embraced Judaism. There are many conflicting stories about the event. The most plausible seems to be that Jews fleeing Christian persecution settled among the Khazars, and when one of their number was eventually elected khan, they decided it was safe at last for all of them to reveal their faith. As was customary, many of his subjects also embraced the khan's faith.

All the Khazar khans thereafter were Jews. They treated all faiths alike. Their courts consisted of a panel of seven judges, two from each faith, and one for the pagan Khazar. In the second half of the tenth century, when the Slavs along the Volga, the Dnieper, and in the Caucasus converted to Christianity en masse, the Khazars were stripped of all their allies. Yet they chose this inauspicious time to tangle with the Christians. Like the Himyarite king four centuries before, they hoped to avenge the persecution of Jewry in Christian Europe, and like the Himyarites, they suffered disastrous results. In 969, the Khazars became a satellite of Kiev, and in 1016, their last resistance shattered, they were completely overrun.

Chasdai ibn Shaprut learned of their existence from Persian and Byzantine Jewish merchants. A letter he addressed to the king of the Khazars reveals his apprehension about the fate of the Diaspora, notwithstanding his own high station.

"Stripped of all honor, degraded and humbled," wrote the Jewish chief advisor to the Spanish Khalifate, "we have no retort to the taunt: 'each people has its state, you alone have none.' Is it true that there is at least one acre on God's earth where Jewry governs itself submissive to none? If this is true, I shall joyfully resign my rank, forfeit my rewards, yea, even desert my family, and cross mountains, valleys and rivers to report to my Lord the King."

His letter reached its destination in 960. It took another several years for the reply to reach Chasdai. By then, the Khazars were being ringed in, and Chasdai was only several years removed from his death.

About a half century after his death, Spanish Jewry produced a piquant figure, of even greater eminence, Rabbi Samuel ibn Nagdela (993-1063).

The Spanish Khalifate, hopelessly entangled in wars with the Christian duchies of northern Spain, had summoned its Muslim brethren, the Berbers of North Africa, to its side. The Berbers descended like locusts. They defeated the Christians, but they also overwhelmed the Arabs, dislodged them, and dismembered the Khalifate into several states, ruled by sovereign emirs who were al-

ways sparring against each other. Samuel ibn Nagdela was for twenty-eight years vizier to two successive emirs of Granada, and in the last decade of his life was virtual sovereign, his emir being too intent on pleasure to attend to his obligations.

Samuel, who had an undeniable penchant for power, was also Granada Jewry's chief rabbi, its nagid, a rank equivalent to exilarch, and a maecenas whose beneficence extended to all Eastern Jewry.

In addition to Hebrew and Arabic, he also knew Chaldee, Castilian, and Berber; his *Introduction to the Talmud* was for a long time an invaluable aid to scholars; his judgments as a rabbi passed review by eminent authorities in Jewish religious law, his treatises advanced research in Hebrew linguistics, and his verse, albeit mediocre, showed technical mastery. He was also a competent astronomer.

What set him apart from other Jewish statesmen at Muslim courts was that he studied military science, personally led his troops into battle, and extolled his feats in triumphant Hebrew verse. For this reason, wars against Granada sometimes attained the frenzy of a jihad, a Muslim crusade to release the "true believers" from the rule of the infidel Samuel. Yet the emirates that rallied these jihads often had Jewish viziers themselves. Jews seemed especially suited for the post. They were astute in handling finance, efficient in administration—perhaps because they had always lived under the discipline of law—and wise in arbitration. Between passionately contentious forces, the Berbers and the Arabs, the Muslims and the Christians, the Jews were a safety valve, averting civil strife, circumventing war.

The golden age of Granada Jewry was brief, paralleling Samuel's twenty-eight year reign. His son and successor Joseph was lynched by a Berber mob, after having been falsely accused of secret dealings with the Arabs. He had only tried to foil a Berber plot to slaughter them. The Jews undoubtedly nursed sympathy for the Arabs who once had ruled them benevolently, and had enlisted them in a great cultural renascence.

121

GRECO-JEWISH RECONCILIATION

Most Jewish religio-philosophical writing for the next two centuries was in Arabic. Even some of the rabbinical Responsa was in that language, partly because their correspondents evidently understood no other, and partly because the Jewish religious thinkers regarded themselves as part of the general culture of their times, and addressed themselves beyond Jewry in a language the largest possible number would understand. These works were later translated into Hebrew for the western Jewish communities, and thus acquired permanency in Jewish thought.

The same renaissance men who wrote on religion and philosophy in Arabic, wrote their poetry in Hebrew. That poetry, still the foremost in all Hebrew literature, reflected the Arabic impact in its form and content. Poets who wrote fervid liturgy, that has been included in Jewry's prayers, also wrote audacious wine songs and richly tapestried love lyrics. Thus, Greece and Judea finally consummated their union under Arab aegis.

Three of Jewry's greatest figures, each of them an astonishingly gifted bilingual author, made their appearance at this time: Solomon ibn Gabirol (1020-1070), poet and philosopher; Judah Ha-Levi (1086-1140?), poet and religious thinker; and Moses, the son of Maimon (1135-1205), or Maimonides, physician, philosopher, and codifier, of whom it has been said: "From Moses to Moses there has been none like Moses."

All three were active in horrendous times, when religious fanaticism seemed the universal mood. Berber Muslim fanatics pouring out of North Africa, Christian fanatics pouring out of Europe, each mounted fierce and merciless crusades. Enlightened Arabs were punished by Christians as infidels, by Muslim fanatics as errant sons. But none suffered more than the Jew from these relapses from civilization.

Ibn Gabirol, Ha-Levi, and Maimonides reflect the full range of the Jews' dilemma in the several centuries of humanity's transition from Islamic to Christian hegemony, when Jewry was caught in a vise between two great im-

perial religions, and was no less threatened with ideological disorientation than with physical extinction.

In Hebrew verse, in the Arabic metric and metaphoric tradition, ibn Gabirol lamented this condition. "Ishmael (Islam) is a lion, Esau (Christianity)—a vulture, one releases us, the other pounces upon us." Yet his philosophical works, all written in Arabic, seem unaffected by this circumstance. Like Philo, the Alexandrian Jewish philosopher, one thousand years before him, ibn Gabirol was a neo-Platonist. Jews accepted neither one's philosophical work. But Philo was a conscious mediator between Greece and Judah, laboring to discover analogies and parallels between Jewish law and custom and Greek thought. Ibn Gabirol, the philosopher functioned as if he were a direct successor to the Greeks. The effect was confusing. When the church fathers adapted Philo's work, they knowingly capitalized on Jewish thought. But when they studied, in Latin translation, the works of one Avicebrol, a distortion of ibn Gabirol, the medieval Christian scholastics were unaware that they were basing themselves on a Hebrew poet and thinker whose verse Jewry recites in its high holiday prayers.

Judah Ha-Levi, born in Toledo, had lived alternately under Christian and Muslim rule. The Jewish elite was still torn, as in Saadia Gaon's day, between the rationalists whose reliance on philosophy ruled out intuitive piety, and the "revelationists," who in reaction to rationalist excess and political persecution turned inward, opposed philosophy, and absorbed some of the intolerance around them.

Judah Ha-Levi rejected all extremism. The Jews were indeed elected at Sinai; their entire history provided successive evidence of their election. The Jewish law, the Jewish people, the Jewish land are interrelated components of the redemptive process. However, Islam and Christianity have their function, too, cleansing the rest of mankind for the day of redemption, and every human of pure heart, generous deed, and honest intent will be redeemed, regardless of his faith.

This man who offered to share redemption with the world was bitterly aware that mankind would not share

with the Jews. He branded as hopeless the efforts of
Spanish Jews to purchase from Christian princes sanctu-
aries for Jewry. Ishmael "pursues us with his hate, we
plead with Esau and he turns upon us," he argued. "This
is not your repose. Have we in all the East or West a place
where we can rest our hope?"

He undertook a perilous journey to Palestine, possibly
as a demonstrative political act as well as a pietist's pil-
grimage. All Jewish communities enroute welcomed him
with enthusiasm. He very likely repeated to them the
warning he had voiced to Spanish Jewry. He vanished
somewhere on the way, or upon his arrival in the Holy
Land.

Maimonides was the greatest and last of the Spanish
Jewish renaissance figures and experienced in his person
the full Jewish Calvary of his times. When he was thirteen,
his family fled from Cordova to escape the invading
Almohades, who began as liberal Muslim reformers and
ended up as vicious Muslim crusaders. Several years later,
the Maimon family turned up in North Africa, source of
the Almohade contagion. Some historians have advanced
a theory, refuted by others, that the Maimons must have
briefly embraced Islam, that being the only alternative to
death for Jews in North Africa at the time.

Maimonides' first legal opinion was a vigorous defense
of Jews who under compulsion pretended to profess Islam.
Islam, unlike Christianity, compels none to submit to rites
that are not pure monotheism or to renounce Judaism, he
argued. Half-hearted verbal concurrence that Mohammed
is a prophet can hardly be adjudged idolatry. The sole
issue, therefore, against reluctant apostates to Islam, Maimonides reasoned, is that they did not choose death, but
then, albeit martyrs may be admirable men, martyrdom is
not an obligation. "And if a person puts to us the question
whether he is under obligation to surrender his life under
such circumstances, we must in all conscience, and in
accordance with the precepts of Judaism, reply 'no.'"
However, he did urge such people to take no comfort in
their impotence, to make no virtue of their circumstance,
and to speedily repair to countries that offered religious
freedom. Thus, Maimonides applied to new circumstance

the opinion handed down in Hadrian's day by the secret tribunal in Lydda under Rabbi Akiba's chairmanship. It has been one of Judaism's cardinal principles that man's natural purpose is meaningful survival, and that he need not forfeit his life even for God, which is the antithesis of Pauline doctrine.

Maimonides finally settled in Egypt, where under Saladin's reign (1174-1193) the Jews still possessed a wide range of autonomy. Maimonides was a member of Saladin's panel of physicians, personal doctor to his vizier, and Egyptian Jewry's chief and nagid.

His monumental compendium of Jewish law was written in Hebrew. Conversely, his Responsa, his commentary on the Mishnah, and his "Guide to the Perplexed," an address on Judaism to wavering intellectuals, were all written in Arabic. Like his Rabbinic predecessors and peers, but with skill unmatched since Saadia Gaon, he was determined to prove the compatibility of philosophy and faith. His influence spread beyond Judaism and beyond his times into Islam and Christianity. The strongest opposition to him in Jewry came from those whom religious persecution had compelled toward mysticism, and also from liberal thinkers who felt that he had overintellectualized Judaism, and deprived faith of its deepest sources.

Even extremists of the other faiths were alarmed by his influence. The leading exponent of Muslim orthodoxy, Abel-Latif, warned that the *Guide to the Perplexed* was "a bad book, calculated to undermine the principles of religion by the very means which are apparently designed to strengthen them." When the first Inquisition was established in Europe (1233) with the Dominicans in charge, Jewish opponents of Maimonides, infected by Christian fanaticism, called its attention to his works. The Inquisitors read *The Guide* in Latin translation and concurred that the book deserved burning because it spawned free inquiry; there could be no greater calamity (1233). The discovery of collusion between the Dominicans and Maimonides' foes shocked all Jewry. The guilty repented, and although the controversy thereafter was just as vituperative, the church was never again enlisted as an ally.

And so in one of the darkest ages in Islamic and

Christian history, a single Jewish genius sustained the traditional dialogue. He also resolved, for his age at least, the dilemma of faith and reason.

However, the pietist opposition to Maimonides was also important to the future evolution of Judaism, for had his conception of God as a detached force and of intellectual attainment as a precondition for immortality been accepted, Jewry's multitudes would have perished in the desert of their despair.

READINGS: CHAPTER SIX

Fischel, Walter Joseph. *The Jews in the Economic and Political Life of Medieval Islam*. London: Royal Asiatic Society, 1937.

Gotein, S. D. *Jews and Arabs, Their Contact Through the Ages*. New York: Schocken Books, 1955.

Halkin, Abraham S. "Judeo-Arabic Literature," *The Jews: Their History, Culture and Religion*, edited by Louis Finkelstein (see p. viii).

Chapter SEVEN

JEW AND
MARRANO

THE IMAGE OF THE JEW IN MEDIEVAL EUROPE AS A FRIGHTENED creature scurrying to the rabbit hutch of the Jewish Quarter, his frail frame succumbing without resistance to the howling mob, or as a possessed martyr, his features blurred by the flames and smoke of the Inquisitorial purge, his exalted voice acclaiming his faith to the last, has been a persistent one. The Christian advanced it to excoriate his obstinacy and prove his rejection by God, the Jew, to celebrate his endurance and enlist compassion on his behalf. But there were other dimensions to Jewish life, rich in compensations and delight that precluded martyrdom from becoming the axis of his fate.

He was sustained, above all, by his relentless conceit in his superiority. This had more to do perhaps with his awareness that he was Better People than with the traditional concept that he was the Chosen People. For several centuries the Jewish Quarter was the one civilized compound in any European city. At first he had retired there voluntarily, for security reasons, and paid for the privilege of shutting it off to instigated mobs. From the sixteenth century on, it became a ghetto enjoined by law.

Confined to one or several streets, it was always overpopulated, its outdoors thronged, tumultuous with loud speech, the shouts of hawkers, and above all other noises the sing song rhythm in which the Jew—in the synagogue, at home, and over the stall in the market place—read aloud to himself the Talmud to better understand it. Because it is, in form, a record of disputations, argument, and counterargument, he would read it like a playscript, first playing the role of one tana or amora, then of another,

127

finally that of one of the later commentators, ultimately re-emerging as himself, a scholar trying to reconcile conflicting legal opinions. There was little, if any illiteracy. Elementary schooling was universal and free for the poor; adult education was widespread through study circles whose interests ranged from the Bible through the Gemara, and scholars were flattered when invited to instruct them.

The congestion inside the Jewish quarter inadvertently favored both adult education and democratic procedures. Scholars pausing in the synagogue or street for even the most casual conversation promptly found themselves the center of eavesdroppers—another means for the uneducated to gather crumbs of learned information.

Jewry's affairs were ruled by an autocracy of learned money lenders and merchant princes, who were only a sliver of a population overwhelmingly comprised of artisans, stallkeepers, and mendicants. Yet crowded conditions, no less than tradition, ruled out class segregation, and the custodians of the communal affairs were everywhere confronted by their constituency. The result was a kind of sustained popular referendum of their conduct. Furthermore, compelled to base their decisions on Jewish law, they were constantly challenged by Talmudists who were plentiful in each community. Anyone who felt seriously aggrieved could, as a last resort, disrupt reading of the Torah in the synagogue by placing his hand on the sacred scroll, and demanding to be heard on "an abomination that has been committed in Israel." This was an automatic injunction against proceeding with religious services until he had been heard, there and then.

The Jewish Quarter was multilingual. It knew Hebrew, and the indigenous language, and an additional Jewish language compounded from Hebrew and the indigenous tongue, Yiddish in Germany, Ladino in Spain. It spoke also varied other tongues. In 1290, Jews expelled from London, brought English with them, and expelled from France three times in the course of the fourteenth century, the Jews carried French to Germany, to Italy, and even to the Muslim lands. They were also, as a result of frequent expulsions and resettlement, among the best informed people

anywhere on the political, economic, and spiritual state of the world.

When the Jews looked about them at the state of Christian Europe, they had no reason to wish to barter away their way of life.

The vanguard of European Jewry were the Judeans who settled in Rome at least two centuries before the Common Era. After the Fall of Jerusalem, additional Judeans, war captives, and refugees fanned out across Italy, concentrating especially in her ports, where they engaged in trans-Mediterranean trade with their kinsmen in Egypt, Persia, and beyond. In the fifth century, after the Vandals ransacked Rome, the Jews migrated northward into the invaders' home base, the underdeveloped Franco-German territories, which were still pagan and offered respite from Christian persecution, and ample economic opportunity to Jewish craftsmen and traders.

The first to comprehend the economic-cultural importance of the Jews to his underdeveloped domains was Charlemagne the Great (742-814), founder of the Holy Roman Empire. Papal policy notwithstanding, he favored the Jews in the classical pattern of Cyrus and Julius Caesar. He named a Jew de facto chief of his diplomatic mission to Haroun-al-Rashid (797), and on his return, received him at the court with formal pomp. When Charlemagne summoned foreign scholars to raise the state of culture in his lands, he remembered to invite Italian Talmudists to settle in Mayence and, ten years later, eastern scholars to establish an academy (yeshiva) at Narbonne, the latter measure may have been intended for either of two antipodal purposes: to strengthen his Jewry's ties with Bagdad for commercial reasons, or to sever that umbilical cord.

Charlemagne's son and successor, Louis I, the Pious (814-840), granted the Jews easements, the like of which they never again obtained in Christendom. The atmosphere at his court was reminiscent of heathen Rome, when its elite had become enchanted with Jewish culture. Because the Jews would not trade on Saturday, and their commerce was indispensable, Louis decreed that the weekly fair be held on Sunday. His second consort, Judith, studied the

works of Josephus and Philo, who defended Judaism from heathen critics; her retinue made a habit of visiting synagogues on the Jewish holidays, so fascinated were they with its simple worship; in discussions of comparative religion, some courtiers upheld the superiority of Jewish over canon law. Franco-German Jewry, remote from the eastern centers of learning, probably knew little of Philo and Josephus, disapproved of what it did know, and while flattered by the empress' attention, was not keen on soliciting proselytes, and experienced an interval of embarrassment and panic when Bishop Bodo, the emperor's confessor, fled to Muslim Spain and embraced Judaism.

Under Louis' successor, the empire collapsed into a score of principalities divided among bishops and barons, and Jewry was trapped on the chessboard of their intrigues.

THE CRUSADES

For two full centuries, from the end of the eleventh through the thirteenth, Europe was trampled by a stampede of predatory self-uprooted multitudes, nobility, and rabble, blessed by the Popes and sometimes led by kings, who sailing under the Cross, in the name of the Saviour, exercised their vilest passion on its sedentary population. The major Crusades, to avenge Muslim persecution of Christians, were interspaced by lesser crusades directed at closer targets, the Christian dissidents. The Jews, however, were always the first upon whom they rehearsed their passion. The Crusades, like the humanity that compounded them, appear to have been an admixture of impulses and cross purposes. They were an enlargement of the long-simmering, intermittent contest between church and state: on the one hand, an attempt to corral under Papal disciplines the recalcitrant Christian rulers, and on the other, the means by which autonomy-minded clerics and states'-righters within Catholicism hoped to compel the Pope himself. Each Crusade was a grab bag for its participants. Impoverished knights hoped to return with loot and glory; debtors were released from their obligations to Jewish creditors, and peasants from serfdom. Presiding over these tumultuous and sanguine enterprises

were psychotic monks, apparently determined to avenge themselves on the world they had rejected. They scored two enduring achievements. They extended Christian territory and trade, and devised for Europe a strategy against the Jews which the anti-Semitic world has preserved to this day.

Caught unaware at first, the Jews soon learned to anticipate and prepare against the enemy. During the first Crusade, in 1096, the higher clergy and the nobles protected them, the Christians of Cologne hid them in their homes, and in an exceptional episode, the burghers of Worms even permitted them to man the ramparts. In most cases, they fought alone from fortresses which they rented from the bishops and barons, together with their arsenals and private guards who deserted as soon as the siege began. In the later Crusades, they were without allies altogether. In York, in 1190, in the harsh month of March, they held out for six full days and took a heavy toll of the enemy, who overwhelmed them only when their water and food gave out. They resisted similarly in Nuremberg that year. In Toulouse, in 1322, having exhausted their arms, they dismantled the towers of the citadel they had rented and hurled its rocks at the enemy.

In many instances, having exhausted both stones and water beset congregations took grim referendums. In congregation after congregation, an awkward minority would walk out to the jubilant mob, announce their decision to apostatize, and be carried off to the nearest church.

The majority voted for collective suicide. This wholesale physical self-liquidation, because it occurred on German soil, invites the facile explanation that the Jews had become infected with the German passion for death Götterdämmerung. But theirs was not a morbid, but a proud and conceited, choice, when they preferred death to apostasy. The Greeks would have understood it. The Jews were certain of their inordinate human superiority over the howling Christian mob with its torches, hatchets, knives, crosses and ikons, bishops and monks. To surrender to these was to yield to a lesser culture. To pass from Jewry to Christianity meant passing from a free into a stratified, oppressively closed society, from life into mere existence.

131

It meant living a lie, forfeiting one's sovereignty. It is this that prevented the majority from crossing over, and that impelled parents to choose for children too young to comprehend the alternatives.

At this time, also, regarding themselves as combatants not martyrs, the Jews formulated a kind of Geneva convention to rule their conduct when besieged by the enemy. Based on the Talmud, reconfirmed by successive generations of rabbis, it provided that "when the enemy states unto you: 'deliver us one, we shall kill him and spare the rest,' rather that none be spared than surrender one; and when he says: 'yield us one woman,' rather that all be defiled than one be surrendered." Later rabbinical opinion adds, "even if she be a public woman," because she is still sovereign of her body. These rules are contained in a moralistic compendium of the thirteenth or fourteenth century. They are hardly a guide to self-immolation, but a testament to human dignity.

From the Second Crusade on, Germany became notable for its anti-Jewish persecutions. Henry II had already scored a first for Germany in 1012 when he climaxed a long period of anti-Jewish violence with an order expelling them from Mayence and other cities. Emperors Henry IV and Conrad III, who were elsewhere occupied during the First and Second Crusades respectively when the Crusaders struck, tried on returning home to repair the injustice by severely punishing the perpetrators of the atrocities. Conrad III, purposing to protect them from the bishops, barons, and mobs, announced that the Jews were henceforth his "servi camerae," chambers servants, the equivalent of serfs. Since the Jews were his chattel, he could also treat their property as his own and if either was damaged, the emperor would demand compensation. This protected Jewry from harm momentarily, but it set an outrageous precedent for more literal-minded rulers.

All kings, bishops, and barons soon classified the Jews as chattel, offered them as collateral for loans, gave them away as gifts to mistresses, and donated them penitentially to the church. At first, they even engaged in rustling Jews from each other like cattle, but later, finding this an unprofitable sport, they agreed to return fugitive Jews, which

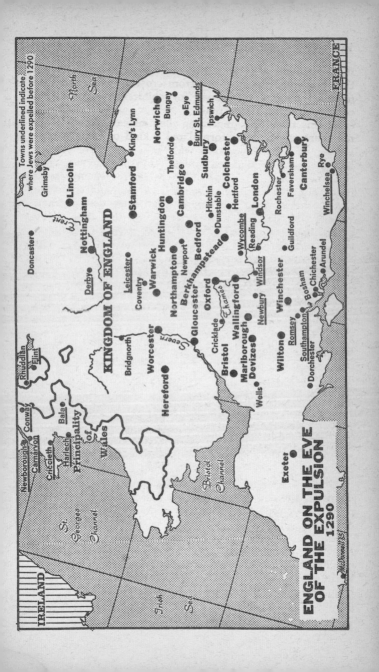

ENGLAND ON THE EVE
OF THE EXPULSION
1290

Towns underlined indicate
where Jews were expelled before 1290

KINGDOM OF ENGLAND

Principality of Wales

FRANCE

IRELAND

St. George's Channel

Irish Sea

North Sea

Bristol Channel

English Channel

Newborough
Conway
Carnarvon
Criccieth
Harlech
Bala
Rhuddlan
Flint
Newborough
Hereford
Bridgnorth
Worcester
Doncaster
Derby
Nottingham
Lincoln
Grimsby
King's Lynn
Stamford
Norwich
Bungay
Eye
Bury St. Edmunds
Ipswich
Thetford
Sudbury
Cambridge
Hitchin
Colchester
Huntingdon
Dunstable
Hertford
Leicester
Warwick
Coventry
Northampton
Newport
Berkhampstead
Bedford
Wycombe
London
Rochester
Gloucester
Oxford
Reading
Faversham
Canterbury
Cricklade
Wallingford
Windsor
Guildford
Rye
Marlborough
Newbury
Winchester
Chichester
Winchelsea
Bristol
Devizes
Wilton
Romsey
Bosham
Arundel
Wells
Southampton
Dorchester
Exeter

cut off European Jewry's one escape. They were permitted to leave only if they left their property behind them; or in the words of the treasurer of Duke Wratislaw II of Bohemia to "his" Jews, as they prepared to depart for safer lands; "sold for a mere pittance (by the Romans, after the Fall of Jerusalem), you have entered this land naked, and naked shall ye depart."

The persecutions confronted Jewry with the dilemma of how to treat those who had apostatized when threatened with death or expulsion, and petitioned to be readmitted when the danger had passed. Gershom ben Yehuda (960-1028), the first ranking rabbinical authority in Europe, whose writ was law to the Jews of France, Germany, and Italy, pondered the dilemma: having surrendered once, these penitents might, under pressure, surrender again. Moreover, their readmission might expose Jewry to the grave charge of proselytizing among Christians. His ruling to readmit them was therefore both liberal and courageous. Whatever the risk, the Jews could not deny spiritual repatriation to forcibly alienated brethren.

Rather than suffer expulsion, Rabbi Gershom's own son joined the Church and never petitioned for readmission. Jewish custom provides that apostates be mourned like the dead. Rabbi Gershom, having never forfeited the hope that his son would return, mourned him only on the day when the church bells tolled his natural death.

Two generations later, Rabbi Solomon Yitzhaki, or Rashi (1040-1105), one of Jewry's greatest teachers, went beyond Rabbi Gershom, ruling that grace, charity, and compassion be extended even those apostates who remained Christians "because fear of the sword compelled them." How different from the relentless policy of the medieval church toward errant sons.

CHRISTIAN DISSIDENTS

The church itself corroborated the Jew's conceit, by imputing to him every heresy in Christendom.

Impeachment of the arbitrary powers accumulated in the Papacy was often the primary, and always an ancillary, objective of the heretical movements. The Jews, albeit

politically unengaged, could not but draw comfort from the discomfort of the Catholic church.

The church charged that the Jewish communities on Germany's eastern frontier abetted the followers of the fifteenth century religious reformer, John Huss, whose rebellion had a double purpose: to recapture Christianity for the common man and to release his Czech homeland from Germanic rule. The Catholic forces which marched to extirpate the rebels rehearsed their violence on the Jews. It is likely, conversely, that fugitive Hussites were fed and sheltered by Jews.

MEDIATOR FOR GREECE

The Albigenses heresy in the south of France, supported by bishops, princes, and the populace had affinity to the doctrine of Averroes, or ibn Roshd, the Muslim philosopher, whose works had been translated by Jews from Arabic into Hebrew, from which Christian Hebraists translated them into Latin. Thus, a heresy was born.

All the insignias Christian Europe had designed, all the devices it had invented to contemn and contain the Jew failed their purpose. Popes, who censured Christians for consulting Jewish physicians, would themselves be treated by none but Jewish doctors; Christian scholars solicited instruction from and collaboration of Jews.

A prodigious pair of translators, Plato of Tivoli and Savasorda, contributed significantly to European humanist thought by translating mathematical and philosophical works from the Hebrew and Arabic into Latin. Savasorda's own work introduced Arabic trigonometry to Europe. Plato of Tivoli was a Christian; his collaborator's real name was Abraham bar Hiyya, a twelfth century rabbi, councilor to the Emir of Catalan. Savasorda means police chief, probably one of his functions at court.

Three successive generations of the Tibbon family of Provence committed their talents to translating Arabic works into Hebrew, and to collaboration with Christians on Latin translations. Samuel ibn Tibbon (1160-1232) introduced Aristotle, and his son-in-law, Jacob Anatoli (1194-1256), introduced Averroes to Europe. The astronomical researches of Jacob ben Makir, the son-in-law

of Moses ben Samuel ibn Tibbon, were studied by Copernicus and Keppler, and the astronomical survey instrument, Jacob's staff, is believed to have been named for him.

Just as the Jewish faith, addressing itself to the Jews, benefited all mankind, so the Jewish translators at this stage benefited all Christian Europe, although laboring primarily for the Jews. Their purpose was to sustain the traditions of Judeo-Arab culture in European Jewry, situated among peoples of inferior culture. This involved transmitting all accumulated scientific and philosophical knowledge, sustaining dialogue and free inquiry, and reclaiming the monumental works of Saadia Gaon, Judah Ha-Levi, and Maimonides, written in Arabic for a generation that knew no Hebrew, and for this reason inaccessible to later generations who knew no Arabic.

In the twelfth century, to advance this purpose, Abraham ben Meir ibn Ezra (1088-1167), scion of a dynasty of Spanish-Jewish scholars and literateurs, descended from Chasdai ibn Shaprut, the first Jewish diplomat at Arab courts, undertook a self-imposed mission to the eastern and western Diasporas, first traveling eastward to Babylonia, then through Palestine and Egypt into North Africa, and from there to Italy, Germany, France, and Britain. A Hebrew poet and grammarian, an author of critical commentaries on the Bible, and an astronomer whose works on mathematics translated into Latin were another bridge between Greco-Arab science and Europe, he was welcomed with reverence, wherever he went, but he also stirred controversy. He bore a celebrated name, possessed great learning, but his "rationalism" put conservatives on their guard. Christian intellectuals attended his lectures in the Jewish Quarters. Ibn Ezra was driven by an inner restiveness, a curiosity about foreign regions and peoples, and, perhaps primarily, by a sense of mission and obligation to communicate to European Jewry the accumulated intellectual riches of the Arab-Jewish era.

The impact of the Jewish Quarters' intellectual vigor on the state of European culture was so great that Joseph Ernest Renan (1823-1892), the French historian, wrote: "One of the reasons why France was slow in gaining from

the great transformation (Renaissance) is that about the year 1500 France had no Jews. The Jews to whom Francis I was forced to have recourse for the founding of his college . . . were Italian Jews."

ECONOMIC ROLE

The Jewish merchant, moneylender, and artisan were no less crucial to the development of the European nations, which is why they were readmitted as frequently as they were expelled. France particularly had a nervous habit of this, and on one occasion, in 1315, justified their re-entry on the ground of "clamour du peuple," popular demand. Protesting a price monopoly that followed Jewry's ouster, the populace acclaimed the Jews as "more honest in business than our fellow Christians."

To retain the Jews as councilors, some of the European nobility took great risks. When Pope Innocent III, backed by the Dominicans and Franciscans, ordered all Christian rulers to dismiss their Jewish officials, contumacious Count Raymond VI of Toulouse and thirteen other barons were dragged naked through the streets and scourged in church before they swore to obey him.

German mobs repeatedly drove the Jew out with a violence unmatched by any other rabble in Christendom. Then, like the French, to break the guilds' ruthless price monopoly, they raised a clamor for his return. Each time he was expelled, or was compelled to flee, the German Jew turned to Poland, which welcomed him. Like the Vandals of the fifth century and Charlemagne later, Poland needed the Jew. Jewish merchants had been crossing the Oder from Germany since the ninth century, buying agricultural products and pelts for the Western markets. Some Jewish fugitives from the First Crusade had even settled permanently in Poland.

Jewish traders roamed eastward beyond Poland, and since the tenth century had been traveling overland across the Slav territories to China, India, Persia, Iraq, Syria, and Egypt. They apparently had been sufficiently visible in eleventh century Kiev to enable its clergy to impute "Jewish influence" to Christian dissidents, who hoped to obtain the "real truth" from Abraham's seed,

as Luther did in his initial explorations. Travelers in those days were adventurous men, and these Jewish traders probably engaged in polemics when taunted by Christians.

ODIOUS OCCUPATION

Jewish merchants traveling abroad could offer a large variety of merchandise of Jewish manufacture. The Jewish Quarter had many skills and professions. It had physicians, cartographers, teachers, interpreters, scribes, and mathematicians—occupations in great demand outside the ghetto. It also had tanners, weavers, goldsmiths, locksmiths, carpenters, shoemakers, tailors, masons, and stevedores. It is the men of these lowly occupations who had great difficulty. The Jewish Quarter obviously was not economically self-sustaining. It could not employ all its labor force. Yet any attempt to offer its skills or merchandise on the larger market was ruthlessly beaten back by the Christian guilds which countenanced no Jewish competition. The Guilds occasionally even forbade the Jewish Quarter to produce certain goods for its own consumption.

Hence, the traveling Jewish traders were no doubt developing markets beyond their lands for the manufacture of their fellow-Jews. Others, circumscribed by the Christian guilds, turned to moneylending. These were few, of course: the men with money.

In turning to moneylending, they at first faced the disapproval of their fellow-Jews, but were from the very first encouraged by the church. The Bible forbade Jews to lend at interest rates to fellow-Jews. It did permit such loans to heathens, however, for this was the latter's way of doing business. The heathens were not impeded by inhibitions when they extended loans at exorbitant rates to Jews. At the time of the amoraim, Jews apparently had begun to lend money at interest rates to fellow-Jews, for there is no other explanation for the frequent indictment of moneylenders by the amoraim. The amoraim had admonished that even in loans to non-Jews, the moneylenders should charge just enough for a modest livelihood, and not be greedy. Adopting the classic Hebrew position, the church declared moneylending sinful for a Christian. Yet, since the European economy required credit, it im-

plicitly assigned this latrine duty to the Jew. This was one occupation in which he was encouraged. Nonetheless, Christian society took care to divest him of his profits. The authorities imposed burdensome taxes on him, the crown disposed of its debts by expelling him and seizing his property, and the lower echelons disposed of their obligations by lynching him.

Yet the Jewish moneylender as a class somehow survived the peril of his high visibility. He also established an enduring institution. W. F. Lecky, the historian, pointed out that "by traveling from land to land till they had become intimately acquainted both with the wants and productions of each" and by "organizing a system of exchange which was then unparalleled in Europe, the Jews succeeded in making themselves absolutely indispensable to the Christian community."

Moneylending was contrary to the Jews' conscience. Yet, in time, reluctant practice became relaxed habit. The Jewish banker, far from feeling embarrassed at his occupation, often began to exalt in his status outside Jewry. His wife and daughters dressed ostentatiously, his sons conducted themselves superciliously, and he boldly interpreted the law to his own purpose, even in the presence of rabbis. There was an undercurrent of discontent among the multitudes, mutterings that the law was incapable of helping them, that it had become the rich man's instrument, the scholar's relaxation.

A GREAT TEACHER

Two measures were necessary, one to curb the arrogance of wealth, another to shore up the people's confidence in its law. Ezra, the leader of the Return from Babylonia, once met such crisis head-on by removing the law from the priesthood and returning it to the people, by convening periodic assemblies at which the Torah was read and interpreted to the multitudes. In the Franco-German territories, during the Dark Ages, a pedagogic genius, the French rabbi Solomon Yitzhaki, better known as Rashi (1040-1105), performed a similar function. Without perhaps realizing its political implications, he launched a monumental adult education program.

There was danger of the people becoming alienated from the law. The Bible, let alone the Talmud, had become obscured by the many commentaries which none but the academically trained could grasp. Every passage, every sentence in the sacred and legal books, became the pretext for fantastic constructions. "Rationalists" squeezed the text for philosophical meaning; legalists used it to demonstrate their talent for sophistry; the mystics tortured the text for all kinds of clues to the Messianic era. The common man could not follow these, and if he could, would end in a state of frustration and irresolution. It seemed as if the sacred books had been returned to the priesthood. Rashi reclaimed them for the people.

His method was no less important than his purpose, which was to establish the literal meaning of the sacred texts. The teacher, he maintained, must relate the matter studied to the pupil's experience; instruction must be made interesting; it cannot be inflicted. In explaining agricultural law, Rashi drew contemporary analogies, probably from his own experience as a Champagne winegrower (the post of rabbi was still unremunerative then), and compared the implements of Biblical times with those of his own day. He interspersed his commentary with notes on gastronomical habits and fashions in clothes. These reconstructions of mood and circumstance endowed the Biblical texts with a "homeyness," vigor, and vividness no commentators before him had even attempted to evoke.

His Hebrew style is precise and succinct. At times, however, he would inject Latin and German synonyms and even complete French phrases to help elucidation. Students of the regional French speech of that time have found Rashi's commentary a veritable mine of information.

Already in his own lifetime, Rashi's commentaries became the most popular of all, accepted by Jewish scholar and common folk alike. His was one of the first two Hebrew books to come off the printing presses. By making the Bible and Talmud accessible to the common man, he made the people comfortable with its law, its past, its great historical figures, and even its god. If injustice was committed in its midst, the people no longer blamed the law and the books, as the Karaites had done, but the men

who perverted them. The custodians of the community's affairs could no longer pretend to be high priests of esoteric learning beyond the comprehension of plain folks.

It was necessary to make the law not only comprehensible, but also flexible. Jewry formally purchased the right to administer its intramural affairs and maintain its own courts, although these institutions were never quite free from Christian intrusion.

The law could not sustain its authority if it were, like the Catholic canon, dogmatic and observed in the breach. Rabbi Jacob Tam (1100-1171) of France, a grandson of Rashi, moved to prevent universal cynicism for all law by initiating periodic assemblies of all rabbis in Germany and northern France to accommodate the law to changing circumstance.

Unlike the Catholic synods and Lateran councils, after which they probably were modeled, these Rabbinic conclaves proposed both relaxation and prohibitions; although stern and unbending in ritualistic matters, they were liberal in the area of social law. Moneylending gave issue to anxiety and debate. The moneylender was often the support of the Jewish community; he purchased its residence franchise, and ransomed Jews captured by pirates. Rabbi Tam realistically refused to proscribe moneylending to Christians at interest rates on the grounds that "king and baron impose burdensome taxes on us, and we are scattered among them, and we must live . . ." However, the synods under his inspiration also very realistically regulated moneylending. They forbade taking Christian vestments and sacraments as collateral, because this often served as a pretext for violence, malicious laws, and expulsions. Allegations that they had defiled the sacraments, or stolen the Eucharist (the communion wafer) from the church, and pricked it with needles to make Jesus bleed again, periodically took a high toll of Jewish lives. They legislated against excessive interest rates on loans to Christians, and advised charity and compassion in collecting debts.

The rabbis' enactments also reveal Christian intrusion into Jewry's affairs, abetted by collaborators inside the Jewish Quarter. "No Jew may summon another before a

non-Jewish court, except by mutual consent, or if the other has refused a summons from the Jewish court; the plaintiff must indemnify the reluctant defendant for damages suffered from the judgment of the non-Jewish court," and "no Jew may solicit from non-Jewish officials appointment to a post in Jewry." Violation of these enactments was punishable by excommunication.

Thus, twelfth century Jewry in France and Germany as well as in England and Spain placed a new interpretation on the ruling of the third century Rabbi Samuel, confidante of the neo-Persian court, that "the law of the land is binding law" in all but religious matters. Matters may have been different in his day and his land, but could the Jews acquiesce in medieval Christian law which put them entirely beyond its pale? Hence, they interpreted his words to mean that "the law of the kingdom is binding, but its rapacity is not," and that the law of the king was not synonymous with the law of the kingdom. This was perhaps the first enunciation in Europe and England of the principles of due process of law and limitation of royal power. From the rabbis of the twelfth century it may have passed on to the authors of the Magna Carta, and through that document to the drafters of the Fifth and Fourteenth Amendments to the Constitution of the United States.

The Jews of Spain, heirs to one of the most vigorous intellectual periods in all Jewish history, and the Jews of southern France, gratuitous beneficiaries of Spanish Jewry's cultural fall-out, were reluctant to confine their fare to law alone. However, their territories having come under Christian rule, its restraining influence on free inquiry began to make itself felt among them as well. The raw nerve was the Jewish community of Montpelier. Situated in southern France, the frontier between eastern or Sephardim (Spanish) and Ashkenazi (Germany) or western Jewries, it was the seat of Jewry's counter-reformation. Its direct target was Maimonides' philosophical work, *Guide to the Perplexed*. Its ultimate goal was to ban all philosophy and science. Maimonides' supporters were read out of Jewry in solemn assemblies, and they in turn excommuni-

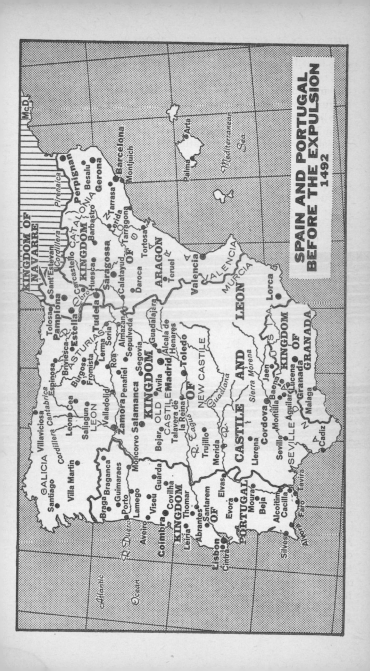

SPAIN AND PORTUGAL
BEFORE THE EXPULSION
1492

cated all anti-Maimonists. Jews on three continents were driven by this war of ideas.

And within this struggle mysticism began to make itself felt. Its roots dated back to Biblical days. Like a throbbing nerve, it always made itself felt in crises. Around the thirteenth century it began its longest tenancy, extending to modern times. It offered an ampler lap and softer shoulder than Maimonides' reason, and encouraged mystical calculations to establish the exact date of Messianic redemption.

OMINOUS CONFRONTATION

Jewry had still another burden to bear. Its rabbis were periodically summoned to publicly debate the merits of Judaism and Christianity. The Christian disputants could blaspheme Judaism all they wished, but the Jews, while holding their ground, had to abstain from any statements that might seem to dissuade Christians from their faith. It was an almost incredible task, but the rabbis were magnificent dialecticians.

These debates were first conceived in Greece in the ninth century. The Jewish participants were offered high office if they would admit defeat and apostatize. In Paris, in 1240, the debates were reduced to interrogations by the king. The Talmud was put on trial as an ominous work, and the ranking Jewish scholars were summoned, individually, without an opportunity to consult among themselves, and subjected to rigorous cross-examination by the king and his clerical mentors.

A new bold style in these enforced debates was set by Spanish Jewry's Rabbi Moses ben Nachmanides (1194-1270), physician, exegetist, and mystic. On July 2–24, on the orders of King Jayme of Aragon, at the royal court in Barcelona, he debated a Dominican friar and apostate from Judaism, Pablo Christiani. Nachmanides appeared reluctantly and demanded immunity or he could not debate. He was granted the request provided he did not blaspheme Christianity. He replied that he knew his manners. He scored impressively, and at the end of the third day, a small but affluent minority of alarmed Jews requested that he withdraw from the debate, even though

it might seem like surrender. His victory, they argued, would have disastrous consequences for the Jews. He replied that he could not withdraw. He must bear witness before the younger generation of Jews to the nobility of their faith. It was inconceivable that the judges should return a verdict in his favor. But he had visibly confused his Christian audience.

Because he circulated a summary of his arguments among the Jews, and transmitted a copy to the Bishop of Gerona, he was ordered expelled from Spain. He was then a man of seventy. He settled in Palestine, declaring repatriation a high privilege for Jews. He had been preceded by others in almost every generation. In a single bitter year for the Jews, 1211, more than three hundred rabbis from France and England emigrated to Palestine.

The most striking characteristic of Spanish Jewry was its proud posture. For two full centuries, from Nachmanides' debate to the eve of their expulsion, the Jews of Spain not only accepted each summons to debate, but produced a voluminous literature which, beyond merely defending Judaism, advanced the superior merits of their faith. Indeed, the official Expulsion Order listed alleged conversionist activities as the reason for banishing them. They were bold perhaps because of their long experience as statesmen, foreign traders, and participants in the general culture under Arab rule. They were probably confident that they were as indispensable to the new Christian rulers as they had been to their Muslim predecessors. They knew the mysteries of finance, were proficient in languages, and performed magnificently as mediators between the realm's diverse religious and ethnic groups. They were proficient still in the arts of war. Alfonso VIII (1166-1214) was so impressed that he knighted them and permitted their youths to join the sons of the Catholic aristocracy in training in the wide range of the arts of war. They repaid him amply in his crisis. Their help was crucial in hurling back an invasion of the Almohades, Muslim fanatics from North Africa. When Alfonso X (1252-1284) was still a crown prince, they helped him seize Seville from the Almohades, and received a village, and permission to fortify it, as their reward.

THE SPANISH WORD FOR PIGS

However, they somehow erred in their calculations. The Christian rulers used and then discharged them. A concomitant of the coercive public debates was accelerated pressure to compel the Jews to conversion. The mobs fell upon them, edicts proscribed their social relations with Christians, and they were ordered to wear the yellow badge.

Unlike German Jewry, they did not accept the badge docilely, but protested and circumvented it in every possible way. It was the badge, perhaps more than the violence of the mobs, that broke the spirit of many of the Spanish-Jewish elite, so that they began to embrace Christianity. Ultimately, Spanish Jewry paid its highest price, not for the many who persisted in their faith, but for the fewer who apostatized and were rewarded with high places in both government and the church.

Eventually, a cry was raised against the apostates, as long ago against the Jews in Pharaoh's Egypt: "They have multiplied and become a peril unto us." Christians who envied their eminence called the new Christians Marranos, Spanish for pigs, accused them of secretly practicing Judaism, and demanded their immediate dispossession. But many of the Spanish nobility were wary of the clamor. The best families had by the late fifteenth century intermarried with New Christians. There was a deep division on Marrano policy among the highest ecclesiastics. The national clergy supported Ferdinand and Isabella, under whom Spain was forcibly united, and urged that the Marranos be inexorably persecuted. The Ecumenical clergy located in Rome advised a softer line. Pope Sixtus bluntly charged that the persecutions were "not out of true zeal . . . but out of greed for their money." After more than a decade of agitation, he eventually acceded to Spanish pressure.

The Inquisition was established throughout Spain in 1483 to investigate and seize "secret Jews." It published a list, "37 Ways to Detect a Secret Jew," by his menu, by the phrase "Praised be the Lord and His Son" deleted from grace, or by a change of underwear on Friday afternoon.

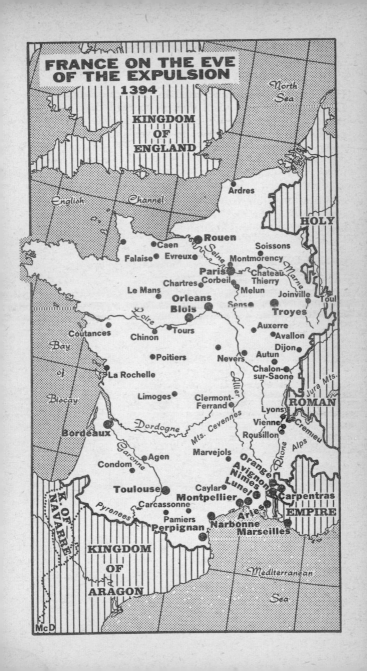

FRANCE ON THE EVE OF THE EXPULSION
1394

KINGDOM OF ENGLAND

North Sea

English Channel

HOLY

Ardres

Rouen
Caen
Falaise Evreux
Soissons
Montmorency
Chateau Thierry
Paris
Corbeil
Chartres
Melun
Le Mans
Joinville
Toul
Orleans Blois
Sens
Troyes
Auxerre
Avallon
Coutances
Tours
Chinon
Dijon
Autun
Nevers
Poitiers
Chalon-sur-Saone
La Rochelle
Jura Mts.
Limoges
Clermont-Ferrand
Lyons
ROMAN
Vienne
Bordeaux
Mts. Cevennes
Rousillon
Cremieu
Alps
Agen
Marvejols
Orange
Condom
Avignon
Nimes
Carpentras
Toulouse
Caylar
Lunel
EMPIRE
Carcassonne
Montpellier
Pamiers
Arles
Perpignan
Narbonne
Marseilles
Pyrenees

K. OF NAVARRE

KINGDOM OF ARAGON

Bay of Biscay

Loire
Seine
Marne
Rhone
Garonne
Dordogne
Allier

Mediterranean Sea

McD

EXPULSION FROM SPAIN

After several years of persecuting only Marranos, the Inquisition turned its attention to the real Jews. Being true to their faith, they could not, like the converts, be accused of infidelity to Christianity. They were accused, instead, of conspiring to reclaim new Christians for Judaism, and were tortured to compel them to name "secret Jews." Many died in agony, their lips sealed to the end. Others named even the guiltless.

Finally, a decision was taken to expel the Jews from Spain altogether, on the ground that as long as they remained, they would bait new Christians back to Judaism. Many Christians intervened against the order. A prophetic plea came from Sicily, then a Spanish vassal. "The Jews spend no less than one million florin a year on food. There are also their taxes. . . . All this revenue would be lost were they expelled. . . . Almost all the working population, consists of Jews . . . and we shall lose all makers of our metal utensils, iron instruments, shoes and all agricultural tools, indeed the makers of everything that is required in the construction of ships. It would be impossible to find Christian replacements within a short time, and those found would charge excessively. Thus we would be lacking in all the necessities of life. Real calamity might befall us were we attacked by the Turks, because albeit the Jews are incapable of actual battle, they are inordinately useful in war because of their labors, such as laying roads and constructing fortifications."

The appeals went unheeded. Ferdinand and Isabella, whose marriage was brought about by a Jewish matchmaker, had spent enormous monies on their wars to unite Spain. The sequestered funds of expelled Jews would erase the deficit.

In 1484, only one year after they had established the Inquisition against the Marranos, Ferdinand and Isabella had named an unconverted Jew to manage their depleted treasury. His financial ingenuity made their military triumphs possible, and they now pleaded with him to convert and remain in his post. Don Isaac Abrabanel (1437-1509), who was a ranking rabbi and author besides, re-

fused. On August 2, 1492, he marched at the head of the columns of expelled Jewry. They were headed for the harbor where an amorphous fleet waited to carry them to the four winds. They took their sacred scrolls with them, and even the grave markers. Their musical bands struck up brisk tunes, so that no Christian might say that the Jews were dispirited. Abrabanel declared that this was a first stage in the unfolding of their Messianic destiny. Catholic clergy mixed with the marchers, hoping at the last moment to persuade some to embrace Christianity. But rabbis appeared alongside the priests to bolster the faith of the weak.

The fleet of expelled Jewry, comprised mostly of leaking vessels, was probably serviced by very competent Jewish personnel. The Jews were eminent then as astronomers, cartographers, and navigators, engaged in many of the important exploration journeys. A Jew, Abraham Zacuto (1450-1510) taught astronomy at the universities of Spain and Portugal; in 1497, he outfitted the astrolabes for Vasco da Gama's expeditions. His almanacs were used on all vessels sailing the high seas. Joseph Vecinho, his pupil, who had been commended by Columbus, conducted navigation studies off the coast of Guinea for the King of Portugal. Jewish science and finance were engaged in all the major exploration of that day.

The vessels were shunted from harbor to harbor. They were preceded by myths of epidemic and sorcery, and stoned by howling mobs everywhere they dropped anchor. Christian princes bid for the services of the celebrated statemen and scientists aboard, who in turn negotiated the admission also of sizable numbers not on the list of preferred human stock.

Abrabanel was enlisted by Ferdinand I of Naples as financial adviser. He later served in the same capacity under Ferdinand's son and heir. In 1494, when the city fell to France, he followed his king into exile, and spent his final years in Venice. There he helped negotiate its treaty with Portugal, which expelled its Jews in 1497. Some of those expelled were admitted into the papal territories.

STRIFE IN CHRISTENDOM

The Holy See was especially distressed when the persecutions of the Marranos in Spain and Portugal continued after the expulsion of the Jews. Their effect was a serious moral derangement in the two Christian empires, and a political imbalance in all Christendom.

The Inquisition possessed virtually independent power in Catholicism. Employing thousands of men as investigators, interrogators, torturers, judges, informers, and witnesses, it could offer infinitely more sinecures than the Popes. Its agents were planted in Marrano businesses and clubs; household servants were encouraged to inform on their masters, and children on their parents. The accused was not accorded an opportunity to meet his accuser, or be presented with a bill of particulars. Arraignment was synonymous with conviction, conviction with death at the stake. Fugitive Marranos were tried in absentia and burned in effigy; those posthumously tried were exhumed and cast into the auto-da-fé. Victims included councilors of the exchequer, royal stewards, ranking theologians, and princes of the church. Informers shared the victims' sequestered estates with the Inquisition and the royal treasury. It was also a convenient way of disposing of political and business rivals.

During the Counter-Reformation the Marranos were singled out as a class, as the Jews had previously been. Philip II (1556-1598) of Spain and Portugal compelled them to wear the Jews' yellow cap. The Bishop Soliceo of Toledo obtained ordinances barring not only Marranos, but even their remote descendants from state and church office—probably the first legislation in Christendom that was based on racist, not religious grounds.

Spain and Portugal benefited from this policy. The sequestered assets enabled them to wage war and develop overseas territories. Papal opposition came from mixed motives. Some of the Popes had been affected by the Renaissance; and Rome was a center of humanist studies. Others feared that the persecutions alienated sensitive minds from Christianity. Pope Paul III (1534-1549) was moved by genuine compassion. He even proscribed per-

formance of the Lord's Passion in the churches, because it inflamed mob passion against the Jews.

Pope Clement VII (1523-1534) contended that the Marranos could not be arraigned for heresy "since they were dragged by force to be baptized (they) cannot be considered members of the church," and that even their children deserve forebearance and patience because "they have been brought up by their relatives in the midst of Judaism."

Both these Popes were engaged in a life and death struggle on two fronts: against emboldened Protestantism and against the secular arrogance, disguised as Catholic religious zeal, of Charles V, Holy Roman Emperor and King of Spain (1500-1558), who ransacked Rome and forced the Pope to flee.

A Marrano lobby in Rome offered to finance the See's defenses if the Popes restrained the Inquisition.

With a boldness of which no Jews in Christendom were capable at that time, it warned the Pope that "if tyranny persists, we would do what none of us would otherwise think of, namely return to the religion of Moses, and objure Christianity . . . we shall seek protection among less cruel people . . ."

The nature and posture of their reaction to Christian persecution was their legacy from a long line of "Josephs at court," dating back to Chasdai ibn Shaprut, the twelfth century Arab-Jewish statesman. Experienced in statecraft. they naturally thought of their relief in categories of political power. The Rome lobby was one means. But they had even more daring schemes.

THE MESSIAH–AMBASSADOR

In February 1524, a slight, dark-skinned man with an armed retinue disembarked from a vessel in Venice. Speaking only Hebrew and Arabic, he introduced himself through interpreters as David Reuveni sent by his brother Joseph, king of a Jewish empire in Arabia, to negotiate with the Pope and the Christian kings of Europe a military alliance to dislodge the Turks from the Holy Land.

One year later, a mad young man became attached to him. He was Diego Pires, scion of a Marrano family, one-

time secretary to the Lisbon courts, who upon hearing of Reuveni's appearance converted to Judaism, changed his name to Shlomo Molcho, and spoke of Messianic visions which had come unto him. Reuveni, who contended that he had come on an embassy, shunned Messianic semantics and fervor. But Molcho, schooled in Jewish mysticism and learned in languages and amenities of European high society, was useful to him. Molcho enchanted Pope Clement VII, who concealed him from the Inquisition, replaced him with an ordinary felon on its pyre, and helped him flee from Rome. Wherever Reuveni came, the Inquisition was ordered to suspend its work as a mark of respect for the Jewish ambassador. Lisbon pledged him an armed flotilla for his war on the Turks. Venice hoped he would help her retrieve her one-time dominance of Levantine shipping and trade.

The appearance of the Jewish embassy had visibly emboldened the Marranos. Agents of the Inquisition were waylaid and put to death. Marrano raiders penetrated her impregnable dungeons in Badajoz, Spain, and released Jewish inmates awaiting interrogation. The raiders, it was established, were not even Portuguese, but Spaniards who somehow had entered Portugal.

These episodes, strung together, presented an ominous façade. Jews concerned over the possible consequences of the Reuveni-Molcho adventure are reputed to have informed the Pope that the two men were impostors. Conversely, the Inquisition contended that they were agents of a far-flung conspiracy, seeking to obtain Christian means for a war not against the Turks, who had received one million Jewish refugees from Spain and Portugal, but against the Holy Roman Empire itself.

This intelligence was in the hands of Emperor Charles V when the two men and their ostentatiously outfitted retinue of councilors and armed guard, carrying the flag of the mythical Jewish kingdom, arrived for an audience with him in Ratisbon in 1534. He had them seized. Molcho was burned at the stake as a heretic, and Reuveni thrown into jail where he perished several years later.

This abortive adventure was nonetheless political action corresponding with the Marranos' experience and compre-

hension. Undaunted by its failure, they were to continue for another two centuries their quest for relief from oppression by the exercise of political pressures. An underground railroad, unparalleled for scope and ingenuity, deposited some of this fugitive Jewish power in the Italian harbors and in Antwerp, just then coming into her own as a trading center.

SERVING THE TURKS

By acquiring Jewish brokers and merchants, these cities assured themselves of a slice of the lucrative Levant trade which in Turkey lay in Jewish hands. Dispersed throughout Turkey's domains—in Greece, Yugoslavia, Bulgaria, and Albania—the Jews were now performing for her as they had first performed for the Arabs, and later for the Catholic kings of Spain, as cultural mediators between East and West, and arbitrators between the ruling people and the ethnic minorities. They were more polyglot than they had ever been, having added to their languages since Arab days. According to one Christian observer, they spoke "German, Italian, Portuguese, Spanish, French, Polish, Czech, Greek, Turkish, Syriac, and Chaldean."

Even before the full scale of Jewry's contribution had become visible, Sultan Bajazet II (1481-1512) declared that "Ferdinand (of Spain) was anything but wise. He enriched us, and impoverished himself."

A Christian, Nicolas de Nicolai, who in 1551 traveled with the French ambassador to Turkey, wrote: "They (the Jews) run the printing presses, hitherto unfamiliar to the Turks, and publish books in Latin, Greek, Italian, Spanish and Hebrew." What seriously disturbed this Christian observer was that "there are good craftsmen among them . . . especially among the Marranos . . . from Spain. To the detriment of the Christian lands, they have taught the Turks (the manufacture and use of) artillery and gunpowder, all the latest inventions of war."

Thus, the prophecy of the Sicilian petition against their expulsion came true. Turkey matched Europe weapon for weapon and held all Christendom in thraldom.

The Spanish Marranos, hard-pressed though they were for a haven, nonetheless stipulated with Turkey the con-

153

ditions under which they would transfer their capital. They demanded, among other things, a guarantee that they could dress as they chose. A sensuous people, they took pleasure in silks, brocades, and scents. Arab rulers sometimes, Christian rulers always, restricted Jewish dress to blacks and greys. Circumvention of these orders by the rich led to collective fine on entire communities. German Jews would never conceive of this as a subject for negotiation with government.

The flight of men and capital from Christendom involved complex smuggling operations centered in the Antwerp branch of the Mendes brokerage firm in Lisbon. Its ships sailed into the harbors of three continents. Its borrowers included Emperor Charles, and Francis I and Henry II, kings of France. The firm's fleet, accounts, and commercial agents were all in the service of the Marrano underground. The guiding geniuses of both the legal and the clandestine enterprises were the widowed Doña Gracia Mendes (1510-1568) and her nephew and son-in-law João Miques, later known as Joseph Nassi.

The Mendeses and Nassis were a single dynasty which since the twelfth century had provided Jewry with rabbis who served simultaneously as physicians, interpreters, and advisers to the Spanish royal courts. The family apostatized in 1492 through its elder, rabbi Abraham Benveniste Senior, patron of Abrabanel, tithe collector to the crown and marriage broker between Ferdinand and Isabella. He could not countenance expulsion in his old age. He and all his kin clandestinely practiced the Jewish rites.

Some of the Mendes' assets had already been secretly removed to Venice, and Doña Gracia herself had moved there when Charles V and Henry II impounded the family's fortunes on the ground that one of its deceased proprietors had been a secret Jew.

Venice, hitherto a safe station of the Marrano underground railroad to Turkey, now followed the example of the others, froze the funds and moved to deliver Doña Gracia to the Inquisition. She fled to liberal Ferrara where she openly reaffirmed her ancient faith.

Joseph Nassi, outwardly unperturbed, stayed on to negotiate a settlement with the royal claimants. He was

urbane, well traveled, and whenever he returned from one of his many multipurposed journeys across the continent, regaled his patroness Maria, ruler of Flanders, sister of Charles V, with the most succulent gossip from the European courts. The emperor agreed to release some of the fortune; the king of France refused to consider any compromise; and Nassi arranged for a special envoy from Suleimann the Magnificent (1520-1566) to carry an ultimatum which promptly obtained the release of the Mendes funds in Venice.

JOSEPH NASSI'S POWER

In August 1552, Doña Gracia entered the Turkish capital, with four stately carriages, forty splendid horsemen, and a large train of attendants. Later that year, having reverted to Judaism and again assumed the Hebrew family name, her son-in-law Joseph Nassi arrived with a host of five hundred Jews—financial councilors, scholars, scribes, trade agents, craftsmen and domestics, the full personnel of the Mendes enterprises in Christendom.

Strong-willed Doña Gracia, who already held in her grasp the reins of complex business undertakings, now gathered up, additionally, the reins of Turkish-Jewish communal affairs.

Joseph Nassi's unfailing intelligence on conditions in the Christian states became the basis of major Turkish economic and military policy decisions, and his generous credits enabled the Turks to pursue their advantages. Suleimann rewarded him with a gift of lands in Tiberias, which set off a rumor in Christendom that he would claim the Holy Sepulchre. On ascending the throne, Selim II named him Duke of the Aegean Sea, and gave him title to a total of twelve islands in its waters.

Christian emperors, kings, and ambassadors seeking the favor of the Porte, were obliged to shower gifts and flattery upon this powerful fugitive from the Inquisition, and address him as "Serene Highness" and "Illustrious Lord."

Emperor Ferdinand I of Austria, suing for peace after an ignominious defeat by the Turks in Hungary, instructed his ambassador to specifically seek this powerful Jew's

favor. A dispirited delegation of Venetians came to negotiate with him. Their Republic which had once tried to deliver Doña Gracia to the Inquisition, had just recently been humiliated by the Turks in a war over Cyprus undertaken by the Sultan on his Jewish councilor's advice, when all others had warned of his defeat by a Catholic coalition which never materialized.

Augustus Sigismund's strained relations with the Pope commended him automatically to the Jewish Duke's favor. Nonetheless, the Polish king thought it wise to mention in a letter to him that Poland would soon introduce additional measures favorable to the Jews.

Joseph Nassi's and Doña Gracia's most audacious political effort for their people was their attempt to break the power of Pope Paul IV. He had established the first ghetto in Rome, corralling all Jews into a few pestilential streets near the Tiber, and ordering their confinement between sundown and sunrise daily, and around the clock on Sundays and Christian holidays. Then the Pope's attention turned to Ancona, a papal seaport. He gave the Marranos, who had developed its commerce, the choice between death on the pyre and public penance and deportation to Malta, where they would be under surveillance for the rest of their lives.

Twenty-four chose death by fire. The others broke away and reached Turkey. At the same time, another group of fugitive Marranos communicated to Constantinople that the underdeveloped seaport of Pesaro admitted them on condition that it would obtain all the Jewish shipping hitherto cleared through Ancona. Joseph Nassi and Doña Gracia, heads of Jewry's greatest brokerage firm, promptly ordered their vessels to sail for Pesaro; at their urging Turkish Jewry, congregation by congregation, voted a provisional eight month boycott of Ancona (August 1556-March 1557), which the rabbinate reinforced with a unanimous decision to excommunicate those who traded with the papal city. Pesaro's harbor, unequipped to handle so much commerce, was clogged with Jewish vessels, while the once-busy Ancona cradled desultory trawlers on its tides.

All the world watched Jewry's economic war on the

Pope. Had this been pressed to conclusion, it might have compelled a reversal of persecution policy in all the Christian shipping states. However, from the Jews of Ancona —only Marranos had been deported—came an outcry that the Pope was holding them as hostages against the resumption of commerce. Two Constantinople rabbis thereupon refused to reaffirm the excommunication order, without which the boycott collapsed; Pesaro expelled the Marranos for not having met its conditions, and Pope Paul IV resumed his relentless persecution of Jews and Marranos alike.

Another great, albeit fleeting, opportunity to avenge himself on Catholic power presented itself to Joseph Nassi when a secret emissary from the prince of Orange reported that all the rebels needed for a successful insurrection against Spain in the Netherlands was a diversionary move by Turkey. The Jewish councilor argued for such a move, but a pro-Catholic faction among the Sultan's councilors now carried the day.

Joseph Nassi toyed intermittently with plans for Jewish statehood; when still in Lisbon, he tried to purchase an island for the Jews from Venice.

Later, as a high official at the Porte, he thought of Jewish statehood under the Turks, as had Chasdai ibn Crescas less than two centuries before under Mameluk rule. He began transforming, for the purpose, Tiberias into an industrial hub to be sustained by a cluster of villages. The city was to manufacture silks and textiles, an old Jewish art, and seize the market from Venice. Arab interposition at the Porte stalled him, and his attention strayed to other preoccupations. He also briefly considered his Aegean Islands and Cyprus as possible Jewish territories, but was diverted each time by other concerns.

When Murad retired him from service, Joseph finally had time but none of the influence required for this purpose. He had been replaced as the Joseph at court by Shlomo Ashkenazi, an Italian Jew, probably of German stock. Not of an imperious presence like Nassi, he was an adviser only to the pro-Catholic vizier, not to the Sultan, and although interceding occasionally for the Jews, had none of the Mendes-Nassi audacity.

THE NEW WORLD

Bold political endeavor did not cease with Doña Gracia and Joseph Nassi. Marrano lobbies at the Holy See and in all the courts of Europe scoured the horizons for new havens. In 1537, Marranos from Spain began entering France, taking up residence in Bayonne, Toulouse, and Bordeaux with whom they had long been trading. In little more than a decade, they had so well proved their worth that when Charles V ordered them to clear out of Antwerp, Henry II offered them lettres patentes and lettres de naturalité, guarantees of rights and privileges to settle in France.

The Antwerp magistrate, appealing against the emperor's order, claimed that the Jews had fewer bankruptcies, gave more honest weight and measure, charged lower interest rates than their Christian peers, and that their departure would cripple the harbor and ruin Flanders' industry. Less than one-half century after their expulsion (1550), Antwerp had shriveled to a dry fig.

For two centuries, wherever they ventured, the Marranos brought international trade and the best medical skills of that day. Amsterdam, capital of Holland, which had snapped the double stranglehold of Spain and Catholicism, was their chief beneficiary. When they first settled in the city in 1593, they were suspected of clandestine Catholicism; having overcome that handicap, they were caught up in a struggle between Calvinists and dissidents who charged the former with favoring Jews over Christians. The effect of this struggle was temporary restrictive legislation which soon evaporated, however.

Jewry discharged in northern Europe the same fermentative function it had previously discharged in Arabdom, in Catholic Spain and Portugal, and in Turkey which now declined through its bureaucratic lethargy and corrosion. Seventeenth century Europe watched with fascination Holland's emergence as contender to Spain and Portugal, and Jewry was credited perhaps beyond its deserve for the gradual alteration in the international balance of power.

Seeking a slice of the expanding ocean trade, harbor cities offered asylum to Marranos with international com-

mercial contacts, but having enticed them, often reneged on pledges to treat them with dignity. The Marranos, cognizant of their worth, would accept nothing less. They were haughty men of extensive commerce, who presided over trade with Spain, Portugal, and the Americas. In 1627, they served a written ultimatum on the senate of Hamburg. They were tired, they wrote, of being molested, pestered, and humiliated, and unless this condition was promptly remedied, would remove themselves from the city. Surely, they would be welcome anywhere. Persecution ceased.

Christian princes boldly offered to barter rights and religious freedom for Marrano science, initiative, and capital. On November 25, 1622, King Christian IV of Denmark addressed an invitation to refugees through the Jewish community council of Amsterdam as though it were the ruling house of Israel. In a sense this was so, for it was relatively secure, and possessed the posture of statesmanship and the skill to use economic power for political ends.

The havens were offered only to Portuguese-Spanish merchant princes and bankers. The majority of Jewish refugees were indigent craftsmen, victims of the Thirty Years' War (1618-1648) and the Ukraine pogroms which began precisely when that war ended. They were the unwanted, because no Christian state was ready to lift the bars so completely that the Jews could apply the full range of their skills and energies.

However, the ancient tribal tradition that every man is his brother's keeper, and that the entity is responsible for the least of its members, had never really ceased in Jewry, so that the Jewish notables of Amsterdam pledged the maintenance of all newcomers. Its ghetto, a cluster of several narrow cramped streets, had a limited absorptive capacity economically and even physically. Its leaders' eyes turned to a new world. Marranos had been settling in Cuba, Puerto Rico, Mexico, and Brazil since Columbus' first journey. They were the New World's first sugar and tobacco planters. Amsterdam Jews held large blocs of shares in the Dutch West India Company; Jewish youth from all Europe volunteered, in 1624, for the Netherlands

159

forces which wrested Brazil from Portugal, and the Company announced boldly that the Dutch would be aided by a Marrano insurrection inside Brazil. The Jews now joined Holland against Spanish-Portuguese Catholic power, as they had joined Islam during its invasion of Spain.

The triumph of Protestant arms in the New World did not always mean immediate free access for Jewish immigration, but it did provide prompt surcease for the resident Marranos from the Inquisition, which had celebrated its arrival in the New World in 1516 by burning New Christians at the stake in Puerto Rico.

NEW AMSTERDAM

In 1654, after a nine year war, the Portuguese recaptured Brazil from the Dutch, and the celebrated first group of Jewish fugitives from the Brazil Inquisition landed in New Amsterdam in September 1654.

There ensued the historic exchange between Governor Stuyvesant and his employer, the Dutch West India Company. The Jews were finally admitted on the condition that they care for their indigent. The Company's instructions to Stuyvesant hint at pressure from the Amsterdam Jewish stockholders, "after long deliberations upon the petition of the Portuguese Jews"; this pressure was a bold ultimatum. If it insisted on barring the refugees, the company was told, Jews might transfer their capital to French and other companies.

The author of that petition and its inspiration was probably Menashe ben Israel (1604-1657), whose regal features are entrapped in his friend Rembrandt's Portrait of a Rabbi. The Amsterdam son of a Marrano fugitive from the Inquisition, he was a dean at the Jewish academy where Spinoza had received instruction in his youth, and a member of the powerful three-man rabbinical court which ruled Amsterdam Jewry with the austere discipline of princes of the church. Like all Marranos, he was at ease in two worlds; his sermons and his books in flawless Portuguese and Latin acquired audience beyond the ghetto. A master also of eight other languages, he moved freely in foreign embassies; a religious rigorist, he was nonetheless a social lion in the best patrician homes; an other-

worldly mystic, he was a shrewd negotiator here on earth. His greatest asset was an imperial self-confidence, barely matched again in Jewry until the appearance at the end of the nineteenth century of Dr. Theodor Herzl, founder of Zionism.

In 1649, as soon as the first refugees from the Ukraine began to descend on Amsterdam, ben Israel initiated negotiations with Britain for the re-entry of Jews. There was a secret congregation of Jews there already which passed as Spanish Christians, engaged in trade with the Levant and India and foregathered periodically for secret worship at the home of the Portuguese ambassador to London. If Jews were permitted to re-enter, this congregation would surface and be immediately able to absorb some of the immigrants.

Menashe ben Israel could truthfully promise that Dutch Jewry would express its appreciation by investing liberally in Britain's overseas trade, if its brethren were readmitted by England. His major theme, however, was mystical, corresponding to his nature and to the high religious fever which then consumed Britain. Puritans adopted Old Testament names, turned Sabbath observers, claimed to be the lost Ten Tribes, predicted the imminence of the Messianic millennium, and Jewry's Return to Zion, where it would of its own free will embrace Jesus. Rabbi Menashe ben Israel, in Latin and English tracts, quoted sacred texts to prove that the Jews could not be reassembled until they had been dispersed among every nation on earth. Britain, he reasoned, has become a deterrent to humanity's redemption. So long as she kept the Jews out, their dispersion would not be complete, their Return precluded.

In 1651, a British mission to negotiate a trade treaty with the Dutch also carried instructions to open talks with the rabbi. The larger negotiations failed, a two year war followed, and it was several years before ben Israel could resume his approaches to London. In 1656, he headed a four-man Amsterdam Jewish delegation invited by Oliver Cromwell to present the case for the Jews' admission. The royalists organized opinion against it. In 1657, his mission a failure, Menashe ben Israel died on his way home from

London. Although he had not brought about the mystical closure of the cycle of Jewish dispersion, he left behind a legacy of political prescience, which his heirs used to good advantage. Approached for loans by Charles II, when he was an exile in Holland, Dutch Jewish bankers obtained pledges that the Jews would be readmitted if he reclaimed the throne. On his return in 1660, Jews began to re-enter Britain, unofficially, but in large numbers.

In 1673, to assuage the clamor of the guilds and the city council, the royal prosecutor arraigned London Jewry for worshiping publicly without formal sanction from the crown. By then they had made themselves sufficiently indispensable to serve notice: If not permitted freedom of worship, they would depart from London. The crown yielded.

READINGS: CHAPTER SEVEN

Abrahams, Israel. *Jewish Life in the Middle Ages.* 2 vols. New York: Meridian Books, 1958.

Bloom, Herbert. *The Economic Activities of the Jews of Amsterdam in the Seventeenth and Eighteenth Centuries.* Williamsport: The Bayard Press, 1937.

Brod, Max. *Reubeni, Prince of the Jews.* New York: Alfred A. Knopf, 1928.

Feuchtwanger, Lion. *Jew Süss,* an historical novel. London: Secker and Warburg, 1927.

Lew, Meyer. *The Jews of Poland in the Sixteenth Century.* London: E. Goldston, 1944.

Marcus, Jacob. *The Jew in the Medieval World, A Source Book.* Philadelphia: Jewish Publication Society, 1938.

Roth, Cecil. *The History of the Jews in Italy.* J.P.S., 1946.
—— *History of the Jews in Venice.* J.P.S., 1930.
—— *A History of the Marranos.* J.P.S., 1932.
—— *The House of Nasi, Dona Gracia.* J.P.S., 1947.
—— *The House of Nasi, The Duke of Naxos.* J.P.S., 1948.
—— *A Life of Menasseh ben Israel.* J.P.S., 1934.

Singer, Isaac Bashevis. *Satan in Goray,* a novel. New York: Noonday Press, 1955.

Chapter EIGHT

DRESS REHEARSAL
FOR
HISTORY

THE VIOLENT TRANSFORMATIONS WHICH EUROPE UNDERWENT from the fifteenth through the seventeenth centuries did not spare the Jew. Uprooted by political and economic upheaval from countries in which he had been settled close to one thousand years, the Jew moved to new and remote lands and was directly or obliquely affected by their cultures. He was also affected by the theological-philosophical schisms inside Christendom which were sometimes the cause, sometimes the result, of its great political alterations. These schisms were not exactly duplicated, but were certainly paralleled in Jewry.

The Mediterranean centers were in decline; Turkey and Holland, successively, were only brief respites for the Jews, whose population shift was in the direction of the East European lands. The Amsterdam community, descended from Marranos, conditioned by the Catholicism that had once been imposed on them, by the Calvinism of their new environment, was wary of all heresy. Italian Jewry mixed cosmopolitanism and mysticism, and in the ancient Hebrew habit of synthesis, increased its spiritual assets by borrowing from the culture around it. German and Polish Jewry, situated among inferior national cultures, retreated into the citadel of its laws and customs, and lived on its principle.

ITALIAN JEWRY

Italy, the universal capital of Catholicism, like all imperial capitals was more relaxed in its habits and comportment than the brooding hinterland. Yet even there, policy to-

ward the Jews was wholly unpredictable, varying from state to state, determined by the relationships among the estates and by whether the most powerful factor at any given time stood to gain from treating the Jew humanely, converting his ghetto into a hell, or turning him out into the fields like a beast.

Yet, throughout these three centuries, there were always at least a few cities in Italy, never the same ones, that ceded the Jew his human dignity.

Among Italian Jews were found individuals patterned after the renaissance Jew of Arab Spain, and after the Alexandrian Jew of Philo's day: like the former, in learning, versatile; like the latter, justifying themselves before their neighbors, and indulging freely in their relaxations. The Alexandrian Jew delighted in the gladiatorial spectacles, which the Judeans denounced as blasphemy. The Italian Jew requested his rabbis to rule whether it was permissible for a Jew to go hunting or to gamble for stakes on the Sabbath, even though monies were not passed. Rabbi Leon Judah ben Isaac Modena (1571-1649), eccentric and inordinately gifted member of the rabbinical tribunal of Venice, dissented vigorously from its ban on cards and dice. He was a passionate gambler who lost fortunes in that city's casinos.

However, these relaxations and preoccupations were confined primarily to the well-to-do: the tax collectors, bankers, physicians, and interpreters. The Italian Jew of more common breed was probably more rigidly observant, too. Burrowing in the cavernous Jewish quarters, where winter dampness and summer humidity were the only certain natural evidences of the changing seasons, he had a few occasions in his lifetime to venture beyond the ghetto, unless he was a runner for a Jewish brokerage firm.

The elite, of course, brought back to the ghetto the scents and affectations of speech, the costume and gesture of the outside world. It induced the so-called frivolous arts. Its ladies took instruction from Jewish dance masters whose clientele included members of the highest Christian society. It produced or sponsored instrumentalists, choreographers, actors, stage directors, playwrights, and composers of popular music who displayed their talents at

least twice a year. They performed in comedy on the most lighthearted of Jewish holidays, Purim, and staged the story of Joseph in Egypt during the Passover season, apparently Jewry's parallel to the Christian passion plays presented during Easter week. Christian aristocrats, attracted by these occasions, would then enlist the most gifted performers for the ducal and papal courts. Since Jewish actors would not perform between sundown on Friday and the appearance of the first three stars on Saturday evening, the Jewish calendar was carefully consulted by Christian nobility planning entertainments.

Performing as a clown to the majority has since become a minority's classical means of insinuating itself into the larger community. The Jewish banker only incurred odium for American Jewry at the turn of this century, but the Jewish vaudevillian obtained prompt and enthusiastic acceptance. The American Negro, too, finds fewer professional and social bars in entertainment than in other areas of American life.

Thus, the Italian theater and probably also the ballet had their beginnings in the Jewish ghetto. There were Jewish instrumentalists in the service of Pope Leo X; a Jewish choreographer, Guglielmo de' Pesaro, was a protege of Lorenzo de' Medici; Salamone de' Rossi, composer of synagogal liturgy, was engaged by the Mantuan court and a collaborator of Monteverdi; and Leone de' Somni Portaleone, a Hebrew poet and an elder at his synagogue, was also the author of popular Italian plays and a book on stagecraft, the first in any modern language.

ANTICIPATING LUTHER

Italian Jewry's contribution went beyond commerce and entertainment. Embracing literature and scholarship, it had an enduring impact on its times and beyond. "If you contemplate love," wrote Cervantes in his preface to Don Quixote, "apply your two ounces of Italian to reading Leone Ebreo's Dialoghi (di Amore)." Christian Europe, afflicted with many schisms, sought surcease from its consuming hates in this testament to universal love by an author who was admittedly an Ebreo, Hebrew. Unwilling to concede such capacity for love to an unrepentant Jew,

it contended he had embraced Christianity. Judah Abrabanel (1437-1509), which was his true name, had accompanied his father, the statesman Don Isaac Abrabanel on his flights and expulsions from Portugal, Spain, and Naples. His one son was snatched away by the church when still an infant, and he could never trace him. Although sorely tried on both scores, he had never forfeited his ancestral faith and his love for man.

Italy, in the sixteenth century, was turning to Hebrew. The Holy See believed that the Jewish writings could offer irrefutable confirmation of Christian myth. The dissidents, the Karaites of Christianity, cited the Jewish Bible to support their charges that the Church had perverted the sacred texts to its own purpose. Both Christian camps, therefore, enlisted Hebrew instructors and translators from the ghettos. These received generous stipends, were occasionally invited to lecture at the universities, and were frequent visitors at the salons of Italian society.

Egidio da Viterbo, General of the Augustine Order and later a Cardinal, maintained a Jewish scholar and his family at his palace for a full decade (1517-1527), providing them with kosher food, while the family head instructed him in Hebrew mystical writings. Count Giovanni Pico della Mirandola (1463-1494), the Italian humanist, similarly received instruction in mysticism and Hebrew from a Jew, with whom he struck up a remarkably intimate friendship. He recommended the same course of studies to a German friend, Johann Reuchlin (1455-1522), who also engaged a Jewish teacher, and eventually became an authority on the post-Biblical Jewish writings, particularly the Talmud, which the Dominicans (1510) had asked to be committed to the flames because it allegedly contained incitement against Christianity. They made the tactical error of proposing that Reuchlin be appointed to a commission to study the issue. Although no friend of the Jews, he ruled in favor of the Jewish literature. However, he soon became more deeply committed than he had contemplated. When the friars assailed his legal opinion, he realized that the Dominicans' real target was free inquiry, classical studies, and Christian humanists like himself. Eventually, he became a defendant in Dominican

litigation before the Pope; controversy raged across Germany and occasionally pitched battles were fought between his supporters and foes.

The controversy set the mood for the emergence of Martin Luther, who drew simultaneously upon Reuchlin in refuting the clergy, and upon the Dominicans in inveighing against the Jews. The Italian Jewish scholar who instructed Reuchlin so well in Hebrew was surely, unbeknown to himself, an element, however infinitesimal, in the Protestant precipitation.

Sixteenth and seventeenth century Italian, like contemporary American Jewry, was very much preoccupied with its public image in Gentile eyes. It produced three genres dedicated to this end. One, in the pattern of Greco-Jewish writing, tried to establish a cosmopolitan tradition for Judaism. Its most illustrious exponent was Azaryah de' Rossi (1513-1578). Another genre was cultivated by Modena, the gambling rabbi who was an admixture of the Pharisee and Sadducee, who handed down harsh judgments against skeptics while tortured by disbelief himself. He was the precursor of some American Jewish writing which ranges from condescending descriptions of the Jew as an entertaining oddball to savage caricatures of him. Modena's contribution was a little book on Jewish customs and rituals which regaled his Christian friends and went through innumerable editions. He offered the customary defense that this was an objective study, written "as if from the outside," but the readers' reaction to what they regarded as "inside information" was very subjective and self-righteous. They did not pause to think that peculiarities of this sort, at one time acquired for very rational reasons, were easily matched in the cultures of all peoples. This stress on oddity served the purpose, one century later, of those who argued that "superstitions" warrant caution in admitting the Jew as a citizen with equal rights of the European states.

A third genre was initiated by Rabbi Simcha Luzzato (1583-1663), Modena's contemporary and colleague on the rabbinical tribunal, who established a new pattern of Jewish apologia, preferred by many to this day. The Greco-Jewish apologists had stressed the cosmopolitanism

of Jewish tradition; the medieval Jewish polemicists counterposed at great risk the merits of Judaism and Christianity; Luzzato reduced the scale. The Jew was no longer a contestant, or a peer. Luzzato pleaded that the Jew be continued in favor because of his usefulness to the city. Its Jewish population numbers only eight thousand, he wrote, yet the ghetto provided jobs for four thousand Christians. Venice would have been economically ruined by British and Dutch domination of the oceans, had her ghetto not appealed to Jewish brokerage firms in other lands for shipping and commerce. This is the kind of argument used today, when humanitarian appeal defaults, to obtain the admission of refugees into the United States. Luzzato also had to contend with the charge of dual allegiance. Surely, if Jewish brokers of other cities cooperated so well with Venetian Jewry, the latter might join them in some international political conspiracy. Luzzato explained that there was no danger of that, because the Jews were ordered by their law to await redemption by the Messiah and not try to hasten it with precipitous human action. He informed his readers that his people had a tradition, as binding as any Mosaic commandment, not to intervene against a government or ruler which has been fair and just to them. This was an implicit assurance that rumors of Jewish assistance to the Protestant cause notwithstanding, Catholic Venice need not fear harm from the Jews.

AMSTERDAM HERESY

In Italy, Jewish mystics could coexist with rationalists and rigorists with "heretics," despite the tensions between them. This was impossible in Amsterdam, however, probably because its Jewish population was primarily Marrano and included a high proportion of former monks, from all the orders—Franciscan, Jesuit, Dominican, and Augustinian. Having defected from absolute Catholic discipline, they sought a corresponding discipline in Judaism, and clashed with other former Catholics who, having cast off the restraints of the church, hoped to function within Judaism without any restraints.

Nothing, neither theology, philosophy, or even the sci-

ences, could at this time escape assault by restless young minds. The Jews were hardest hit, however, or so it seemed to the elders of Jewish Amsterdam. Their ghetto had become a citadel to which flocked refugees from the Ukraine pogroms and the Thirty Years' War, and fugitives from accelerated Catholic inquisitions. They brought with them mixed attitudes: the nervous morale of their hazardous experience, the conceit that their fate was Divine Election, and the cynicism of those who had thrown away the last chip of their trust in humanity, and God. Christian persuaders in Amsterdam studied the fever chart of this chaotic Jewish humanity, and solicited converts diligently.

The reaction to these perils of the former Marranos who were the custodians of public morality corresponded to their early Catholic conditioning. Jewry had long used excommunication, a religious device, as the supreme penalty for violators of its laws, generally applying it to those who digressed from moral principle—loansharks, black-marketeers, and informers. Seventeenth century Amsterdam Jewry used it to enforce maximal religious conformity. It had the official sanction of the city's civil authorities. A ban of excommunication was paced in two stages: first, a provisional or "the small ban" restricted in time and degree, and when this failed to effect penance, "the big ban" was pronounced which forbade even his closest kin to have traffic with the excommunicant. There was always a way back through penance, however, and when the ban was lifted, restoration was complete and unqualified.

The forms of public penance prescribed for those seeking relief from the ban reflected the judges' own experience under Catholicism, and were wholly alien to Jewish tradition. In at least one instance, the Inquisition's penitential procedures were copied rather closely: The penitent was ordered to appear in humble dress in the synagogue and read out to the entire congregation a confession drawn up for him by the tribunal. He was then subjected to flagellation, and ordered to lay down on the threshold, after which the congregants stepped across his prostrate body, digging their heels in his ribs.

169

THE CASE OF SPINOZA

The cause célèbre of all the bans has been the excommunication, in June 1656, of Baruch Spinoza (1632-1677). The philosopher was only twenty-four at the time, and none of his work had yet been published, although his views no doubt were generally known. There is some evidence that his judges were less concerned with his intellectual dissent—Jewry has always debated, seldom outlawed ideas—than with his public deviation from Jewish custom. Judaism being a faith of deeds, not dogma, digression from its custom is the only tangible evidence of defection. The philosopher was accorded more than the customary opportunities to recant, but proudly refused them.

Spinoza taught that God was not beyond, but of the universe, the phenomena of which are manifestations of His imperishable being. Everything is obedient to incontrovertible laws within and beyond itself, and is unable to alter its course. Man is no exception. Thus, in Spinoza, Jewry again encountered the mechanistic concept of the Greeks, to which the Jews counterposed their belief, that man is nature's sovereign, accountable for his deeds, and in a reciprocal relationship with God. However, borrowing from Maimonides, whom he repudiated, Spinoza provided a hairpin margin for choice and virtue: "Blessedness is not the reward of right living, but right living itself." A select few may by vigor of intellect surmount the encumbrances of greed and passion and, although not escaping the irrefragable law of determinism, raise themselves to a plateau of supreme contentment through the knowledge and love of God.

His view of state and law similarly conflicted with Jewish philosophy and Jewish polity. The Jewish view is that authority derives from law; Spinoza's view was that law derives from authority, that authority ceases when its ability to enforce obedience ceases; freedom to think as he chooses and even to state his dissent is every man's right, but his actions are rightly subordinate to the state or ruler who may define faith and heresy. By Spinoza's

own definition, the Amsterdam Jewish elders would seem to have been justified in trying to compel his obedience.

His view of Jewish history was acidulous. The early Jewish state through the era of the judges was a wonderfully harmonious theocracy, the decline of which began with the monarchs; Jewish history since the first dispersion was, to Spinoza, senseless and purposeless. He placed Jesus above Moses, and spoke charitably of New Testament and acidly of Old Testament miracles. His concession that somewhere in the divine scheme there may still be hope for Jewish regeneration was no comfort. Spinoza may well have been the source of Toynbee's dim view of Jewish history, including the codicil that Judaism may perhaps still have a role to play.

GERMANY

The contrast between the Christian Reformation in Germany and in Holland and England is significant. It is pertinent in our own day. It may provide a key to what befell the Jews in Nazi-occupied Europe.

The Dutch and British Reformations were Messianic, universal, perhaps because both these countries, engaged in ocean trade, were in communication with half the world, and many cultures and peoples. Their Reformations, notwithstanding some excesses, spawned a rich diversity of dissenting sects, inquiry into wide fields of intellectual endeavor, launched the secular era, and embraced the Jews and excited Jewish minds. The Prince of Orange, seeking Turkey's intervention against Spain, sent a secret emissary to Joseph Nassi. Cromwell negotiated with Menashe ben Israel. Even Spinoza's heresy is more than vaguely related to the Reformation.

In Germany, the Reformation broke upon an insular people. It was from the outset, and never ceased being, a humorless, ruthless presence. Luther stifled the humanist impulse ignited by Johann Reuchlin. He stifled the Reformation's Messianic impulse by joining the princes in suppressing the religio-Communist Peasants' War (1524-1525). He turned maliciously against the Jews when they refused his Christianity, as they had for centuries refused the Popes'. He gave new incentive to the expulsion of

171

Jews from Germany, which had been going on since the fifteenth century.

The German Jews were chattel under the law, belonging either to the barons or to the emperor. The barons, valuing them as property, tried to protect them. The emperor, for a consideration, permitted city after city to turn the Jews out and seize their property. In 1499, for example, the good burghers of Nuremberg paid the emperor 8000 gulden for this right. Being a parsimonious people they wasted nothing that the Jews had left behind. They even paved the streets with the Jewish grave markers. Luther gave these expulsions his enthusiastic theological sanction and presaged in every detail, except the gas chambers—gas was a latter-day invention—Hitler's final solution. Luther's injunction was clear and specific: that the Jews' assets "be sequestered, their homes razed, their synagogues leveled, (that) they be driven off the roads, quartered in stables, assigned to the mines and quarries, and compelled to fell trees, skin animals and sweep chimneys."

POLAND

This policy paid off in irony. Many of the expelled Jews crossed into Bohemia and Austria, so that during the Thirty Years' War (1618-1648) when both embattled camps were credit-hungry, most Jewish bankers and provision merchants were concentrated in the Catholic territories.

Poland, unlike Austria, did not confine Jewish immigration to financiers and brokers. Jews entered in multitudes, so that by the end of the sixteenth century, Polish Jewry numbered 150,000; in the mid-seventeenth century, when catastrophe struck, the Jewish population was 500,000.

Permitted to engage all their skills and resources, the Jews had an extraordinary, invigorating effect on the Polish economy. Their capitalists became financial agents at the court, leased the royal custom duties' concession, invested audaciously in salt mines and in the exploitation of other natural resources. They established a flourishing international trade by importing finished goods from Frankfurt, Breslau, and the Netherlands, and exporting pelts, agricultural products, and cattle to Bohemia, Mora-

via, Silesia, Hungary, and Turkey. They provided, on the lower economic echelons, physicians and auditors, vegetable farmers, fruit growers, cobblers, tailors, goldsmiths, and jewelers. Serving, as they had elsewhere, as cultural mediators, they established three large printing plants and, in addition, distributed Latin books printed in Venice.

The higher nobility and the kings favored them. The Jews provided loans and revenue. The common folk favored them. Goods were more available and prices dropped wherever Jewish tradesmen appeared. They bid successfully for concessions to collect custom duties, which the lower nobility regarded as its preserve, and hence were resented by it. They were also resented by the Christian guilds whose monopoly they broke and, of course, by their traditional foes, the Germans. The eruptions against Jews were most frequent and violent in Polish cities with large German populations. The triumvirate of lower nobility, the guilds, and the Germans finally compelled the Jews to evacuate the cities and seek their livelihood in the rural Ukraine. This was Poland's eastern-most frontier. Life was austere and dreary there, and the Jews acquired an additional enemy—the Ukrainian serf.

Everything in sight belonged to the Polish barons and bishops—the fields, rivers and forests, the flour and lumber mills, the breweries and inns, and even the Greek Orthodox Churches in which the Ukrainian prayed. The Jew leased it all, except, the churches, from the Polish aristocracy. The absentee landlords were given a sizable down-payment, pledged a share in the profits, and guaranteed against loss. Confident in the Jews' competence, and ever-suspicious that it was being cheated, the Polish nobility spent its income lavishly and pressed the Jew for more revenue.

To meet the Poles' mounting demands and yet sustain himself, the Jew was compelled to squeeze the Ukrainian, while his own reward was only a meager livelihood in primitive surroundings, several days' travel by horse and buggy to the nearest synagogue and Hebrew school. It was

173

a precarious isolation. To the Ukrainians, he had become the embodiment of their horrible fate under Poland.

Polish Jewry, anticipating that this might lead to catastrophe, took steps to enforce ethical business practices and to punish miscreants. But the situation could not be essentially altered because it was not of the Jews' making.

Discipline was enforced by the kahal or Jewish town council, the functions of which were no different from those elsewhere in Jewry through the centuries. It collected taxes for the government, supervised universal elementary education, and either directly, or through voluntary agencies, looked after the needs of orphans, widows, and the aged, and provided for indigent travelers. The larger communities maintained a hospitality house, and even arranged visits to the sick and mourners.

Poland Jewry differed from all other Jewries however in that it maintained, for two centuries, a very elaborate judiciary and parliamentary structure, unparalleled in Jewish Diaspora history. Each kahal had a three-tier judiciary which formed the base of a pyramid of state and federal courts and legislatures. These institutions, initiated in the mid-sixteenth century, endured for two centuries, until Christian authority stripped them of their powers.

The federal parliament, called Vaad Aratzot, the Council of States, also apportioned among the various kahals the combined tax for the royal treasury and Jewish institutions, and legislated on every aspect. It determined the permissible rate of interest on loans, and exorcised ostentatious dress and lavish spending which might incur Christian enmity. Polish Jewry also maintained lobbies— watchdog committees of Jewish notables who attended sessions of the Polish Sejms, or legislatures, both state and federal—to enlist opposition to anti-Jewish bills introduced by the guilds and the Catholic clergy.

HUMANISM IN THE GHETTO

This Jewish self-government was shored up by extensive law which had for long been the major preoccupation of the rabbis of Germany and Poland whose Jewries were as one, before they parted in the eighteenth century. The impression has been that law deteriorated into ritualism,

and resulted in a complete break with the tradition of broad-range investigation that marked, particularly, the era of Jewish life under Muslim rule. This is incorrect. Ritualism was plentiful throughout Diaspora history, and much of it simply gave religious endorsement to significant law, which ranged from the social to the hygienic. It also provided relief from the inescapable, enforced drabness of the Jewish quarters. It was especially necessary interior decoration in Germany and Poland, which were Christian Europe's cultural backwaters.

Ritualism transformed a dull life into a stimulating experience by according mystical meaning to each mundane moment, and transforming the Jew's every movement, however low his earthly state, into divine service.

The jurisprudence propounded and created under these circumstances ranged over wide areas. Its applied social law presaged some of the best contemporary legislation. The kahals' revenue was derived from a graduated income tax. There was frequent conflict between the judiciary, or rabbis, and the oligarchies which governed Jewish affairs, over the latter's attempts to confine suffrage to the highest tax brackets.

The German and Polish rabbis had none of the stimulus of direct environmental challenge afforded Jewish intellect under Muslim rule or in Renaissance Italy. Yet their intellectual preoccupations ranged widely.

A striking example was Rabbi Yehuda Aryeh ben Bezalel Lowe (1515-1609), or Maharal; Czech and Jewish legend credits him with protecting the Prague Jewish Quarter from the mob by creating a giant clay figure, a golem. Whenever the rabble approached the ghetto, he would invest the golem with a Cabalistic amulet which gave him formidable powers that frightened the enemy off. As soon as the peril receded, the rabbi would remove the amulet and return the golem to his inert state. This legend perhaps carried an implied reply to Spinoza, suggesting that authority derives from law, not law from authority.

Maharal's interest in mathematics and physics is startling to anyone who thinks of the Polish-German rabbinate as preoccupied with nothing but ritualism. His

comments on freedom of thought, relations between nations, and national cultures bear comparison with the best humanist thought of the day. At a time when Martin Luther inveighed against all dissenters from his dogma, and several decades before its divisions were to catapult Christendom into the Thirty Years' War, Maharal had this to say on religious freedom: "It is improper to reject that which is contrary to one's views. Everyone should be permitted to express his opinion, however contrary to accepted doctrines of faith, for if people are compelled to keep mute we shall never really know their views and comprehend the faith that moves them."

He analyzed the distinguishing characteristics of Greek, Jewish, and "Edomite" culture. In the Aesopian language of the Jewish writers, "Edom" meant Rome, both Christian and pagan. "Greece is the symbol of wisdom" (philosophy), he wrote. "Her power has been that she penetrated the Palace of Beauty more deeply than other nations," meaning her contribution to art and aesthetics. Judaism advanced moral commitment, "obliged man to his fellow, affirmed the sanctity of human life." The contribution of Rome, representing power, "has been least and inferior; she imposes herself, seeks to devour everything in sight, and cannot countenance the sovereign existence of other nations," yet "even as each object has its space, so is each nation entitled to its own." The harmony of the universe derives from diversity, and to this end each nation is unlike all the others, is conditioned by its own peculiar circumstances, "hence even their languages and their script are different. . . . Because mankind had not yet grasped the cosmic purpose of diversity, nation declares war on what is different in the other. . . ." Because Jewry is singularly different, "The nations hate one another, but hate the Jew most and turn on him like savage beasts." Harmony will eventually prevail because "the enslavement of one nation by another is contrary to natural law."

Of course, there were recessive elements opposed to all investigation. One eminent sixteenth century Polish rabbi Solomon Luria (1510-1573?) was outraged when he found that students at the rabbinical academy were circulating

texts by the "uncircumcised Aristotle," but another great rabbi, Moses Isserles, staunchly defended Maimonides' Aristotelianism and published a commentary on Theoretica, Frohbach's astronomical work. The controversy was anachronistic, because at that particular moment in history this Polish rabbi may have been among the few surviving defenders of the Greek philosopher, the scientific revolution having just disproved Aristotle's science. However, the same rabbi who opposed the "uncircumcised Aristotle" was a liberal jurist. Law must be fluid, every generation is responsible for its own, and cannot escape it by quoting precedent. Each judge must choose carefully among legal precedents, and if he find them wanting, even if their author be Maimonides, must turn afresh to the Talmudic texts for independent deductions. Thus, the exponent of philosophy was a radical in law. Extreme fluidity could lead to chaos, however. He was in fact a student of mysticism which one century later, blown up into a powerful mass movement, almost caused the disrupture of all law.

MYSTICISM

Jewish mysticism persisted since the Second Temple as a low, only seldom strident voice alongside legalistic Judaism. It had both populist and intellectual elite bases. The former, erupting occasionally as Messianic mass movements, was socio-national in impulse, centered on the people, or nation, and sought to achieve the Return to Zion and equity on earth for all mankind. The second was individualistic-ethical in impulse, advocated absolution through esoteric self-denial, and circulated its doctrines to a jealous inner circle.

In the mid-sixteenth century, Rabbi Isaac Lurya (1534-1572), of Safad, Palestine, and his disciples, fused the two trends into a cosmologic theory of the universe. Lurya, like the Greek philosophers, was a peripatetic teacher. He never committed his words to writing. We have only the version transmitted by his disciples.

The combined doctrine of the Jewish mysticism of the period was an admixture of elements, including the gnostic dating to the First Dispersion in Babylonia. The apoca-

lyptic element is already evident in Ezekiel. The doctrine of the transmigration of souls may be Pythagorean. The homiletic portions of the Talmud list an angelic hierarchy whose nomenclature has Persian roots.

The ethical dualism, good and evil, of the aggada portions of the Talmud, evolves into a more dubious dualism in later Jewish mysticism. Even before Genesis, according to this combined doctrine, ten degrees of divine emanations descended through the lower spheres, apparently to purify them. Some of these emanations erupted from their vessels, intermixed, and brought on a horrible disrupture of universal harmony. Like the Jewish people, God himself languishes in exile, awaiting the restoration of harmony. The shechinah, never clearly defined, but vaguely reminiscent of Christianity's Holy Ghost, is awaiting God, as a bride awaits her groom, and when the two are mated, supreme delight, hence full harmony, will have been achieved. Israel is to perform a special function by somehow raising itself to high levels of being, and drawing the rest of salvageable mankind with it. The people and the land of Israel are indispensable to the redemption of the universe, and hence to God's own fulfillment. Thus, unlike Christian doctrine, it is not God's son who redeems the universe, but God and mankind who redeem each other through some reciprocal action.

Sixteenth century humanity seemed like clay in the hands of an erratic maker, as power shifted and Christendom split. Chiliasm, the doctrine that the chiliad, or millennium, was on hand when Christ himself would rule on earth, turned sensitive Christian minds, seeking a key to history, to Jewish mysticism which offered striking analogies to Christian semantics. They found similarity between the shechinah and the Holy Ghost, the contaminated emanations and Original Sin.

Jewry had even more reason to seek comfort in esoteric teachings. The Spanish expulsion was a searing memory, as Jews were still being tossed from land to land. The mystical movement had a cosmopolitan élan in Italy and Holland where there was association between Jewish and Christian mystics. The mystical tradition of Spanish Jewry, from whom these communities were descended

was of a philosophical predisposition. Conversely, German and Polish Jewry was obsessed with a demonology which had both ancient and immediate environmental roots. The mythology of the German and Polish peasants who still secretly called on their nature gods to protect them from the ambient malignant forces, could not but work its awe also upon the Jew.

Itinerant Jewish preachers, whenever catastrophe threatened, drew upon demonology to chasten the women and the am haaretz towards penance. It comforted the isolated Jew to think of himself as potentially a divine emanation awaiting redemption from the contaminated Ukraine environment. This folkloristic mysticism was advanced in books in Yiddish, a language whose base is an amalgam of German, Hebrew, and Slavic elements. Yiddish manuscripts, which began circulating in the fourteenth century, fell into three general categories: fiction and travel, translations and interpretations of the Bible, and moralistic tracts. Demonologic mysticism belonged to the latter category. None of the learned read it. Like the itinerant preachers, the authors addressed themselves to the women and the inadequately lettered menfolk; in this manner, those of simplistic faith became a factor in shaping the East European Cabala.

UKRAINE CATASTROPHE

In the mid-seventeenth century the scene was set for the conversion of Jewish mysticism into a political force. The trigger-event occurred in 1648 when Bogdan Chmielnicki (1595-1657), a Ukraine Cossack chieftain, launched with the Tartars a rebellion to sever his country from Poland. The rural Jewish leaseholders and agents, the visible embodiment of Polish feudalism, were his first victims. He then marched on the towns and cities, everywhere perpetrating horrendous crimes against the Jews who defended themselves furiously. They fought by the side of the Poles, and when the latter betrayed them, fled in panic, or deserted (a Polish commander crossed over with his entire force to the enemy), the Jews still held out until thirst and hunger felled them. It was an amazing exhibition of endurance, valor and martial prowess that aston-

179

ished even Jewry, for it had been assumed that the Polish and German Jews, unlike the Spanish, were too resigned to their exilic fate to be capable of resistance.

The Ukrainians' allies, the Tartars, either compassionate or practical-minded, or both, did not kill the Jews, but delivered them instead to a Jewish central committee in Turkey which, acting for all Jewry, ransomed the captives by the thousands. It is an interesting footnote to history that a similar Jewish committee functioned from Turkey in the 1940's hoping to ransom Jews en masse from the Nazis.

Poland, invaded from all sides by the Germans, the Swedes, and the Russians, was bleeding from many wounds. The Russians matched the Ukrainian brutality toward the Jews. Of the German behavior, there is no record. The Swedes were correct and honorable, content with imposing taxes, the classical custom of the conqueror, which the Jews dutifully paid. The Poles, whose ranks were riven by deserters, called it collaboration with the enemy; when they recaptured territories from Sweden, they were as bestial to the Jews as the Ukrainians and Russians had been. Half of Polish Jewry, approximately 250,000, was decimated in the eight years of war.

The savagery of the Chmielnicki forces had no parallel in all previous Jewish history. It was surpassed only by the Germans in World War II. However, it may be said that the Cossacks acted from passion, out of a real, albeit misdirected, grievance, while the contemporary Germans performed dispassionately with calculating precision; the Cossacks raped in hot heat, the Germans systematically forced women into brothels; the Cossacks devastated more than they carted away, the Germans utilized even the corpses of their Jewish victims, drawing the gold from their teeth, collecting their hair, transforming their fat into soap bars. The Cossacks spared those Jews who agreed to embrace the Orthodox faith; the Germans offered no alternative. It is significant, on the other hand, that of all the peoples in Nazi-conquered Europe, none collaborated more diligently than the Ukrainians in the German liquidation of European Jewry.

Refugees from the Chmielnicki pogroms poured into

Germany and Holland, and ransomed captives settled in Turkey; Jewish communities everywhere contributed to their relief, and all Jewry partook vicariously in the Ukraine trauma.

Jewry turned for explanations to the Cabalists in Safad, Palestine, who had long been admonishing Jewry that its endeavors and achievements "abroad" were like chaff in the wind, and that it should reassemble in Zion. The Cabalists were embarrased, for they had previously predicted that 1648 would be the year of Jewry's deliverance. Conversely, the Christian mystics, who had calculated that the chiliad, Christ's millennium, was imminent, saw their faith confirmed. The Ukraine tragedy had been Jewry's last purification. Reports began to circulate in Christendom that huge Jewish forces had marched forth from the Libyan and Arab deserts, were advancing rapidly despite antiquated chariots and obsolete weapons, and already had brought down the wall of Mecca with a single blow of the ram's horn.

In Amsterdam, a serious Christian scholar, Peter Serarius (1580-1669), leader of the Dutch Protestant Chiliasts and a friend of the deceased Rabbi Menashe ben Israel, collated all rumors and passed them on to fellow Chiliasts of other lands. Christian ambassadors in the Near East gravely included these rumors in their diplomatic dispatches. Scotland reported that during a storm a ship carrying a huge detachment of the Jewish mythical force had stopped there for shelter. London correspondents requested more detailed information.

THE "MESSIAH"

It was in 1648, after the arrival of the first refugees in Turkey that Sabbatai Zvi (1626-1676), an Izmir Jewish scholar, confided to friends that he had been informed by a visitation that he was the chosen Messiah. His confidences aroused neither interest nor scandal, because he was a peculiar young man, still unmarried at 22—a late age for that time!—and given to deep depressions and sudden elations. In his elated mood, he would prance, clap his hands, and sing psalms joyfully, in beautiful voice, through the long night. Later, seemingly having

181

forgotten his "call," he settled in Jerusalem and became a traveling fund-raiser for Palestine charities. In 1665, he was joined by Nathan Benjamin Levi (1644-1680), a Gaza scholar and healer, proficient in the Cabala and possessed of a felicitous pen, who announced that he had been divinely informed that Messianic redemption was on hand, that Sabbatai Zvi was the anointed Messiah. Sage Cabalists from Safad and Jerusalem were unable to shake his story. A young woman appeared out of nowhere, claiming that she had been divinely instructed to mate with the Messiah. Reports that she had once been engaged in the world's oldest profession did not perturb Nathan. He confirmed her claim, and she was wed to Sabbatai Zvi.

Almost at the outset, the Jerusalem rabbinate excommunicated him. But popular enthusiasm could not be arrested. Pepys recorded that Jews on the London exchange were offering odds of ten to one "on the chances of a certain person now in Smyrna being acclaimed King of the World and the true Messiah." The Jews of Yemen and Persia, who had followed impostors before, responded with their customary enthusiasm. But even the sophisticated were deeply stirred.

The Marrano-descended Jews of Amsterdam were conditioned to mysticism, and also had always sought political solutions to the Jewish problem. Sabbatai Zvi corresponded to their disposition, as he did to that of Italian Jewish scholars. Catholic interest in the Cabala and Protestant Chiliasm indirectly confirmed him. Polish and Ukraine Jewry, having virtually experienced the Apocalypse, was now more than ever in the grip of folkloristic mysticism. Even skeptics held their tongue.

The Messiah from Izmir had become the focus of a multipurpose revolution, internal, within Jewry, and external, against a universe of oppressors. The Jews' preparations to return to Zion were an audacious challenge. Their departure would be an irreparable capital loss to Christian Europe. They would take their talents and, by divine protection, also their assets. Their return would mean that Turkey would be forced to yield Palestine to the divine legions. Both Turkey and Europe were determined to frustrate the Messianic plan, if possible. The

Messiah's movement gathered to it all the abortive eruptions against the oral law and the populist mutinities against the ruling oligarchies that had plagued Jewry since the days of the Second Temple. Sabbatai Zvi went beyond these revolts. He flouted the written law to confirm his legitimacy, for will not all law be abolished when the Redeemer came? Thus he lifted the Pauline torch within Jewry. The Cabalists of Safad who themselves had set the mood for this movement were alarmed. Vigorously and desperately they denounced him. They could not dam the tide, however. All opposition was violently silenced as the multitudes gathered about him, including ranking rabbis. This was the nervous breakdown of a people exhausted both by persecution and self-restraint.

All the disciplines that had sustained Jewry dissolved. Sexual orgies and wife-bartering spread like an epidemic. Most significant was the conduct of the wealthy oligarchs. The movement, stressing egalitarianism, threatened their status and wealth, yet they joined it enthusiastically, and anticipating the ideal order, began to distribute their wealth. It was as though the German princes had joined the Peasants' War. This happened perhaps because no affluent Jew was ever certain of his possessions: he more often lost them through Christian dispossession than through business error. Amsterdam Jews met daily, in the community hospitality house, refugees who had been as wealthy and prosperous as they themselves until Chmielnicki struck.

In 1666, Sabbatai Zvi sailed to Turkey to demand from the Sultan the surrender of Palestine, was seized on arrival, and taken to the fortress at Gallipoli. There, far from appearing like a prisoner, he received in regal manner pilgrims from all corners of the world. The local Turkish officials prospered on the pilgrimages until the Sultan demanded that the pretender be brought to Constantinople. There, the audience was brief. Informed that he was guilty of subversion, for which the penalty was execution, but would be spared if he embraced Islam, the "Messiah" first denied his mission. He blamed his disciples for imputing it to him, and finally agreed to Islamize.

183

The multitudes promptly disclaimed him. However, thousands still remained faithful to him, including, some of the elite who were unwilling to admit their error. Furthermore, from their experience with the Marranos, Jewry generally came to regard apostasy as not necessarily a definitive act. Yesterday's apostates were today's custodians of communal affairs.

Sabbatai Zvi's most tenacious disciples, even after his defection, were among the Marranos. His defenders reasoned that the Cabala presaged his temporary apostasy, for the most divine emanations must descend into the lower depths to retrieve other deeply sunk emanations. Had not David pretended to serve the Philistines, Joseph served a Pharaoh, and Moses been raised at an Egyptian court? The ranking authority on Sabbatai Zvi and Jewish mysticism, Professor Gershom Scholem, points out that the Marranos saw his defection as a vindication of their own one-time defection. They now rationalized that their own one-time desertion had been a predestined passage through Christian subordination toward Jewish redemption; as they had been redeemed, so would the Messiah be redeemed.

In 1676, he died a Muslim. His followers went underground. The law reasserted itself. Jewry had survived its greatest crisis.

His movement had several enduring effects which outlasted his times. The first effect was of a paradoxical nature. The movement created divisions within the separate Jewish communities, but disenchantment with it united the Jews as a people. The Chmielnicki horrors had only been vicariously experienced by most Jews. The exhilaration of Sabbatai Zvi's promise and embarrassment of his default were universally experienced by all strata of Jewry alike: the unctuous merchants of the Turkish bazaars, the crude rural Jewish innkeepers of Poland, and the worldly brokers of Amsterdam. Many Talmudists were swept along. Few could hereafter claim greater wisdom, caution, or even security than the others. Only their common insecurity could account for their indiscriminate acceptance of the impostor.

The second result was that, having experienced egali-

tarianism and release from ritualism, the multitudes were not ready to surrender again to the firm rule of the patricians, nor even to the authority of the rabbis. The masses justified their misdirected enthusiasm for the impostor on the ground that they had followed the rabbis who should have warned them, and should certainly not have erred themselves.

Jewry also recalled with delight how apprehensive Christian kings, and how stunned the Christian rabble, had been by the Jews' contemplated exodus to Palestine. This sensation of political action lingered on.

The year 1666 had been the great dress rehearsal for several intramural Jewish revolutions—Hassidism, Zionism, and Secularism.

Chapter NINE

JEWRY'S DESEGREGATION

THE EIGHTEENTH CENTURY IN EUROPE WAS AS CRUCIAL IN THE history of the Jews as their several dispersions from Palestine. In the feudal order which compartmentalized society into three estates—the clergy, the nobility, and the bourgeoisie—the Jews constituted a distinct and separate fourth estate. When the old order was abolished, Christian-Jewish relations required a new basis if the Jew was to survive at all in the new order. The nations which had absorbed the estates were neither ready to absorb the Jew as well nor to permit him to remain, as he had for centuries, a closed society with its own self-governing institutions. The debate and struggle for a new status and relationship lasted well into the nineteenth century.

After an agitated two year debate, France granted him equality reluctantly (1791) and with humiliating reservations. He was first pledged equality not in Europe, but by Roger Williams in Rhode Island in 1652, before even a single Jew had settled there. The first voice raised in the old world for the enfranchisement of the Jew also spoke English. It was in Britain, in 1714, the voice of a great nonconformist Irishman, John Toland. Holland, in 1798, was the first state in all Europe to name a Jew, Isaac de Costa Atias, President of its Assembly, or Parliament, to a high government position, two years after granting them equality.

Germany held out longest against equality. The Jews' opponents included two giants of German kultur: John Wolfgang Goethe, defender of the old aristocratic order, and Johann Gottlieb Fichte, spokesman for the new democratic order. Yet even before they were fully emancipated

in the mid-nineteenth century, the Jews already contributed to Germany's new eminence in science. They
produced physicians, mathematicians, physicists, and
chemists. Even before they had achieved admission into
German universities and state-subsidized laboratories and
research institutes, Jews and half-Jews laid the foundation
of Germany's powerful chemical industry which, in the
service of Adolf Hitler, produced the gasses that ex-
tinguished the lives of six million European Jews.

The Jewish impetus in science did not derive from
Germany, for when it began, Germany was herself just
developing. Its roots were in an infinitely older tradition:
in the Talmud with its substantial anatomical, botanical
and mathematical data; in Maimonides' medicine, Zacuta's
astronomy and cartography; and in the Marrano physicians whose activities ranged from the papal courts to
Goa, India.

Unlike Christendom, the Jews had never really experienced a Dark Ages. Some fitful attempts in Jewry to
banish science and philosophy hardly got beyond circum-
scribing such studies for anyone below twenty-five years
of age. And even these limited bans did not endure.
Eastern European Jewry in the eighteenth century was
reputedly the heartland of rigorous orthodoxy, opposed
to all free inquiry, yet the ranking exponent of this conservatism, the Gaon of Vilne, foremost Talmudist of his
day, relaxed with mathematics, astronomy, and physics,
and while wary of philosophy, recommended enthusiastically the pursuit of medicine and the natural sciences,
i.e., anything that can advance the physical well-being
of mankind.

Hence, the emancipation of the Jews, wherever it took
place, was a political act. The Jewish intellect did not
require release from any ghetto. It had always lived
beyond it. In the eighteenth century Jewish history in the
making was dispersed, as never before, on numerous
stages, all performing simultaneously, each performance
complete in itself, yet complementing all the others. In
general terms, the preoccupation of the East European
Jewries still living in feudal lands appeared to be the
preservation of Jewish custom and culture, then beginning

187

to decline among the Jewries west of the Oder whose task seemed to be to develop for Jewry channels of communications with the Christian world.

As the Jewries of Central and Western Europe were acquiring, albeit slowly, political equality, the East European Jewries suffered grave setbacks. Poland was the prime example of the latter. Invaded, partitioned, divided against herself, Poland was in bitter mood, and the Jew was a convenient scapegoat.

POLAND

The Poles specialized, from the sixteenth through the seventeenth centuries, in the ritual murder libel, an invention traceable to the Greco-Egyptians at the commencement of the Common Era. A corpse found anywhere in Poland around Easter time was Godsent, serving several useful purposes: It automatically committed several Jews to the pyre, put the Sejm, or parliament, then in spring session, in a favorable frame of mind for the consideration of guild-sponsored legislation against Jewish competition, and endowed some decrepit or remote church or monastery with a martyr's remains which, on permanent display, provided a guaranteed annual revenue from pilgrimages and spared its inmates excessive self-abnegation.

In the 1750's, Poland produced at least one ritual murder accusation a year. Of the Jews' guilt there was no doubt; whenever tortured, they confessed. As far back as 1698, Stefan Szuchovsky, a Jesuit priest, published a judicious opinion on the art of torture and confession: "Men whose counsel we hold in high regard, instruct us that it is necessary, when torturing the body on the rack, to apply a burning wick to its shadow on the floor, because the scheming devil may sometimes transpose the body where the shadow seems to lie."

For more than a century, the Jews fought desperately against the libel; they cited old papal bulls in their favor, enlisted the intervention of the Roman heads of the Dominican and Carmelite orders, and in 1758 dispatched Jacob Zelig, financial agent and seasoned court Jew, to plead directly at the Holy See. After a formal investiga-

tion of the charge, a report vindicating the Jews was confirmed by Pope Clement XIII. But pressure from the Polish prelates prevented its publication.

RUSSIAN DILEMMA

However, thrice-partitioned among Austria, Germany, and Russia—1764, 1793, and 1895—Poland was erased from the map even before the century had concluded. Each of her successors received a portion of her Jews.

Jewry's previous contacts with Russia had been fitful. All Russo-Polish trade treaties through the sixteenth and seventeenth centuries carried, at Moscow's request, a clause barring Jewish traders from entering Russia.

When King Augustus Sigismund, perhaps at the request of his friend Joseph Nassi, proposed deletion of the clause, Ivan the Terrible (1530-1548) could not conceal his exasperation: "I have written you several times my view, that the Jews had dissuaded our people from our faith and poisoned our medicinal herbs." The reference was to two episodes in earlier history: the charge that the Jews were behind the agitation of the Christian dissenters and the failure of a Jewish physician, summoned from Italy, to save the life of a Muscovite prince.

In 1563, when he temporarily occupied the Polish city of Polotzk, Ivan gave its Jewish population a choice between drowning in the river and embracing the Russian orthodox faith. History records that all chose drowning. Yet it is conceivable that some chose life, apostatized, and settled in Moscow. There was indeed a Marrano colony there in the days of Peter the Great (1672-1725). It consisted of men of high station, and perhaps dated back to Ivan the Terrible.

When Peter visited Amsterdam in 1698, a delegation of Christian burghers, at Jewish request, proposed that he open Russia to Jewish refugees. They would benefit him, as they had benefited Holland. His reply was: "It is too soon to bring these two peoples together, the Russians and the Jews. Tell them that I appreciate their offer and know how valuable they can be. But I could only feel pity for them if they settled among the Russians." Nonetheless, he had several Jews in his immediate coterie. They

189

may even have accompanied him on his visit to Holland. Israel Hirsch was his banker, Sundel Hirsch supplied the silver for his mint, and Jacob Lacoasta, not an overt Jew, but a Marrano, was invited from Hamburg, where the Czar had seen him perform, to become Peter's court jester.

Even before Poland was partitioned, there were small settlements of overt Jews in the peripheral Czarist domains, in the Ukraine, seized from Poland in the seventeenth century, and in Riga, the commercial and shipping center, severed from Sweden in 1710. The German guilds of Riga would not tolerate the Jews as business rivals, but solicited them as customers. Hence, although they would not permit the Jews to reside in the city, the guild-controlled magistracy of the city and the provincial administration protested vigorously when Russia, overzealous, banned Polish-Jewish traders from Riga's annual fairs. The Germans argued desperately that unless the ban was lifted, the city would lose all her export trade.

A similar condition developed in the Ukraine. The Jews who had apparently survived or returned since the Chmielnicki wars were expelled in 1727, yet one year later they were invited to attend the annual fair as wholesale merchants, several years later as retail tradesmen, and eventually to resettle as permanent residents. The Christian population, having obtained their expulsion, discovered that prices had soared, and that retail trade in some towns had stopped altogether when the Jews departed; consequently, they began petitioning that the Jews be permitted to return.

Catherine the Great revealed that when she ascended the throne in 1762 her senate was almost unanimously convinced that Russia could benefit immeasurably from Jewish commerce and incentive, and was ready to vote that they be admitted. However, reluctant to provoke the clergy before she had properly seized hold of her reins, Catherine obtained a deferment of the senate vote. In the meantime, she unofficially instructed her officialdom not to molest Jews who entered Russia illegally.

Ten years later, it was no longer necessary to take any kind of vote or to smuggle the Jews into the country with

royal concurrence. When Moscow annexed White Russia after the first partition of Poland, 100,000 Jews were automatically annexed; each successive annexation increased their number. There were too many, too densely concentrated, cut off by the annexations from their previous economic hinterland. Catherine pondered the "Jewish Question," a habit to which Russia is addicted to this day. She dared not admit them into the interior because of clerical protests, yet that is where their incentive was most required. She kept them where they were.

Catherine first tried Jewish self-government and retained the kahal, the Jewish municipal structure, a legacy from Poland, with its three-tier judiciary. She later circumscribed the kahal's powers, but compensated the Jews by according them burgher status, which graded them, corresponding to income in the merchant guild, or the lower middle class of petty traders, artisans, and clerks. With this came the right to vote, some seven years before they achieved it in France. They took full advantage of the privilege. The White Russian elections of 1784 turned in 25 Jewish mayors, councilors, and judges. The Christian guilds were stunned. Measures were devised to preclude future Jewish triumphs of this order.

The status of the burgher had its handicaps. Graded as urban population, the Jews were ordered to evacuate the villages. This meant the ruination of thousands of Jewish families who made their living as brewers, millers, lumber-haulers, and innkeepers. The inns were combined general stores, taverns, and hotels. There was an economic interdependence between the rural and city Jew; they served as each other's consumers, suppliers, borrowers, lenders, and agents; if either rural or city economy collapsed, the entire Jewish structure would crash, impoverishing 100,000 Jews overnight. Petitions and delegations were dispatched to Moscow. Christians also joined in these intercessions; the barons who leased to the Jews and the menial laborers who worked in their enterprises were seriously concerned.

The danger was staved off by an evasion that was to become the custom of every successive Czar. The evacua-

tions were slowed down and eventually deferred, but never permanently abolished.

This was the beginning of Russia's apartheid policy against Jewry.

The Jews were confined to one region, primarily cities, and forbidden to travel except on a permit difficult to obtain, or to settle, unless they had considerable financial means, beyond the frontiers of the Jewish Pale. This was the consummation of tribulations that attended the life of Polish Jewry throughout the seventeenth century, as the country was being torn limb from limb.

The shuttling of populations and the transfer of territories from one power to another, the wars that preceded each partition, and the economic chaos and disseverance of families that followed it, gave rise to profound despondency among Jews. Even rabbis seemed to lose faith in the law and turned to Cabalistic writings. These were irrational times, and the search was on for irrational solutions. The Sabbatai Zvi movement might have died under normal circumstance, but in this apocalyptic setting his faithful lingered on, bequeathing to successive generations their faith in his Second Coming. Some of the lay elite founded sects that stressed sensualism and advanced trinitarian doctrines without, however taking the final and irreparable step—conversion to Christianity.

HASSIDISM

It is against this background that Hassidism arose, an egalitarian religious reform movement which in our own day, through the agency of Martin Buber, and deprived of its spontaneity, has had an impact even on Protestant theology. Its cradle was the Ukraine, a rural region. Its Jewish population paralleled the Galilean am haaretz whom Jesus had addressed seventeen hundred years before. Its early followers were artisans and innkeepers who had acquired the gruff manner and awkward speech of their environment, could comprehend neither the Law nor the convoluted Cabala, indeed, could barely read anything but their prayers and Yiddish entertainment. Treated superciliously by the city Jew, ignored by the scholar as though lack of learning were an unshrivable sin, feeling

the hot breath of the peasants' hate on their necks, and always in danger of expulsion from their leaseholds, they had never lost the common man's capacity, which endures past all adversity, of deriving pleasure from the daily and mundane, from wholesome food and spontaneous song (the folk music still played at Jewish weddings originated among them) and their simplistic faith in a personal God whose intervention they petitioned on every malignant occasion, from the illness of a calf through the perils of a pogrom. Their world, like a peasant's, was peopled by demons, made radiant by miracles, and charmed by amulets, sometimes inscribed by secret Sabbatai Zvi sectarians, and distributed by the baal shems, or miracle healers, who visited the rural communities.

It is among these people that the founder of Hassidism, Israel Baal Shem Tov, (1700-1760) Possessor of the Good Name, revealed himself in the thirty-sixth year of his life. A man of little learning by the severe standards of that day, seemingly a ne'er-do-well, and a jack of all trades, he was treated as a pariah by his learned rabbinical in-law. He was twenty-nine when he removed his wife and children to the Carpathian mountains where he worked in the clay pits, lived among the crudest Christian peasants, and acquired the reputation of a baal shem. Seven years later, his "spiritual apprenticeship" completed, he received his "call," and was henceforth called Baal Shem Tov to connote his superiority over all other healers.

He was a peripatetic teacher, who spoke in parables and set down nothing in writing. His teachings, transmitted in his disciples' words, were an admixture of pantheism and Cabala, yet essentially different from both. It has been suggested by an eminent author, Professor Gershom Scholem, that he was probably familiar with texts circulated by residual followers of Sabbatai Zvi. Unlike Spinoza, he did not deny God a personality, and unlike the Cabalists he did not regard that personality as splintered, dispersed, and awaiting redemption through man's absolution and piety. His God is whole, yet ubiquitous, reflected in everything, yet invisible in his totality. Man is in a special and significant relationship with God, and not a captive of impersonal law. Divine justice is

spontaneous, fluid, and responsive to man's supplication which, however, must not be melancholy and ascetic, but, in deference to God's wonders, must celebrate the joys of being.

Israel Baal Shem Tov, unlike the Karaites, had no quarrel with the law, but he disputed its application in a manner that inhibited spontaneity between man and God. Authentic religious response cannot be commanded by mere learning, or induced by mere ritualism. It is within the reach of the sincere, regardless of rank. He was clearly the spokesman for those who could offer nothing but their hearts. This was a social revolution. It threatened the patricians who had denied the underprivileged not only voice in community affairs, but also status before God. It erased the caste distinction based on learning, and raised the self-esteem of the rural and other humble folk.

Within a generation, Hassidism lost its spontaneity. To the rabbi-legalist it counterposed the tzadik. The rabbi was an interpreter of God's law which all learned men, the ordained and lay alike, could examine. His opinions could be judged by The Book. The tzadik was a priest. He pretended a special relationship with the divinity and presumed to act as intercessor between God and the supplicants. He was a charismatic leader, risen among the people, subject to no ordination, abiding by no prescribed rules of conduct. However faulty this kind of evolution of leadership might be, it nonetheless opened up new sources from which Jewry could draw its mentors and guides. It compelled social mobility. But like all revolutions, Hassidism was eventually perverted from its purpose by those very persons who contended they were its custodians. Dynasties and a chain of hierarchy evolved. Some tzadikim maintained lavish courts wholly unbefitting a movement whose mythical heroes were saints disguised as tailors and cobblers. At first, Hassidism had heightened class tensions, but in its latter stages it ameliorated them. The royal courts maintained a vast rabble of dependent hangers-on. The monies came from affluent supporters who, as they entered the ranks of the tzadik's disciples, were perforce committed to Hassidism's fraternalism.

Hassidism might have degenerated into a superstitious

know-nothing movement, had it not been challenged by the Misnagdim, the rabbinical legalists who, recovering from the first shock, charged that Hassidism's unlettered and undisciplined spontaneity led to lawlessness and moral chaos as in the days of Sabbatai Zvi. Hassidism, to enlist the affluent and learned elite, had to meet the test of learning; the tzadik had to shore up his authority by qualifying as a scholar. Conversely, the rabbi, to qualify as their mentor, had to address himself to the multitudes in language and terms they could understand.

The class issues evaporated from the struggle between Hassidim and Misnagdim. The issue now was the infallibility of the leader, the tzadik, versus the immutability of the law. The struggle engulfed all the former Polish territories and spilled across the frontiers of Russia, Austria, and Germany.

The class struggle within the East European Jewish communities was soon to assume a secular form. But in a profounder sense, and still in religious guise, it was pursued along ethnic lines between Jewry's "haves," the Yahudim, or old-time residents of Germany and Austria, and the "have nots," or Ostjuden of Russia and the Polish territories annexed by Germany and Austria. The Yahudim were ruled by an elite of brokers, bankers, and suppliers. These were indispensable to the German and Austrian emperors. Their counsel, monies, and provisions were desperately needed. Yet they were treated with contempt. For a steep price, they were permitted to reside in petty numbers in the capital, Berlin, and in Austria. They were classified in several categories. Each paid a different price and was entitled, correspondingly, to a different number of privileges. These rights had to be renegotiated annually. The number of families and the total number of persons were restricted. They kept a strict watch against "undesirable" Ostjuden who might attempt to enter the capital precincts, although they were generous in their contributions to relieve starvation inside the Ost territories.

The authorities knew no distinction, really, between Ostjuden and Yahudim, between the household masters and their retinue. Both were ruthlessly taxed, unconscion-

ably humiliated. They were taxed for birth, marriage, burial, and for staying, when they traveled, in the only inns permitted them, the segregated "for Juden only" hotels; and the toll bridge charge to them was "the same as for heads of cattle." Only one out of five Jewish families in Vienna was permitted to own a house. Only one young person in each Jewish family in Berlin was permitted to marry. Others were compelled to emigrate if they wished to marry. The intention, like Pharaoh's, was to prevent the Jews from multiplying.

There sometimes was a discrepancy between government conduct and popular custom. As late as 1808, Vienna's court Jews still paid 60,000 gulden each for the privilege of residing in the capital. In a petition to their sovereign, they offered to generously reward the royal treasury if henceforth, in official documents, they were addressed not as Jude (Jew), but, like all other citizens, as mister, and if that was impossible, without honorific at all. Yet at the same time, courtiers attended musicals at the homes of these very same Jews. In the German-speaking countries, in fact, social mixing between Christian and Jew began early in the eighteenth century, so that law lagged behind custom. This social intercourse considerably influenced the habits and popular culture of the Jews. The court Jew determined the trend. The rest of the Jewish community, admitted as his retainers, dependent on his benevolence, merely followed. The court Jews abandoned the orthodox kaftan and took to wearing ordinary or "German" garments. They went hunting with their Christian neighbors. Their womenfolk kept lapdogs, another custom alien to Ostjuden.

The German and East European Jewries, however sharpened the divisions between them became, had in fact once been a single community. The East European Jewish communities were founded by German refugees. They still maintained close commercial contacts. In a world that legislated against him, and kept him within the confines of certain occupations, Jew traded with Jew, one Jewish loanbroker with another, one Jewish supplier with another, across national frontiers. Hence, German Jewish custom also spread to Eastern Europe.

THE ENLIGHTENMENT

This spreading of "the German habit," no doubt, was a factor in the evolution of the Haskalah, or Jewish Enlightenment, in the eighteenth century. The Haskalah was the obverse side of the Hassidic coin. Both were revolts against the extremes of rabbinical discipline. Yet they were at cross purposes. Hassidism was a social revolution within Jewry. Its base was the lower classes. It was anti-intellectual in execution and stunted free inquiry. The Haskalah was largely an upper-class movement. Acceding to Gentile argument that the Jews were "backward," it sought to qualify them for equal rights through the promotion of general studies, to which Hassidism was fiercely opposed. In the process of opening for Jewry "windows on the west," Haskalah launched the modern Hebrew renaissance and Jewish secularism.

An earlier generation of Jewish historians, either German or German-influenced, credited the Haskalah to one person, Moses Mendelssohn (1729-1786), grandfather of the composer. He was no doubt a giant figure. Risen from the ghetto, self-educated in philosophy and science, he was a social lion in Berlin's literary salons when only "privileged Jews," few in number, were permitted to reside in the capital. He was one of the great German stylists of his day, an author of philosophical works and literary criticism, a hero to the assimilating Jewish upper bourgeoisie. Then, having acquired his laurels, he turned his full attention to matters of Jewish concern, although he displayed some interest even earlier. He launched the first modern Hebrew periodical, initiated Judenwissenschaft, investigative research into Hebrew history and culture, and was a factor in the evolution of the Reform movement in Judaism—although he might have deemed some of its later manifestations as rank heresy.

All this is credit enough for one man. However, he has also been credited with reintroducing the concepts of free inquiry and general studies into the Jewish community. These concepts had never ceased, although they had suffered a serious setback in the aftermath of the Chmielnicki pogroms and the Sabbatai Zvi trauma. Two ranking rab-

binical authorities of that day, Mendelssohn's own contemporaries, Jacob Emden of Germany and the unchallenged Elijah, the Gaon of Vilna, pursued general studies themselves and sharply criticized the practice of training the Talmudic student in sophism instead of analysis. The Gaon argued that a knowledge of mathematics and the natural sciences could only further the ultimate ends of the Torah. He also studied Hebrew grammar and sentence structure. Jacob Emden boasted that he read philosophy and science in several languages and audaciously discoursed, in his many works, on matters that were taboo. For example, of pre-Pauline Christianity he commented: "It is therefore a customary observation with me that the man of Nazareth brought a double kindness to the world; on the one hand, he fully supported the Torah of Moses . . . on the other, he brought much good to Gentiles. . . ."

However, circumstances were such that Germany was the first stage on which the Haskalah fully unfolded. East European Jewry was preoccupied with intramural issues of greater urgency. The rabbis were engaged in restoring the authority of the law, which veritably meant order out of chaos, in the Jewish community. Sabbatai Zvi sectarians, in various disguises, were still engaged in disruptive activity, including the advocacy of apostasy to Christianity as a "prologue" to Messianic Redemption. The Hassidim had to be stunted in their anti-intellectual crusade. The Czarist authorities were also engaged in pursuing the Jews with carrot and stick to inveigle them into conversion. These were not circumstances conducive to pursuing the delights of the Enlightenment. Furthermore, there was no move toward Enlightenment in the cultures of the peoples among whom the Jews lived. Matters were different in Germany. There was no divisiveness in German Jewry. Its custodians were the court Jews who had paid for the residence privileges of all the other Jews. They also freely adopted, as has been pointed out, the social customs of the Christian upper class. This kind of conduct would have been suspect, at that time, in Jewish communities burdened with guilt over the Sabbatai Zvi hoax. For some inexplicable reason, however, the Sabbatai Zvi movement had leaped across Germany;

consequently the inhibitions that were its aftermath did not prevail there. The result of this complete lack of inhibition was some apostasy among the Jews, which of course was well rewarded by church and state. There was yet another important factor. The Renaissance had skipped Germany. Luther had suppressed its incentives. Now, under French influence, Germany was experiencing a belated Renaissance. One of its lesser manifestations was an interest in Hebrew culture among Christian intellectuals. It is these perhaps, curiously of anti-Semitic disposition for the most part, that in fact laid the foundation for Judenwissenschaft.

All these circumstances set the stage for Mendelssohn. He sought to stem apostasy by instilling in Jews greater pride in their cultural heritage and reconciling German-Jewish custom with Jewish faith and tradition in the classical manner of Saadia Gaon and Maimonides who faced similar situations in their times and countries. From the vantage point of an East European rabbi, living amidst sectarian dissension, Mendelssohn's activity might have seemed disruptive. He counterposed anti-Semitic Judenwissenschaft with Jewish research. He translated the Bible into German, printed in Hebrew script, as a means of bringing Enlightenment to the ghettoized Jew. He wrote apologias and polemics in German to ward off anti-Semites and to reclaim Jews so assimilated that they no longer knew Hebrew. Like all enlightened figures of that age, he believed that education was a panacea, that an educated humanity would be free of all bigotry. Hence he urged Jewish youth to help advance that day by studying the sciences and humanities.

Some of his disciples perverted his doctrine. Their Reform of the synagogue broke more radically with tradition than he had anticipated. They preferred to blame their own brethren rather than the German authorities for German Jewry's disabilities. Hence, they concluded that their full legal emancipation was deterred by the disrepute suffered by all Jews from the presence "elsewhere" of "unenlightened" Jewish multitudes. They decided that something drastic must be done to remedy the situation, and petitioned the imperial governments of Austria, Ger-

many, and Russia to forcibly impose religious and educational reform on the Jewish multitudes. One Mendelssohn disciple enthusiastically hailed a "tolerance edict" published by Joseph II of Austria which relaxed some restrictions, but still held down the numbers of Jewish residents in Vienna, and provided for a policeman to be stationed under the canopy at every Jewish wedding to make certain that the vows, customarily uttered in ancient Hebrew, should be uttered in German, and declared null and void all contracts and wills written in Yiddish or Hebrew. To Mendelssohn's overzealous disciples this evidently was proof of good intentions to "integrate" the Jews.

There is no evidence in the works of Mendelssohn and his disciples of intramural socioeconomic struggles. Yet there were such struggles, pointing to interaction between the gentile environment and the Jewish community. It is significant, for example, that the lower classes within the Jewish communities in Germany, although dependent on the court Jews, began to protest tax policies and demand greater voice in communal affairs. Evidence of this is provided in the Responsa of Rabbi Jacob Emden. He ruled that taxes must be equitable and that all were entitled to a voice in communal affairs, and not only the big taxpayer. The rabbinical legalists in Germany spoke for the lower classes.

FRANCE AND EMANCIPATION

In France, the class division in Jewry was between the Jewish aristocrats of Bordeaux, descended from former Marranos, and the German Jews of French-annexed Alsace-Lorraine. The former had for several centuries dealt with French kings; the latter lived among an illiterate Jew-baiting German rabble. Bordeaux Jewry had once been lobbyist for all Jewry. Now, however, its spokesman Isaac de Pinto, banker, economist, author, drew invidious distinctions between Jew and Jew, by assuring a French provincial governor (1761) that "we are from the tribe of Judah. . . . We do not intermarry or otherwise associate with the children of Jacob. . . . Our interests and self-esteem preclude that." When Voltaire stated in the *Dictionaire Philosophique* that a high birth rate and

monetary greed were Jewry's only talents, Pinto respectfully informed him that the Portuguese and the German Jews "are two completely different creations."

The Jews of Bordeaux behaved no better at the French National Assembly which debated intermittently, for two years, a motion to naturalize the Jews. Opponents of the motion called Jewry a nation within a nation, a state within a state, encumbered by peculiar superstitions, bad habits, and repulsive customs, and not yet housebroken for civilized society. Even some of its defenders called Jewry a delinquent whom compassion could retrieve.

The Jews of Alsace-Lorraine had no courtly experience. Profoundly orthodox, ruled by the disciplines of rabbinical Responsa, and steeped in the rich and sophisticated Talmudic tradition, their spokesmen argued with cogency and precision that there could be nothing incompatible between the oldest surviving law and French civil law. Indeed, they told the Assembly, they were stunned that so ancient a people should now be asked to defend and redefine itself. Theirs was a vigorous statement for cultural pluralism beyond the comprehension of their time. It contained one element, however, that added to the Assembly's confusion. They requested both civic equality and the continuance of their autonomous institutions, which were a residue of the old order based on the estates. The Assembly could not permit Jewry to straddle both the ancient and the new order. Jewry, conversely, had not yet devised new vessels for the preservation of its collective personality. The Alsace-Lorraine delegation would rather forfeit emancipation than self-government.

The Jews of Bordeaux, bankers and merchants, had been uncomfortable from the first at being paired off with these Yiddish-speaking petty traders and loan brokers. Now they felt justified in quietly moving to have their petitions separated. They asked the Assembly to simply confirm the "patents," "letters of naturalization" issued more than two centuries ago to the "merchants of the Portuguese nation," their ancestors. The Assembly was cornered. The motion was granted.

The Jews of Alsace-Lorraine and Paris alone remained without rights. The two were different from one another,

yet hewn from the same hard ghetto rock. The Parisians were secular young men who had broken with Jewish religious discipline, but had been apprenticed nonetheless in the Talmudic academies. Nor were they novices in the techniques of political action. They were Polish Jews, and Jewry there had for two centuries maintained its own legislatures, judiciary, and lobbies. They were also Parisians, members of the imminent fraternity of mankind whose common bond was reason, and had witnessed the eruption of that formidable anonymous power called the people's voice. They persuaded their orthodox brethren to delete the demand for self-government from the petition. Next, they engaged a Christian attorney to plead their case before the Paris Commune as well as before the Assembly, and seated themselves in the audience: fifty young Jews in the uniform of the National Guard.

Yet even so, it took two years before the Assembly voted that all Jews who take "an oath of allegiance which means that they also foreswear their previous rights and privilege," be admitted to citizenship "without exception, pretext or further delay." It was a parsimonious resolution. The Jews were arraigned collectively, and had to qualify for citizenship individually. Another resolution, passed at the same time, released Christian borrowers of one-third of their indebtedness to Jewish loan brokers, and implied additional exemptions for those unable to meet even the reduced obligations. The emancipation of French Jewry was not a solemn act.

The Jews had in the past paid the nobility and church for "privileges." They now paid "the people" for citizenship. Four decades before France voted it, a Whig Parliament in Britain, in 1753, naturalized the Jews but was compelled by mob violence to denaturalize them several months later.

AMERICA

Events in America at the time have been accorded insufficient Jewish attention because they involved an infinitesimal number, yet continental Christian liberals did not overlook what was taking place there. In arguing in favor of Jewry's parliaments, they cited the great American

example. That example was less perfect than it appeared to be. The Declaration of Independence, like France's Human Rights Declaration, was an eloquent statement of principle. Both required legislative flesh to concretize their promise.

When the Constitutional Convention met in 1787, only two states, New York and Virginia, had admitted the Jew to full civic equality. When Congress discussed the First Amendment in 1789, a third state, Georgia, had been added. Pennsylvania and South Carolina joined the roster in 1790, and Delaware in 1792.

Fortunately, the Jews were not alone. Several Christian minorities were in the same circumstance, and the Jews were less visible than the others. "It is well within the realm of possibility," writes Dr. Jacob Rader Marcus, contemporary historian of American Jewry, "that if the Jews had been the sole minority religious group, they would not have received complete equality in the Federal Constitution and in some of the state constitutions." Some American colonies had their relapses. Roger Williams granted the Jews equality when Rhode Island was founded and had no Jews; but in 1719, Rhode Island barred Jews from naturalization; it was not until 1842 that it completely removed the last religious test.

Fortunately, America had no nationally established church. America was not composed of corporate estates— nobility, guilds—with fixed and reserved interests threatened by mobility.

The character of the early Jewish pioneers was also a factor in the determination of Jewish status in America. The American Jewish pioneers were peddlers, general storekeepers, business brokers, artisans, and shippers, poorly tutored, with not a single eminent scholar among them, who wrote to Amsterdam or London when they required an authoritative rabbinical opinion. The American Jew was perhaps the first in many centuries compelled to function on his own, outside the corporate body. The disadvantage, he had none to mediate for him, was counterpoised by an advantage; he was not impeded by collective agreements between corporate Jewry and corporate Christendom. Each time he protested a religious test, he protested a private

grievance. Each time he won his case, he established a constitutional precedent for all Jewry. The traditional Josephs at Pharaoh's court had been replaced by the common man acting as his own ambassador to Christendom.

Only a special kind of individual could endure in this daring enterprise. Moses M. Hayes was of this special breed. A man in his thirties, owner of a general store in Newport, he was summoned in June 1776 to take a loyalty oath, before members of the General Assembly of Rhode Island, which was required of all suspected of opposing the American Revolution. On July 11, he was again summoned, one of seventy-seven Newport residents, four Jews among them, denounced by their neighbors. Hayes refused to take the oath, stating:

"I always have asserted my sentiments in favor of America and confess the War on its part just. I decline subscribing the Test at present from these principles, First that I deny ever being inimical to my country and call for my accusers and proof of conviction, Second that I am an Israelite and not allowed the liberty of a vote, or voice in common with the rest of the voters though consistent with the Constitution, and the other Colonies, Thirdly because the Test is not a general test and consequently subject to many glaring inconveniences, Fourthly, Continental Congress nor the General Assembly of this nor the Legislatures of the other colonies have never in this contest taken any notice or countenance respecting the society of Israelites to which I belong. When any rule, order or directions is made by the Congress or General Assembly I shall to the utmost of my power adhere to the same."

On December 23, 1783, a group of Philadelphia Jews filed a petition that Pennsylvania amend the law requiring a Christian oath from members of the General Assembly. The petitioners made it at the outset clear that they were not motivated by aspirations for public office, but by deep hurt. Recalling the contributions of Jews to the wealth of other nations, "Holland and England have made valuable acquisitions of men who, for their religious sentiments, were distressed in their own countries," they served notice that Jewish immigrants to America hereafter "might de-

termine their free choice to go to New York, or to any other of the United States of America, where there is no such like restraint."

In eighteenth-century American Jewry there were still many former Marranos with the ineradicable evidence of inquisitorial torture on their bodies. Abraham Israel Abrahams, a New York businessman who performed the rites of circumcision without gratuity as a religious devotion, received a letter, dated September 6, 1767, from Aaron Lopez, a fugitive from the Inquisition who became one of the largest shipowners in Newport. "I have the singular pleasure of addressing you on the joyful occasion that presents me the arrival of a brother of mine from Portugal with his wife and three sons. . . . Therefore earnestly entreat your devotion lead you to be the meritorious instrument of their Covenant."

There were Jews who fled Austria and Germany, especially from the annexed former Polish regions, where Jewish marriages and births were restricted by law. The first Jewish settlers in Georgia were an admixture of Portuguese and German Jews, shipped from London by British court Jews who were apprehensive that the influx of impoverished Jewish refugees would imperil their own status. In 1732, General Oglethorpe solicited Jewish members of the London stock exchange for funds to establish Georgia as a refuge for prisoners released from debtor's jail. The Jews responded generously, in addition to which they chartered a vessel and sent off a shipment of Jewish refugees, without even inquiring of the company. They knew that its policy excluded Jews.

Concern for Palestine asserted itself early in American Jewry. The first fund-raiser for Palestine institutions, a Safad rabbi, arrived in the United States in 1759; some two decades later, another Palestine fund-raiser helped polish the grammar on a Hebrew congregational prayer for the welfare of the newly installed first government of the United States. So began the relationship between American Jews and the State of Israel.

READINGS: CHAPTERS EIGHT AND NINE

The United States

Blau, Joseph L. and Baron, Salo. *The Jews of the United States, A Documentary History, 1790-1840.* Philadelphia: Jewish Publication Society, 1963.

Davis, Moshe. "Jewish Religious Life and Institutions in America," *The Jews: Their History, Culture and Religion,* edited by Louis Finkelstein (see p. viii).

Glanz, Rudolf. *The Jews in American Alaska.* Privately Printed, 1953.

—— *The Jews in the Old American Folklore.* Privately Printed, 1961.

Goodman, Abram Vossen. *American Overture, Jewish Rights in Colonial Times.* J.P.S., 1947.

Grinstein, Hyman B. *The Rise of the Jewish Community of New York, 1650-1880.* J.P.S., 1945.

—— *The Times of the Jewish Community of New York, 1650-1880.* Philadelphia: J.P.S., 1947.

Handlin, Oscar. *Race and Nationality in American Life.* New York: Anchor Books, 1957.

Knox, Israel. *Rabbi in America, the Story of Isaac Mayer Wise.* Boston: Little, Brown and Co., 1957.

Korn, Bertram Wallace. *American Jewry and the Civil War.* J.P.S., 1951.

Makover, A. B. *Mordecai M. Noah.* New York: Bloch Publishing Co., 1917.

Marcus, Jacob Rader. *Early American Jewry.* 2 vols. J.P.S., 1951-1953.

—— *Memoirs of American Jews 1775-1865.* 3 vols. J.P.S., 1955-1956.

Pool, David de Sola. *Portraits Etched in Stone, 1682-1831.* New York: Columbia University Press, 1952.

Schappes, Morris Urman. (ed.). *A Documentary History of the Jews in the United States: 1654-1875.* New York: Citadel Press, 1952.

Europe

Cohen, Israel. *Vilna.* Philadelphia: J.P.S., 1943.

Greenberg, Louis. *The Jews in Russia,* Vol. 1. New Haven: Yale University Press, 1944.

Herzl, Theodor. *The Complete Diaries.* 5 vols., edited by Raphael Patai. New York: Herzl Press and Thomas Yoseloff, 1960.

Hess, Moses. *Rome and Jerusalem, A Study in Jewish Nationalism.* New York: Bloch Publishing Co., 1918.

Patkin, A. L. *The Origins of the Russian-Jewish Labor Movement.* Privately Printed.

Sokolow, Nahum. *History of Zionism 1600-1918.* 2 vols. London: Longmans, Green & Co., 1919.

Szajkowski, Zosa. *The Economic Status of the Jews in Alsace, Metz and Lorraine, 1648-1789.* New York: Editions Historiques Franco-Juives, 1953.

———— *Poverty and Social Welfare Among French Jews 1800-1880.* New York: Editions Historiques Franco-Juives, 1954.

Teller, Judd L. *Scapegoat of Revolution.* New York: Charles Scribners and Sons, 1954.

Chapter TEN

THE NINETEENTH CENTURY

THE NINETEENTH CENTURY JEW WAS CONFRONTED BY OLD FOES and ancient challenges in transparent disguise.

Lutheran Germany, Catholic Austria, and Orthodox Russia were the new embodiment of Christian state power which inflicted experiences upon the Jew that ranged, as in the past, from oppression to disaster.

France was transfused Greco-Roman power, and the relationship between the Jew and this new Hellenism was as ambivalent as it had been almost consistently since the third century before the Common Era.

The votaries of the Religion of Reason (1793-1794) who raided churches and dishabited priests and ministers were complemented in Paris by Jewish intellectuals who publicly scored the rabbinate as "hypocrites seeking to perpetuate absolute and absurd customs." These Parisians were a reincarnation of the Judean Hellenists who had raised the Roman eagle over the central Temple gate in Jerusalem.

Napoleon's policy toward the Jews followed the curve of Greco-Roman-Jewish relations. But, in his own lifetime, the French emperor covered its entire spectrum. He began like Julius Caesar, summoning Jewry to aid his conquests of the East (1799), and ended like the mad Caius Caligula by publishing (1808) his "Infamous Decree" which reimposed restrictive legislation on French Jewry only seventeen years after its enfranchisement.

The French forces had trampled Egypt, seized El Arish and Gaza, and were preparing to scale the fortress of Acre and to besiege Jerusalem. The chief adviser to the Pasha of the former city was a Jew, Chaim Maalem Farchi. In

the Holy City, exhorted by their rabbi, the Jews were helping the Turks erect barricades. Napoleon hoped to instigate the Jews in both cities to treason, and to inflame the entire Turk empire with Jewish rebellion. Like Julius Caesar, he promised to reward them with sovereignty in Palestine. His proclamation, worded in solemn accents, told them that "the time has come, and it may never recur again . . . to reclaim your . . . political status as a nation among nations . . . your unqualified natural right to worship Jehovah publicly and forever."

The Jews probably remembered that Turkey had accorded them hospitality when Christendom, France included, expelled them like beasts. They remained loyal to Constantinople. Within a few years, Napoleon began accusing them of performing in France as a nation within a nation. His policy toward them, his utterances about them, were a web of paradoxes, as he sought to bend the Jews now to one purpose, now to another. The Soviet Union in our own day has been almost duplicating Napoleon's vacillations and cross purposes on the Jewish issue. Napoleon, too, wished to parade abroad as a great defender of Jewry (Moscow long claimed to be the champion of the international struggle against anti-Semitism), while suppressing Jewry on his homegrounds.

The German-Christian rabble of Alsace-Lorraine compounded his confusion. Petitions from the Rhine provinces were piling up on his desk, most of them demanding that the Jews be restricted, even disenfranchised.

The Jews were not without complaint. They found themselves circumscribed in commerce and the professions by spiteful bureaucrats and popular prejudice. A leader from the Rhine provinces, where prejudice was most violent, complained in correspondence to his peer that the emancipation "has been only a paper, perhaps we lost more than we gained through this new freedom." The Jews volunteered in large and enthusiastic numbers for army service, but discovered that their life was unsafe in the barracks. So they altered their names and passed as Christians. When the emperor took a quick census, the number of Jewish servicemen seemed far smaller than it actually was.

NAPOLEON'S SANHEDRIN

Napoleon contrived a stratagem to restrict Jewry in France, and still enlist pro-French sentiment among the Jews of Germany and Russia. He convened an assembly of French Jewish notables, rabbis, and laymen hand-picked by his prefects. They chose discriminately and well, so that the Hellenist elements prevailed and responded to a series of questions submitted on his behalf with a virtual redefinition of the Jewish people. This redefinition reduced universal Israel to almost a French national church, suggested that the difference between a French Jew and Christian was ritualistic and nothing else, and that Napoleon had neither obligation nor emotion for Jews beyond France's frontiers. However, the assembly refused to guarantee that it would so regulate marriage among Jews that one out of three would be an intermarriage.

Napoleon then requested that it convene a great sanhedrin to confirm its decisions as religious law. Its composition was almost the same as that of the assembly. He had just asked these notables to disavow Jewry's transnational nature; now he asked them to pretend to restore an institution which had ceased to function some nineteen hundred years before, and had been in its day the legislature and judiciary of universal Jewry. He hoped that a sanhedrin would focus global Jewish loyalties on Paris. It would arouse Messianic enthusiasm for himself and the French armies among the Jews of Germany and eastern Europe, territories against which he was about to campaign.

Metternich, then Austrian ambassador to France, was deceived and advised Vienna to keep a watch on all Jewish correspondence between Austria and France. Czar Alexander I of Russia was sufficiently worried to twice rescind orders expelling the Jews from the rural areas. Only the Jews seemed unimpressed. The Russian Rabbi Schneur Zalman of Liadi, one of the great Hassidic leaders, said that Napoleon "is our worse enemy, he is out to entrap our souls." A British Jew bitterly inquired of the sanhedrin who had accorded it the mandate to

legislate for all Jewry; but in the United States, a one-time Jewish business associate of Thomas Jefferson, apparently impressed, presented him with a copy of the sanhedrin's proceedings.

In 1808, one year after the sanhedrin had completed its assignment and been discharged, Napoleon, while still exhorting the Jews of Russia to collaborate with his "liberation forces," published his "Infamous Edict." It impoverished and partially disenfranchised French Jewry. Jews were forbidden to move from or into the Rhine districts. They could not engage in trade except by special permit, good for one year and granted only upon the submission of affidavits which satisfied the authorities that the applicant was "morally qualified" to engage in commerce. Their annual renewal required the same humiliating procedures. All debts owed Jews by women or soldiers were automatically and retroactively cancelled provided the borrowers swore they had acquired the loans on credit without either the consent or knowledge of their husbands or officers, respectively. Thousands of Jews were reduced to penury; the effects on the general economy were so disastrous that Napoleon was compelled to cede to popular pressure and exempt entire districts of Jews from the provisions of his Decree.

JEWS "IN THE BLOOD STREAM"

When the law had run its ten year course, the French Parliament deferred a motion to renew it (1818), thus restoring the Jews' rights; under Louis Philippe (1830-1848), they entered the French arts, and their rabbis became salaried employees of the state, on an equal footing with the Protestant and Catholic clergy; under Emperor Louis Napoleon III (1852-1870), they entered French politics at the highest level and assumed the incentive in developing the country's economy. The Pereira brothers, of old Bordeaux stock, backed by Rothschild capital, began constructing the French railroad system. They also branched out into Austrian, Balkan, and Turkish railroads. Jewish capital took risks none others dared. They had been attracted to transportation since the sixteenth century, when their capital and science were involved in

every major navigation-exploration enterprise of the time. Furthermore, they always were in danger of losing their money, whether they risked or saved it. They lost it in France, by government decree, twice within a century, once in 1791 when the National Assembly cancelled one-third of all debts owed Jews, and again sixteen years later, under the Napoleonic decree. Their capital was always at risk.

Louis Napoleon solicited both their credit and their counsel. Jewish political commitment ranged from conservatism to socialism; some in the latter camp were ardent advocates of a reconciliation between the emperor and labor. Jewish politicians also favored the unitary state in juxtaposition to regional parochialism, which stunted economic growth and prevented incentive. Although they were unconcerned with, and uninformed on, matters Jewish, they unknowingly performed in a Hebrew tradition. The ancient Judeans on the one hand were indisposed to all government, but on the other believed that a firm imperial presence was the only guarantee against the chaos created in the region by their malicious, bellicose neighbors.

Only fifty years before it had been charged that the Jew was alien and unassimilable. Now the cry was raised that he was too assimilable and had become a disease of the French national blood stream. The utopian Socialists on the Left agreed unanimously with the clergy and dishabited feudal nobility on the Right that something had to be done to dispose of Jewish influence in commerce, politics, and culture. Among the radicals relentlessly opposed to the Jews was Charles Fourier (1772-1832), whose socialist doctrines enthused Horace Greeley and inspired the establishment of experimental communal societies in nineteenth century America. Fourier recommended "strict measures" against Jewry: "compel them from commerce, bar them from the frontiers and the coast." The anarcho-syndicalist Pierre Joseph Proudhon (1809-1865), who denounced monotheism and sided with the Confederacy in America's Civil War, warned that the United States was "reverting to Israel, and the Bible will yet drive her mad."

Jewry now acquired a statesman in the style of the sixteenth century Joseph Nassi and the seventeenth century Menashe ben Israel, and who alone among ranking French politicians of Jewish descent committed himself wholeheartedly and openly to his people's concerns. He was Adolphe Cremieux (1796-1880), a centrist in politics, parliamentarian, lawyer, orator, and minister in Republican governments. In his brief first term of office (1848), he abolished Negro slavery in the French colonies and capital punishment for political offenders; in his second term, twenty-two years later, he published the Cremieux Decree (1870) which accorded French citizenship to Algerian Jews. This enabled them in our own time to escape to France from the anti-Jewish terrorism of French and Muslim extremists during the civil strife which preceded that country's independence.

JEWRY'S DEFENDER

Cremieux restored the high style of Jewish diplomacy, the carrot and the stick, from the relapse it suffered during the Assembly's emancipation debate (1789-1791) when, at one time, three separate Jewish delegations presented petitions, each contradicting the other.

His first appearance for a Jewish cause was in defense of a group of Damascus Jews charged with an alleged ritual murder. Jews everywhere protested, and enlisted their governments' support. Austria's Metternich was a ranking figure in pressing for justice for the Jews.

For French Jewry, the caste was more complex. When he discovered that the French consul in Damascus was implicated and had effected a "confession" from one of the accused by means of medieval torture, Cremieux appealed to King Louis Philippe who pledged to investigate, but reneged under the pressure of cabinet members who believed that they were protecting France's international reputation by shielding the consul. French complicity in the affair recalled a painful analogy. Paris, in 1242, had been the first city in medieval Europe to burn the Talmud on a public bonfire. Now, the Talmud was again in the docket as the alleged source of instigation to ritual murder. Cremieux, aware that he was inviting the charge

of disloyalty, declared for all the world to hear: "France has turned on the Jews; France has betrayed us!"

Such boldness was unique in emancipated Jewry of that day. It must have shocked the Rothschilds who were deeply and publicly committed to the defense of the Damascus victims although, in the words of Jewry's foremost historian Heinrich Graetz, "they appear to have adhered to the principle not to throw the power of their riches into the scale on behalf of their co-religionists and their faith."

Bolder still was Cremieux' role as President of the Alliance Israelite Universelle, a post he held with but brief interruptions from 1862, two years after its founding, almost until his death. As its name implies, it was to have been a world-wide association of Jews. Modeled after a Protestant organization with a similar name, its purpose was to provide philanthropic and political assistance to destitute, undereducated, and persecuted Jewish communities everywhere. However, other Jewries refused to join, or joined and then quickly reconsidered, fearful lest any organization of global scale convey the impression of a Jewish conspiracy. Their abstention did not deter anti-Semitism, however. Anti-Semites, touting the myth of Jewish "world dominion," inevitably cited thereafter the Alliance as exhibit number one. Actually, the Alliance in earlier years did far more to advance French than Jewish culture among the Jews in Africa and the Orient.

No such daring concept as Cremieux' was again advanced until the Viennese journalist, turned Jewish secular Messiah, Dr. Theodor H. Herzl, founded the World Zionist Organization in Basel in 1897, giving Cremieux' design even greater vision—the restoration of Jewish statehood in Palestine.

BACK TO MEDIEVALISM

The Greco-Roman world ended on the west banks of the Rhine. Across the river began medieval Europe, embracing Germany, Austria-Hungary, and Russia.

When the French armies retreated, Germany, where the Jews had enjoyed a brief respite, reverted to her old custom. Her states not only denied civic equality to the

Jews, but intruded into Jewry's intramural affairs, as few Christian states dared do even in the Dark Ages. Some German states now instructed the Jew to promptly update and reform his rituals; others forbade him to deviate from orthodox custom. The Prussian authorities were uncertain, sometimes preferring the Jews to be orthodox, sometimes preferring them to be reform. In 1836, predating by a full century Nazi legislation, Prussia forbade them to take the same names as Christians. This caused confusion. Since Protestant Germans also took their names from the Old Testament, it almost seemed as if the Jews would have to resort to Greek mythology and numbers, until the Prussians, in a generous moment, passed an amendment that applied the ban only to New Testament names. The Jews might have, of course, easily established their claim to these as well.

It was not until 1871, when Germany was united under Prussia and a federal constitution, that the Jews were enfranchised in all her domains. On the issue of German unity, Jewish politicians helped Bismarck, the Iron Chancellor, even as their French counterparts helped Louis Philippe. Edward Lasker, the Liberal leader, and Ferdinand Lassalle, the Socialist, lined up their respective parties for a unified Germany, in the belief that it would erase the violent parochialism of its separate parts. Lassalle even hoped that Bismarck would help advance socialism, and the welfare-state features which the latter introduced were probably inspired by the Socialist.

The secular united German state excluded the Jew no less than the disparate Christian states had. Previously, this was done on religious grounds, now because he was a member of an "alien nation." Herman von Trietschke, historian and ideologian of Bismarck's Germany, explained that the state had "a personality . . . its omnipotence is the highest moral law," which was contrary to the Jewish placement of law above state and ruler. But it mattered little whether or not Jews endorsed his definition, unfortunately, because they were "foreign matter" which was unassimilable into the "state-personality." Von Trietschke, being a compassionate man, would not think of disenfranchising them. He would only restrict them.

They were restricted in astonishing ways. The authorities could not order the opposition parties and newspapers to oust Jewish leaders, editors, and contributors. There was not much objection to Jewish playwrights and actors. The smug bourgeois society could maintain a patronizing attitude toward them. They were after all pariahs, tolerated for their capacity to entertain their superiors. But a Jew could not obtain a civil service position on any level, not even to teach elementary school. The Jews were blocked wherever the state determined matters, and public incitement by Adolf Stoecker, the royal court chaplain, caused them to be publicly condemned, abused, and beaten. Notwithstanding this, and discrimination at all levels of academic life, the Jews and half-Jews pioneered in experimental and applied physics, in chemistry and physiology, presaged the principles of wireless and x-ray and the advent of Einstein's theory of relativity, which like Freud's psychoanalysis was largely a Jewish movement, founded the German potash and dye industries, and laid the basis for I. G. Farben.

The very prevalence of Jews in science suggests a crisis in the younger generation's relationship to Judaism. Neither Christian nor Jew, in that generation of scientific rationalists, took religion seriously. Many of the German Jewish elite therefore saw no reason why they should not leap the barrier from Jewry into the church, since it automatically opened all opportunity to them. Conversely, a remarkable generation of Jewish encyclopedists arose in Germany at this time. Disciples of Mendelssohn, they hoped to arrest apostasy by presenting a rational sequence of Jewish intellectual endeavor through the centuries and to reconcile, as Saadia Gaon and Maimonides had done in their day, the conflict between faith and reason.

RELIGIOUS REFORM

As researchers, the encyclopedists succeeded astonishingly well. They branched off into history, biblical criticism, and linguistics, and reconstructed centuries of Jewish social and economic circumstance. They collated classified and interpreted materials that for two millennia had been dispersed on several continents, in innumerable languages,

embedded in the history, politics, customs of scores of peoples, and came up with a coherent composite of Jewish civilization. However, they failed in their second purpose —to stem apostasy. The clue to their failure is implicit in the proceedings of numerous assemblies these men, most of whom were rabbis, convened to consider religious reform. They charged that the orthodox rabbi was obsessed with ritualism. Yet their own deliberations were similarly obsessed. Motions to excise prayers, suspend outdated observances, and introduce greater decorum into the synagogue were debated passionately and caused schisms. But few of the participants, and none of the assemblies, dealt with the true issues of the day that fermented revolution in Europe, such as class tensions and relations between the state and its citizens. Had the Jewish religious reformers conceived their function to be the formulation of a policy statement on these unresolved issues, they would have been compelled to base themselves on the Talmud and generations of Responsa literature, which had always concerned itself with social law and the relations between man and his rulers. Since this was not their purpose, some of the reformers scornfully dismissed the entire corpus of Jewish jurisprudence as anachronistic.

They also made themselves wholly irrelevant to their times. There was no difference, in this, between the orthodox and the religious reformers in German Jewry. Both seemed determined to persuade the German people that Judaism was the supreme expression of loyalty to the German state, and nation, even as there is a similar tendency among American Jewish organizations, not necessarily synagogues, to present Judaism as synonymous with contemporary America. The reformers disavowed the credo of Messianic redemption in a restored Palestine as impugning the blessedness of the Jewish circumstance in Bismarck's Germany. There was general agreement that some prayers should be recited in German, since few of the congregants knew Hebrew. However, some extreme religious reformers proposed that all the prayers be recited in German on the ground that it was a nobler vehicle for supplication. They even carried their battle to Amer-

ica where they sought to impose German, while excising Hebrew and excluding English from the synagogue service.

It was only later, in America, that the Jewish reform movement acquired the passion of a social gospel. At its beginnings, while proclaiming its universalism, it was only seeking to accommodate Judaism to Germanic parochialism; consequently, assimilated or apostatized Jews, disenchanted with the German promise, did not return to the Temple, but railed against it.

RENEGADES AND PENITENTS

The most bitter voice, speaking in enduring hate, was that of Karl Marx, born a Jew, converted in childhood, descended from a long and venerable line of Talmudic exegetes dating to Rashi. His father, not his mother, had leaped the barrier for the opportunities denied a Jew; their son shuddered at the grotesque admixture in himself of the Prussian and the Jew. Throughout his lifetime, he labored to obliterate the memory of his origin by fantastic allegation and by horrendous invective against the Jews.

He accepted as prototypal Jews the high society members of the Reform Temple. They were no worse, no better than others of their class. Like Marx himself, they wished to appear as more Prussian than the Prussian. He evolved a thesis that Jewry was the spur of all capitalist evil, that through the centuries it had enslaved society, not been enslaved by it. The roots of his anti-Semitism, apart from his inner conflict, were German Lutheranism, the writings of the French Utopian Socialists Proudhon and Fourier, and debates on Jewish emancipation which, commencing in the French Assembly in 1791, raged in Germany and all Europe throughout the nineteenth century. His own comment on the subject was ambiguous: "the social emancipation of the Jew is the emancipation of society from Judaism."

Yet he could not escape the stigma of his Jewish origin even within the First International which he had founded. In a contest for leadership of the organization, the Russian anarchist Mikahil Bakunin accused Marx of plotting with Rothschild, "I am honestly convinced (they) hold

each other in high esteem . . . this sect . . . today constitutes a major power in Europe."

Even in his theories Marx was trapped between Jewish tradition and its antipodes. Determinism is Greek, yet Marx sees its denouement not in tragedy, but in mankind's redemption, which is the Jewish concept. He sees economic laws working toward a purpose that cannot be altered, which is Protestant predestination, yet mankind may redeem itself through egalitarianism. The Old Testament is preoccupied with such "mundane" matters as the equitable distribution of land among the tribes. Judaism views sin primarily as social injustice and its corrective had been the concern of Jewish law from the Bible through eighteenth and nineteenth century rabbinical literature. His view of history as essentially purposeful and unfinished is also Jewish; Christianity sees the purpose as already accomplished in Christ. However, his class war recalls Gnosticism's combustive vision of the war between the forces of light and the forces of darkness, Christendom's anti-Christ, and, of course, Germany's apocalyptic Weltanschauung.

Marx's search for absolution through flaggelation of his origins was within a tradition dating back at least to the first century of the Common Era, to Philo's nephew Tiberius who had been Roman procurator of Judea, had led a mob on the Jewish Quarters of Alexandria, and had served on the staff of Titus during the siege of Jerusalem. Two contemporaries, on familiar terms with Marx, were, conversely, Josephs at the court of the liberal and radical movements of their day, Heinrich Heine, the poet, had apostatized as a youth to obtain larger opportunity, and never forgave himself. Moses Hess, an egalitarian utopist descended from rabbis, worked on the first drafts of the Communist Manifesto, but his pristine humanitarianism precluded a sustained relationship with Marx and Engels. Both Heine and Hess had reached the conclusion that underneath its liberal façade apparently all Germany was committed to persecute the Jew and bar him from dignified assimilation. Like Marx, both renounced the German Jewish upper class but for different reasons; they saw it as a reprehensible break from the historical

Jew, its posture imitative of the despicable Prussianism which expectorated the Jew. Both turned reverentially to the medievally garbed Jew of the annexed former Polish territories, and celebrated his authenticity, custom, and ritual. Heine, admittedly, was unable to make that way of life his own, and, in his words, was torn by the ancient conflict between Hellenism (pleasure) and Judaism (obligation). Hess found the transition easier. In a brochure "Rome and Jerusalem" which presaged an inevitable collision between Jew and German, he predicted the restoration of Palestine as a Jewish state, based on a kind of religious socialism and radiating its moral influence to all the world.

AUSTRIA

Emperor Francis Joseph I (1848-1916) of Austria, a benevolent autocrat, was regarded by his Jewish subjects as their protector. They could indeed rise to high rank in the army, which was under imperial control, but could make little headway in the civil service which was under the control of a bureaucracy drawn from the bourgeoisie and the clergy, and supported by some of the nobility. As in Germany, they were a power, however, in professions which obtuse minds relate to entertainment, or the clown's role in society. They were the poets, novelists, playwrights, and critics, who from the mid-nineteenth century on gave Austria her eminence on the stage and in letters. They were also editors of the opposition journals, which exacerbated feeling against them.

Another element adverse to Jewish interests was the pluralism of the Austro-Hungarian empire. In the United States, pluralism connotes immigrants from many countries; in Francis Joseph's empire, it meant many nationalities and their ancestral lands bunched together forcibly under Austrian rule. Their territories having become intermixed, these nationalities clashed at election time, as each tried to obtain more offices and mandates than all the others.

In Galicia, today the Western Ukraine, when the returns were in, Ruthenian politicians charged that the Jews determined the outcome by voting for the Poles; the latter, conversely, sent pickets into the streets to deflect cus-

tomers from the Jewish shops to the Polish co-operatives. In 1848, the leader of the liberal Hungarian independence movement, Ludwig Kossuth, went on record against enfranchising the Jews and even rejected their volunteers; he relented only when the imperial forces pinned him down and his cause was beyond retrieve. His enemies—the Czechs, Croats, and Serbs—did not quickly forget the Magyar-Jewish alliance.

Vienna and Budapest were Jewry's last western frontier. Here, the forces of Jewish orthodoxy and religious reform clashed as nowhere else. The reform group qualified psychologically, if not always occupationally, as court Jews. Within reach of opportunity as no other segment of Jewry, they produced a rising spiral of apostates. Believing that absolutism was their last bar to equality, they became implicated in the 1848 liberal constitutionalist insurrections.

The orthodox had no stake in these revolutions. From the evidence on hand, they began to regard rights as a stimulus to apostasy. Commanding orthodoxy's defenses in Hungary was the venerable Moses Sofer or Shreiber (1763-1839), ranking Talmudic authority, better known as Chasam Sofer, the name of his six volume collection of rabbinical Responsa. It was the custom among Jews to call their great thinkers by the names of their major works.

Chasam Sofer was a rigorist in matters relating to religious ritual. In social law, conversely, he was left of the insurrectionists fighting in the streets for a constitution. "Whoever alters a single custom," he ruled in relation to ritualistic amendments, "or waives a single observance, even if its source be neither the Talmud, nor the Bible, but only popular usage, deserves excommunication from Jewry." This conservative, however, once ruled that "the laws of the state are not binding law." He was responding to a particular circumstance. Budapest had been buffeted by invasions, goods and credit were scarce, and the government countenanced profiteering by bankers and wholesalers, while imposing inequitable taxes on petty traders. The latter inquired of the rabbi whether it would be sinful to conceal their true assets from the tax collector.

His reply was brought to the attention of the royal courts. The city was under martial law. Fortunately, some friends interceded for him directly with the emperor. His religious conservatism was no doubt cited in his favor.

RUSSIA

Another ranking spokesman for ritualistic rigor and social radicalism was Malbim (1809-1879), the initials of Meir Leibush ben Yechiel Michel, the author of a revered biblical commentary which acquired the unique distinction of being placed, in his lifetime, alongside Rashi and other ancient exegeses in many of the new editions of the Old Testament. Born in Posen, former Polish territory annexed by Prussia, he spent a long and harassed career as rabbi of Jewish communities in the Czarist domains. Because of his eminence, the affluent custodians of the Kahals, or Jewish community councils, solicited him for their communities. But when, upon taking office, he promptly demanded that the rich produce merchants lower their prices so that the poor would not be wanting in the necessities of life, the same men who had outbid all others for Malbim's services moved with dispatch to rid themselves of him. They had the police forbid his sermons as a disturbance of the peace, and on two occasions, when he seemed reluctant to depart, they had him seized as a political agitator. He was released only after Moses Montefiore, the celebrated British philanthropist, had petitioned the Czar.

Nicholas I (1826-1855) was perhaps the worst of all the Czars. He had one obssession, the mass conversion of Russia's overwhelmingly orthodox Jewish multitudes. Nothing could deter him from this purpose. He seized their religious books and burned those found "subversive." He interdicted the kaftan and beard which Jewry anyhow abandoned wherever it achieved emancipation. In Russia, however, the Jews were still confined to the Pale. Nicholas conceived of a devilish plan to seize the Jews in their youth and convert them. He therefore lowered the army conscription age for Jews to twelve. He demanded of each Jewish community a set quota of juvenile conscripts, and when it was necessary to fill it, even

children under twelve were drafted. The job was entrusted to a gross breed that had replaced the once honorable and distinguished leadership of the Jewish community councils. The same kind of breed served, in our own time, on Hitler's judenrats. The conscripted children were driven on foot across the steppes into the Russian interior. Half of them perished. The survivors were quartered in the homes of regular army men who worked them like slaves. The children were beaten and compelled to kneel before ikons, make the sign of the cross, and partake of forbidden foods. Many of the children survived these tortures without submitting. When they were eighteen years of age, they were conscripted into regular service. The term was twenty-five years for all conscripts, Jews and Christians alike. The term of juvenile service was not deducted.

Even after their discharge, they were not permitted to take up residence freely, but were compelled back to the Pale. Here they were a distinctive breed—of powerful build, with coarse peasant features, Russian-accented Yiddish, and astonishing guilelessness. Their children and grandchildren were of the same physical type. They later formed Jewish defense units against pogroms, and some sailed for Palestine where they joined the Zionist armed guard, Shomrim, which preceded the Haganah from which the Israel army evolved.

About one and a half decades later, Nicholas I announced that in order to advance education among Jews he would establish government-subsidized Jewish parochial schools which would include Hebrew and other Jewish subjects in the general curriculum. He also announced the establishment of two government-supported rabbinical seminaries. He expected an enthusiastic reception for this plan from the Jews. Instead, they reacted apprehensively. It was inconceivable that a Czar who could kidnap Jewish children from their parents and compel them to convert would suddenly become so benevolent. Indeed, they were right. Governmental archives that have since been published reveal, in the Czar's own handwriting, that these schools, including the rabbinical seminaries, were to serve as a ruse to condition Jewish students for conver-

sion. One of the latter-day disciples of Mendelssohn's, had been brought from Germany to conduct these schools. He was enthusiastic about the assignment, but left abruptly when he accidentally learned its true purpose.

The Russian maskilim, however, were more guileless. They trusted the Czar, despite his record. They trusted him because, like the German maskilim and court Jews, they suffered from an agonizing inferiority complex and readily conceded that the Jews as a people did not yet merit equality before the law and must first acquire education and "civilized habits." They even concurred in the myth that the Jews wilfully engaged in unproductive occupations. The fact is that thirty per cent of East European Jews were engaged in "productive," or menial occupations; they constituted seventy to eighty per cent of Russia's artisans. The fact was also, however, that confined to the Pale they had no markets for their skills and products. As a result, about one-fifth of the Russian Jewry was the recipient of charity provided by the other four-fifths who were themselves near privation. The Jews were accused by their enemies of being traders because this was an easy way to turn a ruble, and of being too indolent to work the soil. The maskilim shared this estimate. Yet the anti-Semitic governors of Russia's frontier provinces always opposed proposals for the expulsion of Jewish traders from their regions. The Jews, they contended, were the cornerstone of the local economy. On three separate occasions, under Alexander I and Nicholas I, the Jews were offered free land in Russia's virgin territories. Each time, prepared to become farmers, they responded enthusiastically. Each time the offer was rescinded or curtailed.

Although suffering from the same self-deprecation, the German and Russian maskilim worked toward separate ends. The German disciples of Mendelssohn were concerned with halting the tide of apostasy. They believed that by "Germanizing" the synagogue and bringing its rituals closer to the austere Protestant pattern, they might accomplish their purpose. The Russian maskilim had another purpose. Russian Jewry was clinging to its ancient tradition, and had to be forced out into the daylight. A

sure way of making the Jew suspicious was to tamper with his synagogue rituals. Hence, the Russian maskilim dared not tamper with these. They sought no alterations in the order of prayers. Furthermore, there was nothing in the primitive, peasant-based Russian orthodox Church to commend its adaptation by the synagogue.

SOVEREIGN CULTURE

Yet the life of this people of "bad habits" was rich and dynamic, in sharp contrast to the monotone of German Jewry which was predictably centrist-liberal in its politics, upper class in its tastes and prejudices, reform in its faith, and superpatriotic.

The Pale maintained its own network of educational and charitable institutions. If his capacities warranted, a poor man's child was assured free education from the elementary level through rabbinical ordination. The Pale also provided dowries for brides of poor families, sitters and nursing for the sick, comforters for the bereaved, food and lodging for transients, and free loans for needy who refused charity. It was engaged, further, in several simultaneous kulturkampfs. The debate still continued, although with abated passion, between the Hassidim proponents of populist emotional religion, and the Misnagdim, advocates of discipline learning as the consummate form of worship. The maskilim wrote, translated, or adapted to Hebrew works of science, philosophy, and history, which spread the "scientific heresy" in the yeshivot, the Talmudic academies.

A new folk literature flourished in Yiddish, branching off from entertainment and moralistic preachments in history, popular science, instruction in foreign languages, and political agitation.

The Pale was sovereign even in its foods and hobbies, a sure gauge of a people's inner independence. Jewish weddings were entertained by bands and a badchan, a kind of calypso singer. Among these musicians, the synagogual cantors, and the Hassidic assemblies, a rich liturgy and folk music evolved which endures to this day. The most striking phenomena of the times was the secularization of the Pale's relaxation. Wine cellars, that had be-

come the fashion in the larger towns among the food-loving Southern Russian Jewry, presented performance by itinerant companies of singers and comedians, forerunner by several decades of the Yiddish theater founded in the 1870's. They catered primarily to the unlearned, the artisans and their apprentices and to the demimonde, another stage in the social mobility initiated by Sabbatai Zvi and, later, Hassidism which had legitimized levity and endowed the repressed classes with boldness.

Since all Jewry, poor and rich, was closely packed in the Pale, fashions, both good and bad, spread infectiously up and down the rungs of the social ladder. The combustive proximity of Jewry's socioeconomic graduations precluded wide qualitative differences in dress, food, and custom. Housing ranged from the mudhut, on the lowest level, through the rich man's brick structure, but even the latter was modest not to arouse envy. Distractions notwithstanding, the synagogue like the Forum in ancient Rome was still, however, the focus of all activities. It is here that the day commenced with prayer and, at vespers, closed with study circles which were adult education designed for all levels of the population.

LAST COURT JEW

Like all sovereign nations, East European Jewry had its allies. The greatest at this time was Sir Moses Montefiore, the compassionate autocrat who traveled to Damascus to defend its Jews from a ritual murder libel, visited Palestine several times to initiate and supervise his philanthropies for its residual Jewish communities, and twice came to Russia to intercede for its Jews directly with the Czar who was then seeking development loans. However extensive his charities, his banking power was not sufficient to serve as political leverage. That is perhaps why his missions failed. Only the Rothschilds possessed such capacity, and they would not contemplate using it. Even their philanthropies, until the last two decades of the nineteenth century, were very moderate; except in the Damascus case, they shied away from any public gesture that might suggest their concern for fellow-Jews. Russian Jewry embroidered the myth about the Rothschild wealth

but intuitively hung Sir Moses Montefiore's image in its parlors, on the eastern wall, in the direction of Jerusalem.

AMERICAN BOLDNESS

Sir Moses was the last great "court Jew." The ordinary Jew was now beginning to speak for himself, and nowhere more forcefully than in America. Its Jewish population was sparse—10,000 in the first two decades of the nineteenth century, and 50,000 on the eve of the Civil War—but possessed men and women who were sufficiently bold and tough to meet any challenge. Such were Mordecai Manuel Noah (1785-1851), playwright, journalist, editor, flamboyant politician, and Commodore Uriah P. Levy (1792-1862), salty shipmaster and naval hero, who began his career at sea as a cabin boy at the age of ten. Both were fifth generation Americans, descended from Marranos.

Noah, then just turned thirty, had been recalled from his post as U.S. Consul to Tunis by Secretary of State Monroe because as a Jew he was allegedly persona non grata in a Muslim land. Fighting back, Noah pointed out that the Muslim courts welcomed even Jewish ambassadors, and were themselves represented in Christendom by Jews. After three years, he received a written apology from President Madison who disclaimed any prejudicial intent, which is easily supported by Madison's previous successful efforts barring a religious test from both the Virginia state and Federal constitutions. Levy, a retired captain in his sixties when he made his charges, maintained that he was removed from the active officers' list solely because of religious bigotry. He obtained restoration and eventually promotion to Commodore, the highest U.S. naval rank, and was put in command of the Mediterranean Squadron.

Both were Jews fighting singly, but tenaciously, for what they felt was a cause greater than their own vindication. They were not backed by a battery of lawyers, press agents, and researchers from Jewish defense organizations as would be the case today. The United States was still raw-mannered, blunt-spoken. There was a thou-I relationship between the common citizen and the highest

offices in the land. Also, both men were of bold Marrano stock. Their utterances are imperial beside the memoranda which Sir Moses Montefiore, imperious under other circumstances, submitted to the Czar of all the Russians.

"The citizens of the United States who profess the Hebrew religion have merited . . . the rights which they enjoy," Noah wrote. "There was (also) something insufferably little," he recalled, "in adding the weight of the American government, in violation of the wishes and institutions of the people, to crush the nation (the Jews), many of which had fought and bled for American independence, and many had assisted to elevate those very men who had thus treated their rights with indelicate oppression." He was defending America. "It is not . . . to satisfy the Israelites in this country that I notice this subject. They are capable of defending their own rights, but is done to prove to the Jews in Europe, who have great commercial connections with the United States and are capable of serving or injuring us, that this act of intolerance, of which I had so much to complain is not the act of the people."

Noah's experience propelled him forever into Jewish affairs and to concern himself with Near Eastern developments. Fitfully, from 1818 on, he urged that the disintegrating state of the Turkish Empire presented an opportunity to restore Palestine to the Jews. His histrionic gestures impugned his intent. In 1825, wearing splendorous robes of his own design, he laid the cornerstone for "Ararat . . . a temporary and provisional" Jewish state on Grant Island, N.Y. He never again returned there, perhaps because there was no response to his proclamation, circulated to all Jewish notables and rabbis abroad, which proposed a global Jewish annual per capita tax for maintaining Ararat as a temporary settlement for Jewish refugees: "The Jews should and never will relinquish the just hope of regaining possession of their ancient heritage." He signed himself "governor and judge of Israel. . . ." This theatricality may be the reason why there was not even a ripple among Jews—although Christian interest was stirred—when Noah, in 1837, proposed pur-

chasing Palestine outright, for cold cash from the Pasha of Egypt.

Commodore Levy sought no role for himself in Jewry when four decades later he told a naval court of inquiry, convened to hear his charges, "My case is the case of every Israelite in the Union. . . . Are all these to be placed under the ban of incapacitation? . . . Are the thousands of Israel and the ten thousands of Judah, in their dispersion throughout the earth, who look to America as a land bright with promise, are they now to learn to their sorrow and dismay, that we too have sunk in the mire of religious intolerance and bigotry? And are American Christians now to begin the persecution of the Jews? . . ."

OLD-NEW ISSUES

Some of the issues that were raised in the nineteenth century endure with American Jewry to this day: discrimination against American Jews by foreign governments, Sunday closings imposed on Sabbath observers, and religion in the public schools.

Today, it is the Arab states that discriminate against American Jews. In the 1850's, the U.S. Government was considering a treaty with Switzerland in which the latter stipulated the exclusion of U.S. Jews. Although Switzerland's federal law did not discriminate against them, it could not override the law of the separate cantons which did discriminate. American states-righters had a ready comprehension of the sacredness of canton law. Moreover, Switzerland was an excellent market for their tobacco. Jews protested to no avail. The Swiss people themselves resolved the issue on January 15, 1866 when they voted in plebiscite to extend civic equality to all, regardless of religion.

The same issue was raised in respect to Russia in 1864. After one-half century of futile protests, American Jewry learned in 1907 that Secretary of State Elihu Root had tacitly concurred with the Czar's discrimination by instructing the U.S. Passport Office not to clear Jews for travel there "unless it has assurance that the Russian government will admit them." European countries had earlier compelled the Czar to alter his policy in relation

229

to their Jewish citizens. The first firm action by the United States was taken in 1912, when President Taft retaliated by abrogating the Russo-American Treaty.

The issue of Sunday closings and Sabbath observers has endured since colonial days. The issue of religious instruction in the public schools was dramatically raised in the first half of the nineteenth century when Catholics were indignant over Protestant teachings in New York's schools. Firmly told by the New York Board of Education in 1843, that this being a Christian country, it would continue to use Christian textbooks, the Jews withdrew their children and enrolled them in parochial schools that were immediately founded. A decade later, the Board of Education modified its position, and ruled that each ward could vote whether or not it wished religous instruction in its schools. The Jewish wards voted to excise it from the curriculum, and since parochial schools were too costly for a community of its size, New York Jewry returned its children to the public schools.

CIVIL WAR

During the Civil War agony, the Jews in America were small in number, yet they loomed sufficiently large in the public eye because, American society being Bible-conscious at the time, all parties—Abolitionists, Unionists, Confederates—solicited witness from and impugned the motive of the People of the Book.

Rabbi Arnold Fischel probably expressed the view of the majority, who lived in the North, when he wrote after Lincoln's election that "hitherto, state legislatures have been less liberal than the Federal Government, which gives us good cause to apprehend should the present constitution be changed and another one adopted by the seceding states. . . ." This was, instinctively, the position of Jews everywhere, in France and Germany earlier still, whenever the issue of states rights versus federal or unitary government was involved. Such a position was perhaps rooted in the ancient Judean experience dating from the Macabbees, who invited the protection of a great imperial presence from their small and malicious neighbors.

The rabbis were almost all Unionists; several were rabid Abolitionists. Eccentric individuals joined both camps. August Bondi, an untutored German immigrant, was a sharpshooter with John Brown; Eugenia Levy Phillips was a Confederate agent. Judah P. Benjamin, a probable apostate, the "brains of the Confederacy," was called "Judas Iscariot" by embittered Southerners, and an exemplar of "Jewish treason" by extreme abolitionists. The Seligmans, emigrants from Bavaria who began their career in this country as peddlers in the 1830's, floated in Europe a $200,000,000 Union Bond issue. It was crucial for Union victory. No other banks were willing to assume it. *Harper's Weekly* charged that the Rothschilds were the Confederate purse, and the U.S. Consul in Frankfurt refuted the charge.

German political refugees in 1848, liberal on all other issues, were sometimes vituperative in respect to Jews and Catholics. Germans serving with the Union forces had sometimes vandal sport with Southern Jews. The American Jew was discomfited but not alarmed by these events. History had immunized him to prejudice in small doses. Furthermore, he was irrelevant to America's distemper. The primary targets, besides the Negro, were the Germans and the Irish.

The German immigrants in America, like the Jews in Germany, were treated as a formidable, superior conspiracy. However, whereas the Jew in Germany sought acceptance as a full German, the Germans in America formed enclaves, which disparaged native American culture and predicted Der Tag when German kultur would hold full dominion in America.

The Irish Americans were treated like ghettoized Alsace-Lorraine Jewry when it pleaded for enfranchisement by the French Assembly. They were castigated as "superstitious, ignorant, ruled by the Pope." Native labor charged that they depressed wages, surfeited the market, and caused unemployment. The New England Brahmin confounded the Irish with the factories, constructed by nouveau riche Yankees, that defaced his bucolic landscape. He rightly sensed that they would reorder his fastidious custom and succeed to his political power.

THE CLASSIC ROLE

The Jews performed in America their classic economic role as middlemen. It was the happiest performance in all their history in Christendom, because American society was fluid; no class alliances that had previously excluded them existed here, and supply fell short of demand. The appearance of a Jewish peddler with a sack on his back, or the establishment of a Jewish general store, was not met with the jeers and hate of guildsmen and competitors. Wherever he turned, he was a pioneer. The peddler saved the country people a trip to town, and the general store made it possible to order by catalogue from the big city. The Jews were early engaged in the Indian trade. They were among the first settlers in Alaska. During the 1850's, the Jews joined the California goldrush, not as prospectors, excepting eccentric individuals, but as shopkeepers.

A contemporary newspaper account notes with appreciation that "merchandise, from the time it is freighted on the clipper ships until it is consumed, passes principally through the hands of Jewish merchants . . . without them trade would become almost stagnated in the state (California). The Express Companies of the interior depend mainly on their support. . . . This position they have not acquired without great attention, honesty, industry and personal sacrifice, and by unremitted prudence and civility."

When he became a clothing manufacturer, he still kept prices down and sought his profit through volume.

Yet the Jew was still haunted even here by self-deprecation and self-indictment. He could not easily shake off the myth, propounded by Christians and even his own maskilim in Russia, that his occupations were parasitic, that trade was sinful, and that agriculture was the only honorable alternative. One can imagine in what desperate economic plight American Jewry would be today, and how irrelevant to the American economy, if it had in the nineteenth century turned en masse to farming. However, in the 1830's, 1840's, and 1850's, New York Jews repeatedly founded societies purposing to settle on the lands. One or two of these even realized their plans, settled up-

state, but did not endure. There was wise counsel which challenged the wisdom of these experiments. These men argued that there was nothing immoral or unproductive about urban occupations, not even trade. Moreover, Jews were engaged as carpenters, cigar-makers, plumbers, shoe-makers, tailors, bricklayers, blacksmiths, butchers, and in many other occupations. The country was parturient with resources and possibilities. It welcomed incentive and skill. No serious application, in whatever field, was without merit.

REBELLIOUS RABBIS

American Jewry experienced the difference between old and new circumstance in every area of private and public life and Jewish community effort.

Central and Eastern Europe offered the nineteenth century Jew only two alternatives: the synagogue or apostasy. Even in Britain, before the last civil disabilities were removed, the rate of apostasy was high. Apostasy was everywhere in Europe, in Heine's words, "a ticket to admission." In America, there was no established church to compel dissidents, including the Jew. There was not one dominant Christian denomination that could pledge converts certain professional or social success. A Jew, in America, his heart set on apostasy, had to do comparison shopping among the various churches.

Jewry here was a conglomerate of immigrants from many lands, with disparate customs. Two new types of Jew, now universally common, emerged for the first time perhaps in nineteenth century American soil: the secular Jew who shunned the synagogue, but was otherwise engaged in all Jewish public effort, especially charity, and the Jew who married out of his faith but wished to retain his synagogual affiliation. Jewish religious law disqualified neither one. Conversely, the constitutional provisions of the individual synagogues were a law unto themselves.

Since there was no universal Jewish discipline in America, there could be no rebellion against tradition, only a drifting away. The sole rebels against custom were rabbis, who formed in the mid- and late-nineteenth century

the three major divisions in American Jewry, known today as Orthodox, Conservative, and Reform.

The Orthodox Jew altered nothing, neither procedure of service, prayerbook, nor ritualistic observance.

The Conservative Jew introduced only slight modifications, excised a few obscure prayers, introduced English sermons, and included an English translation of some prayers. They were for observance of the Sabbath and the dietary laws. Like the Orthodox, they believed in Jewry's restoration to Zion.

The Reform Jews were an amazing cauldron of factions and paradox. The moderate Reform Jews were not prepared to disavow all Talmudic, or rabbinical Law, and would not venture in synagogue decorum beyond introducing mixed Choirs. The extreme Reform regarded the Talmud as "prison walls." The Reform consensus favored the excision of all reference to Zion and redemption from the prayerbook. Some called "Washington—our Jerusalem, America—our Zion," in a profound religious sense. They accused nascent Zionist movements abroad of excessive pessimism over the plight of European Jewry. Rabbi David Einhorn, violently opposed to any implication of feeling for Zion, was a direct heir, however, to Sabbatai Zvi's radical disregard of Jewish law. He, too, brooked no custom. He transformed the observance of Tisha B'av, the ninth day of Ab when the Temple was destroyed, into a joyous celebration, because, he said in a special "thanksgiving prayer," the Lord had delivered Jewry from its physical bondage to Zion and dispersed it among the gentiles to instruct them in its prophetic mission. He found most ancient Hebrew customs incompatible with modern times, but he saw nothing archaic in retaining the German language prayerbook in the American Temple.

In retrospect, Einhorn cuts a ludicrous figure. Immeasurably more important historically were two other German-born leaders of religious reform in American Jewry, Isaac Lesser (1816-1868), forerunner of the Conservative movement, and Isaac Meyer Wise (1819-1900), founder of American Reform Judaism. Both were ministers, journalists, editors, translators, speakers, polemicists, indefatigable travelers across the land, initiators of rabbinical

synods, convenors of conferences and drafters of schemes to form one central organization of American Jewry, which efforts are optimistically pursued to this day.

These two men, unlike some of the Reform rabbinate in Germany, did not seek to copy a model Christian decorum nor to adjust to Christian custom, but sought instead to accommodate the synagogue to the new American Jewish circumstance. They either adumbrated or founded some of the religious educational institutions that play a significant role in contemporary American Jewry. They appeared on the American scene when the dominant role in Jewish affairs had passed on from the elder Sephardic, or Spanish-Portuguese families, to the German-Jewish immigrants. The Sephardic community functioned like a Catholic diocese. All communal activities, education and charity included, were centered in the synagogue. The Germans dispersed Jewish effort. Influenced by the Protestant tradition, they retained the synagogue as a house of worship, but functioned culturally and philanthropically through other, secular agencies, such as the newly founded fraternal orders. Lesser and Wise worked to sustain the role of the synagogue against its diminution within the framework of a German-conditioned Jewry.

But in Wise's lifetime, and fifteen years after Lesser's passing, American Jewry was overwhelmed by immigrants of another culture—the East Europeans, primarily the Russians. Until the early eighteenth century these Jewries had been at one with German Jewry. Then their ways briefly separated; when they met again on American soil, the East Europeans were an "Arab" or "Mongol" invasion of a sedate German-American Jewry; 1881 was the year this invasion began.

Chapter ELEVEN

MANY FACES
OF
FREEDOM

THERE IS A TENDENCY TO ATTRIBUTE ALL MAJOR EVENTS IN contemporary Jewish history to three traumatic experiences. American Jewry came into being, this view contends, only because no other country would admit the Jews fleeing from the Czarist pogroms of 1881. Dr. Theodor Herzl, a Viennese journalist, founded the Zionist movement and advanced the idea for the restoration of Jewish statehood in Palestine, because he was shocked by the frame-up against the French Jewish officer Captain Alfred Dreyfus whose trial and sentencing for treason he had covered in 1894 as a correspondent for one of the great continental newspapers. Finally, the revelations of the full scope and horror of the German's persecution of European Jewry compelled guilt-ridden Christian nations to atone by granting the Jews a state in Palestine.

This thesis arranges causes and effects too neatly. It denies the Jewish people all incentive and initiative. When a people loses these, it ceases to be altogether.

The fact is that Russian Jewry did not drift to America on a life raft, but sailed by compass. Other lands had admitted them, but the refugees were determined to move on to America's more remote and alien shores. Jewish philanthropists offered the immigrant asylum in Latin America, but they still moved on to the United States where they were no more welcome than in Britain and elsewhere.

Herzl's preoccupation with the Jewish problem preceded the Dreyfus case, and Zionism preceded Herzl. Already in the 1930's, the Jews had a shadow government in Pales-

tine which engaged in an underground effort to compel Britain to advance them toward statehood or surrender her mandate. Their campaign was suspended during World War II, and resumed immediately thereafter.

The thesis of catalytic disaster deletes altogether the inner development which paralleled the historic Judean and Hellenist divisions in Jewry and immeasurably influenced all other events. The Judean tradition produced Yiddish and modern Hebrew literature, the American Jewish community, the State of Israel, and numerous ideologies which, although tailored for parochial use, had an impact beyond the Jewish environment. The Hellenistic disposition provided western civilization within the past eight decades with intellectuals who, variously alienated from their tradition, nonetheless performed in historic patterns; the ancestors had dissented from Christian church civilization, the progeny from Christian secular civilization. Einstein and Freud are among the foremost exemplars of the Hellenic tradition.

YEAR OF DISENCHANTMENT

The Year of Czarist pogroms, 1881, was not a catalyst; it was only the climax of Jewry's disenchantment with the promises of the Age of Reason. This was already apparent in Adolph Cremieux' cry, "France has betrayed us!"

The emancipation had disrupted Jewry's immemorial dialogue with the civilizations around it. The orthodox, alarmed by the ravages of assimilation and apostasy, would have no traffic with infectious ideas. The Hellenists, seeking dissociation from their imprecated people, fled to the church or shouted more loudly than others the super-patriotic slogans of the various European nationalisms.

In the 1880's and the 1890's, the dialogue was resumed. The Judeans feeling that events had proved them right, capitalized on the Hellenists' confusion. Jewry now spoke in many voices. Orthodoxy had re-entered the mainstream of culture by its rapprochement with secularism; Zionism projected a somewhat reluctant Jewry onto the stage of world affairs, and many of the painfully bruised assimilationists, rejected by the various nationalists—French, German, Russian—flocked now either to Zionism or So-

cialism. Dr. Max Nordau, critic of Western society and colleague of Theodor Herzl in Zionism, forewarned that "anti-Semitism will compel the Jew to destroy among all peoples the idea of a fatherland."

PROLOGUE TO HISTORY

On March 3, 1881 Alexander II of Russia was torn to shreds by a bomb thrown by populists. It could also have been thrown by ultrarightists. Both extremes opposed the constitution which the Czar had pledged his people. The left called it a subterfuge; the right knew it would be its undoing.

The guiding spirit of the extreme right was, as always in Russia, a ranking member of the Russian Orthodox clergy. Konstantin Petrovich Pobiedostzev, Procurator of the Holy Synod, feared the penetration of Western ideas, as Stalin was later to fear them, hated Catholics and Protestants, and seriously proposed that the "Jewish problem be resolved by expelling one-third, forcing 'the best third' to convert, and letting the remainder starve to death." It was probably his circle that conceived a plan for deflecting popular attention from the pledged constitution and disposing simultaneously of both radicals and Jews by pinning the Czar's assassination on "Jewish nihilists." A cry went up: "Kill the Jews who killed our Lord Jesus and our little father, the Czar!"

A circular signed by the emergency directorate of Narodnaya Volya, the populist underground organization that had engineered the bombing, joined in the murderous festivities by calling on the peasants to show no partisanship and to kill alike "the barons, Jews, and Czarist officials." Its authors later explained that they regarded it as the best means of disproving the reactionaries' allegation that the revolution was synonymous with Jewry. Indeed, there were very few Jews in Narodnaya Volya.

The pogroms began on Easter Sunday, 1881, and by harvest time Jews in 160 cities and towns of the Pale has been pillaged, wounded, and killed. A week's press agitation preceded each pogrom whose duration was approximately forty-eight hours. A cadre of lynch specialists traveled openly by train from target to target, arriving

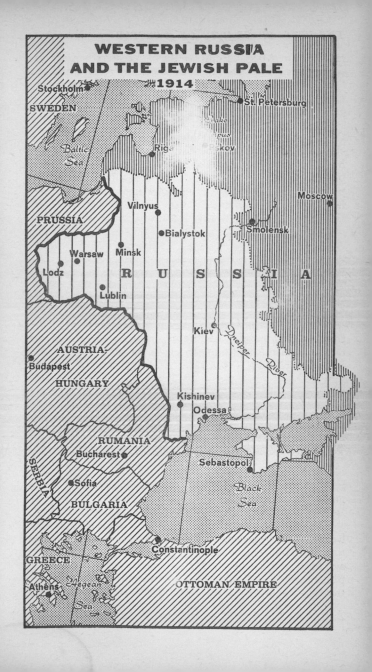

WESTERN RUSSIA
AND THE JEWISH PALE
1914

Stockholm

SWEDEN

Baltic Sea

St. Petersburg

Lake Peipus

Pskov

Riga

Moscow

PRUSSIA

Vilnyus

Bialystok

Smolensk

Warsaw

Minsk

Lodz

Lublin

R U S S I A

Kiev

Dnieper River

AUSTRIA-HUNGARY

Budapest

Kishinev

Odessa

RUMANIA

Bucharest

SERBIA

Sofia

Sebastopol

BULGARIA

Black Sea

GREECE

Athens

Aegean Sea

Constantinople

OTTOMAN EMPIRE

just before the press campaign commenced, and moving on as soon as the pogrom was over. From May 1882 on, Russian Jewry was virtually snowed under by regulations designed for its discomfort. No Jew was permitted to take up residence in a village except by special and costly dispensation. Old residents were by ingenious devices transformed into new ones as a means of expelling them; Jews lost their status as an old resident if they moved from one house into another, if they had been away serving with the army, or if their suburb had been reclassified as villages, or if the latter had been renamed.

Even Jewish pharmacists and midwives had been encouraged to settle in the interior of Russia when it was lacking these professions. The pharmacists were told that they could no longer practice outside the Pale, although they could continue living there, and midwives were told that they could reside and practice, but that the dispensation did not include their families.

The Jews, having overcome their inhibition about secular education in government schools, were faced with a quota system both in high schools and universities. They surmounted the first by tutoring themselves, and the second by traveling abroad, where they skimped on the allowances from home and took any work available to pay their university tuition. Returning home, they discovered that a new ordinance disqualified foreign graduates.

THE EXODUS

Jewish philanthropists in Russia and abroad proposed to relieve the problem by teaching the Pale productive occupations and by settling Jews on the land. The first plan was self-defeating because the Pale had more artisans than it required, and the second was rejected by the Czarist government. Baron Maurice de Hirsch (1831-1896), German-born Parisian who made his millions in Brussels railroads, turned in mid-life from racing horses to aiding Jews. He had spent a fortune on teaching the Jews of Austria trades, and now proposed to resettle Russian Jews on the land in Argentina. He was both compassionate and supercilious in his Jewish philanthropies. He told Dr. Theodor Herzl: "No, no, no! I don't want to raise the

(Jews') general level at all. All our misfortunes come from the fact that the Jews want to climb too high. We have too many intellectuals. My intention is to keep the Jews from pushing ahead." In his peculiar savage way, it was also the Czar's intention. The baron on his precarious perch in European society was strangely unaware that it was perhaps the splendor of the Hirschs and Rothschilds that accelerated anti-Semitic myth. The roots, of course, went deeper. The contest had been underway for more than three thousand years.

So the Jew of Russia began to move en masse on their own in 1891. Alexander III (1881-1894), perhaps fearing his reputation abroad would be impaired, forbade them to leave, which is analogous to the Russian policy today. However, in Czarist days Russia's frontiers were porous, her guards venal, and the fleeing Jews were ingenious and desperate. As the deluge of humanity erupted into the continent, the De Hirschs and Rothschilds could not escape association in the public mind with the displaced multitudes. Pharaoh's courts throughout the world were watching the descent of Jacob's sons upon their brother Joseph. American Jewish philanthropists rushed to Brussels to consult with their European peers on how to help the Russian émigrés, and also how to arrest their embarrassing descent.

Emissaries of the philanthropists traveled to Galicia, an Austrian province on the Russian frontier, which was the sieve through which the refugees poured in to persuade their leaders that immigration must be planned. The East Europeans, conditioned by Jewish egalitarian law, deferred to learning but not to wealth. Having only recently emerged from the Hassidic revolution, they were already under the spell of secular socialism, and replied that if the "Jewish princes" were not prepared to assist them, they would still proceed in shabby disarray to Britain and to the United States.

However, the Jewish barons and lords, for all their titles, sashes, and medals, were themselves not too far removed from the ancestral tradition. They would not think of using the immigrants' obstinacy and defiance as a pretext for withdrawing from their responsibility. The

dictate "I am my brother's keeper" is deeply ingrained in the Jew.

STRANGER IN THE GATES

The philanthropists had accurately anticipated resistance to this downpour of Jewish refugees. Through the 1890's opposition mounted and, at the turn of the century, Britain's Prime Minister James Arthur Balfour (1902-1906) proposed legislation to restrict immigration. The spur of the agitation was the trade union movement which charged that imported cheap labor was undermining British wage standards. The Rothschilds for once swung into action behind the scenes to prevent passage of these laws.

Balfour is remembered in Jewish history for something of greater and different significance. Later, in his capacity as wartime Foreign Minister, he was the author of the declaration bearing his name, which on November 2, 1917 pledged his Majesty's Government to facilitate the establishment of a Jewish National home in Palestine. By peculiar coincidence, on the same day as the Declaration was issued, the British ambassador to Washington, on Balfour's instructions, addressed a memorandum to the U.S. Secretary of State opposing the sending of condensed milk for infants in Poland, because "the large and influential Jewish element in Poland is to a great extent actively pro-German." Yet it was to win all Jewry to the allied cause that the Balfour Declaration was issued in the first place.

In America, also, opposition to immigration came largely from labor. Each tidal wave of immigrants—the German, Irish, Poles—had been similarly greeted. The arguments were the same as in Britain: The newcomers would undermine American wage standards. There were other ingredients, too, in the American agitation. The Boston Brahmin blamed all immigrants for the disrupture of the genteel tradition; populism subscribed to all the classical myths about the Jews, blamed them for the vagaries of international marketing, for the drop in the price of wheat, cotton, and hogs, the export staple of the Southern and Western states which nurtured populism.

At least one Brahmin, Henry Brooks Adams, grandson and great grandson of Presidents was as violent about the Jews as the most obstreperous populist rabble-rouser. "We are in hands of the Jews," he wailed, "They can do what they please with our values. . . . The Russian Jews and the other Jews will completely control the finances and government of this country in ten years. . . . In a society of Jews . . . I have no place." Generally, the Brahmins were not hysterical, but disdainful.

Henry Cabot Lodge, U.S. Senator, urged restrictions on the entry of East and South Europeans—he did not single out the Jews, but they were the overwhelming majority of entrants from East European lands—because they lacked "the nobler abilities which enable a people to rule and administer and to display that social efficiency . . . without which all else is vain." Like Lord Balfour, he has gone down in Jewish history not for his immigration restrictionism, but for his Zionism. He spearheaded, over State Department objections, a joint Congressional resolution which committed the United States to the principle of a Jewish National Home in Palestine. Paradoxically, he also led the campaign which kept the United States out of the League of Nations, which had been entrusted, inter alia, with supervising Britain's administration of the Palestine mandate.

Populist phobia and Brahmin contempt were welded together in the voluminous testimony which a commission of American eugenicists and sociologists, appointed by President Theodore Roosevelt, placed before him much to his embarrassment. These men based themselves on the new racist "science" advanced by Count Arthur de Gobineau and his British interpreter William Houston Chamberlain, son-in-law of Richard Wagner and forerunner of Nazi racism. They measured the skull and limbs and studied the skin pigmentation of the various ethnic groups entering America and discovering that it differed from that of the older stock determined that that difference was evidence of inferiority. This phrenology fermented in American thinking until eventually, in 1921, it became the gauge for determining the national quotas for immigrants into the United States, thus according America

the invidious distinction of having implicitly written racism into its law more than a decade before the Nuremberg laws were promulgated in Germany.

Compassion for the refugees from Czarist persecution and apprehension that they might become an affliction on American society was the counterpuntal theme of President Benjamin Harrison's message to Congress on September 9, 1891, which warned that the influx from Russia was "likely to assume proportions which may . . . seriously affect the labor market. . . . A decree to leave one country is in the nature of things an order to enter another —some other. This consideration, as well as the suggestion of humanity, furnishes ample grounds for remonstrances which we have presented to Russia."

The Rothschilds, Montefiores, and De Hirschs had their counterpart in America. He was Jacob Henry Schiff (1847-1920), German-born banker, who angered the newcomers by trying through his philanthropies to order intramural Jewish affairs, yet caused them also deep satisfaction by using his banking powers to penalize persecutors of his people. While Alfred Rothschild, a director of the Bank of England, boasted of his Austrian and Prussian decorations, "High, what? Royal Orders, first class!," and hesitated about colonization in Palestine "because Palestine sounds too Jewish," Schiff disdained such honors as below him. He was a strange admixture of a Joseph at Pharaoh's court and a man of the people, like Noah and Commodore Levy. In 1905, during the visit here of Count Sergius de Witte (Czarist Prime Minister, 1905-1906), Schiff was the ranking figure among five signatories to a memorandum which bluntly warned the Czarist government that it should not expect "that the influence of the American Jew upon public opinion will be exerted to the advantage of the country which systematically degrades his brethren-in-race, making their fate almost unbearable."

EARLY ZIONISM

Several months after his 1891 message to Congress with its admixed concern for Russian Jewry, a citizens' petition was submitted to President Harrison which proposed that the Government of the United States convene an inter-

national conference "to consider the condition of the Israelites and their claims to Palestine as their ancient home, and to promote, in all other just and proper ways, the alleviation of their suffering condition." Signatories included a Representative from Ohio who six years later was to be sworn in as the Twenty-third President of the United States, William McKinley.

Initiator of the petition was a Reverend William Blackstone, who no doubt was moved by the impulses that gave rise to the Christian Gospel, American Christendom's wonderful direct response to social inequity. Among the petitioners' considerations must have also been the dilemma to which President Harrison referred and which since the mid-nineteenth century had given rise on the continent to a Christian Zionism of mixed Messianic and geopolitical origin. George Eliot (Mary Ann Evans) and Benjamin Disraeli had published Zionist novels; the private secretary of Napoleon III, Ernest Laharanne, argued in a book on the Oriental Question that "continental conditions . . . patently require the re-establishment of the Jewish State . . . as a mediator between Europe and the Far East in opening roads to India and China," and several English orientalists and military strategists, unbeknown to one another, urged similar schemes unsuccessfully on the Rothschilds and Montefiores. Two rabbis representing two antipodal traditions in the rabbinate, petitioned "Jewish princes" with corresponding ineffectiveness. Yehuda Alkalai (1798-1878), a Cabalist from Sarajevo, once within the heartland of the Sabbatai Zvi movement, tried to persuade Montefiore, and Cremieux and Hirsch Kalischer, a legalist and Maimonides "rationalist" from Thorn, Prussia, approached in vain the Berlin Rothschilds.

THE PEOPLE ACT

But the initiative had already begun to pass from the Western Jewish bankers and magnates to the East European masses. The boldness of Moses Hayes, Mordecai Manuel Noah, and Uriah Levy was having a late burgeoning in the Russian and Galician ghettos.

Its soil, of course, was richer. Its confidence grew out

245

of a profound internal revolution which these Jewries had experienced in less than three decades since Nicholas I. Jewry's capacity for assimilating Hellenic culture into Pharisee tradition had again reasserted itself. Some rabbis defended secular education, the need to explore the "wisdom that was Greece," even if the price for free inquiry was banishment from their posts; the wives and daughters of Hassidic tzadikim studied foreign languages and music and ordered continental fashions; pietists sent their sons to universities abroad, and a new generation of maskilim broke with their predecessors' derogation of their own people. Having explored the Hellenic perimeter, and having even considered socialism and Russian populism, the younger maskilim now turned from the adoration of Russian to the celebration of Hebrew and Yiddish as literary vehicles.

They also sought to redefine the Jew in comprehensible modern terms. Peretz Smolenskin (1842-1885), essayist, novelist, editor, who like many other Talmudic prodigies instructed himself in secular studies, called the Jews a distinctive "spiritual nation," and after the 1881 pogroms proposed that several million Russian Jews be resettled in Palestine, thus giving the "spiritual nation" a material base. Leon Pinsker, born into the Sadducee tradition, published anonymously in 1882 a German-language brochure, "Auto-Emancipation" which proposed the establishment, somewhere or anywhere on God's earth, of a sovereign domain as the only escape from anti-Semitic persecution. He was promptly offered and accepted chairmanship of the semi-clandestine Lovers of Zion societies which also had effete branches in Britain and the United States, and had been exploring the possibility of establishing Jewish colonies in Palestine. These societies were an amalgam of Pharisees and Sadducees, the revered orthodox rabbi Shmuel Mohliver, the formerly Russified physician Leon Pinsker, and once radical Jewish students who became forever disenchanted from the Russian *folk* when the peasantry, celebrated in populist myth, raised its scythes against the Jews.

Five hundred Jewish students from Russia enlisted for resettlement in Palestine. Some four decades after Mor-

decai Manuel Noah first made the proposal, they sent a delegation to Constantinople to negotiate the purchase of the Holy Land from the Sultan, but got nowhere. Forty of them did establish in 1882, however, the first of a series of Jewish settlements in Palestine, and the Paris head of the House of Rothschild, the baron Edmund de Rothschild (1845-1934), alone among the family, immediately judged them worthy of his charitable support. However, from the start the colonist began to protest his paternalism, or that of the custodians of his philanthropies, and decided to turn also to the peoples themselves for financial support.

THEODOR HERZL

It took another fifteen years before this disparate and amorphous effort was given distinctive form and raised as an issue before the chancelleries of the great powers. It seems as if Canaan had been waiting for its Joseph at Pharaoh's court, Goshen for its Moses. He presented himself in 1896. His name was Theodor Herzl, a journalist and playwright, a member of the Viennese Jewish bourgeoisie. He could not be decried by the latter as either a radical or a "ghetto schnorer," for he was neither. They could only mutter that he was a mad man. He fit perfectly, however, the East European image of a deliverer, a "prince among princes." Actually, he was not quite that. His several moderate stage successes did not merit his inclusion among the literati, and despite his widely read, perfectly stylized columns on random subjects, ranging from book reviews through travelogues and political comment, in his own words, "the editorial writers . . . looked upon me as a chatterer." Even his slender, bearded appearance did not quite conform. It had a Semitic cast and restlessness. In the words of Martin Buber, it was "a countenance lit by the glance of the Messiah."

In 1896, Herzl shocked his social circle and electrified East European Jewry and some Jewish intellectuals in Western Europe, Britain, and the United States with a short book, *The Jewish State*. It was originally planned as an address, or memorandum to the Rothschilds who he hoped might finance his plan—a Jewish state. He pre-

sented the Jewish problem as an agony transcending national frontiers. The rebuffs suffered by the socially ambitious upper Jewish bourgeoisie in Germany, Austria, and France, and the petty persecutions that were the daily fare of East European Jewry are of one fabric, he explained, part of the universal Jewish condition. He eventually presented Zionism as a panacea also to all the ills of the continent. The retirement of large numbers of Jews to Palestine, he told Czarist ministers and the German Kaiser, would attenuate anti-Semitism which, in turn, would reduce the disposition among young Jews to join radical movements.

A year after his book appeared, he convened the First World Zionist Congress. The audience that assembled in the Basel Casino on August 27, 1897 for the opening of the historic Congress was the Jewish people in microcosm. They had come even from Russia, Africa, and America, and by every means of transportation—train, cart, on horseback, on bicycles and on foot. But they were not really delegates. They were, for the most part, self-mandated enthusiasts bearing the petitions with the names of 50,000 Rumanian and 10,000 Galician Jews, hardly a consensus of global Jewry. Aligned against him were almost all the reform and orthodox rabbis, although some of both persuasions attended the Congress. The elders of the Jewish community of Munich protested publicly against holding the Congress in their city, as had originally been planned. Yet when the Congress opened in Basel, diplomats of many nations were in the loges and boxes, instructed by their governments to follow its proceedings which they suspected perhaps would be of a conspiratorial nature.

Herzl was the perfectionist stage director. The people on the dais were in full dress, as was the custom of European parliaments. He unfolded to his delegates a "Jewish flag!" Jewry had none before this, having come into the world in time to present the Decalogue, but far too early to attach importance to colors. Proposed by one of his colleagues, the flag's white background and blue stripes were the pattern of the Jewish prayer shawl. He even contemplated "the yellow badge" as a Jewish Legion

248

of Honor boutonniere, and "a coffin ship to bring our dead." More than fifty years after his passing, the ashes of Hitler's victims were flown by plane to Israel, as were Herzl's remains.

Even before the Congress was convened, he was in negotiations with the ranking statesmen of his time, seeking their influence with the Sultan for "a charter" that would grant the Jews the right to colonize Palestine. Later, failing in this, he considered in talks with the British such alternatives as the Sinai Peninsula and El Arish as a springboard for Palestine, and also East Africa, as a temporary asylum.

In his diaries, he compares himself without embarrassment to Sabbatai Zvi. He also confides that three years before writing *The Jewish State* he had considered a radically different plan—proposing to the Vatican that he would propagandize the Jews to convert their children in return for a pledge from the Pope to protect from harm all adults who remained within their faith. He even envisioned the baptism ceremony in precise, exacting detail. On Sunday, at mid-day, at Vienna's celebrated St. Stefan's Kirche, the Jewish parents would "lead our children (to baptism) before they reached the age of independent decision, after which conversion looks like an act of cowardice or calculation."

It is sometimes only his triumph that spares the great leader the ignominy of going down in history as an impostor. Herzl's audacious initiatives often brought him close to that precipice. He assured the Sultan that Jewry would reciprocate Turkey's favors by stabilizing the Ottoman empire's finances. He behaved as if all the wealth of the mythical elders of Zion were at his command. Not a single great Jewish financier, however, was prepared to endorse his political program. His many talks with the Rothschilds had come to nothing.

He attracted, as David Reuveni in the sixteenth century had done, both guileless romantic figures and seedy adventurers. To the first class, that of enamored innocents, belonged the Reverend William F. Hechler (1845-1931), chaplain to the British embassy in Vienna, a Christian mystic who believed that the publication date of Herzl's

book significantly confirmed his own Cabalistic calculations about the Jews' Restoration. His excessive fervor at first repelled Herzl. But Hechler proved both dedicated and helpful. He introduced Herzl to members of the German royal house which eventually led to an audience with the Kaiser.

Philip Michael Newlinski, a Polish down-at-the-heels aristocrat who doubled in journalism and intelligence and published a diplomatic newsletter which could inflict great damage, offered his services to Herzl. He promised to arrange for him an audience with the Sultan, and sent him on at least one fool's errand to Constantinople. Herzl was on his guard at all times. At the very outset, he remarked in diaries upon Newlinski's "great Slavic charm" and "intellectual qualities," that he nonetheless "produces a suspicious impression"; on his passing, the Zionist leader wrote "he cost me a great deal of money . . . (and) I don't know to this day whether he did anything for us . . . nor if he was even in a position to help us."

Unlike his present-day mediocre successors, Herzl was not maintained by his movement, but spent his own modest fortune on it, leaving his widow and children unprovided.

A meeting with the Sultan was finally arranged for Herzl by a fellow-Hungarian, Arminius Vambery (1832-1913) who was born of orthodox Jewish parents, had converted to several faiths including Buddhism and Islam, qualified as Europe's leading authority on Central Asia, performed as a confidential agent for Disraeli, and was an intimate of Sultan Abdul Hamid. In his old age, Vambery became a practicing Protestant. On the faculty of Budapest University, and at work on his memoirs, he still occasionally took time out to freelance as an eminence gris. He instructed Herzl gratis, simply as a fellow "Zeidemeber" (Hungarian for "Jewish man") in the intricacies of the Sultan's court.

Herzl and his immediate circle designed in the Zionist leader's lifetime all the instrumentalities of the Zionist movement—its executive, judiciary, and fund-raising organs—which had carried it through the establishment of the Jewish State. His inordinate political prescience fore-

saw problems that Israel faces today, and also means for their solution.

He comprehended even then the importance of the Negev, the southern part of Palestine which Israel is now laboring to develop. He proposed construction of a railroad across the country, from the Mediterranean to Akaba, the Red Sea outlet, as an alternate for the Suez Canal. He favorably considered proposals from Zionist engineers for the exploitation of the Dead Sea minerals, today one of Israel's major export items. He also showed enthusiasm for their proposal to harness Mediterranean, Dead Sea, and rain waters to provide the country with electric power and irrigation. Israel has repeatedly been pressing this plan, and the Arabs have been hampering it.

The hero in his utopian novel, *Old-New Land*, published in 1902, a Jewish scientist evidently bespeaking the author's thoughts remarks: "Now that I have lived to see the restoration of the Jews, I should like to pave the way for the restoration of the Negroes." Israel's technical aid program to Africa is patently a realization of this Herzlian dream.

Stopping in Egypt when visiting Palestine, he remarked of the oppressed, disease-ridden Arab peasantry: "I am resolved not to forget them when I have any power." The State of Israel's official spokesmen have repeatedly stressed that if the Arab states were willing to accept its co-operation, living standards could be raised in the entire region.

Herzl's career lasted only eight years. It ended on a Lincolnesque note of tragedy. The Sixth Zionist Congress in August, 1903, almost split over the issue of an East African territory which the British had proposed to Herzl. He called it a temporary asylum, but the Russian Zionists accused him of having abandoned Palestine. He was even shouted down as a traitor by one of them. They repeated their long-standing charge that he was frittering away the movement's priceless energies on a fruitless, grandiloquent diplomatic pursuit after a charter, instead of laboring to establish more colonies in Palestine. Herzl replied that before he proceeded with colonies, a charter from

the Sultan was required, providing the Jewish colonists with legal claim.

The Seventh Zionist Congress, in 1905, rejected the East Africa proposal. By then the British had also reconsidered their offer, under the pressure of their white colonials there.

Herzl had passed away the year before, on July 2, 1904, broken by eight years of strenuous Zionist effort and near-rejection by the people who at first had so quickly and enthusiastically acclaimed him. He was forty-four when he died. Jewish multitudes mourned him in Vienna, New York, Warsaw, and throughout the Jewish Pale. The mourners were primarily East Europeans. Mourning with them were also members of the Jewish elite that had been attracted to his movement—a handful of reform rabbis in the United States, the eccentric sons of several aristocratic Jewish families in Britain, and scattered Jewish intellectuals everywhere.

Among the Jewish upper classes there may even have been some anticipation that the Jewish problem which he had so tumultuously unveiled for all the world to see, would fade away again into the Russian Pale. It did not fade away. His death reunited the movement.

The Russians' schism with Herzl was part of the continuing revolution inside Jewry of the East European havenots against the Western have's. It was also within a historical pattern beginning with the revolts against Moses in the desert: the Jewish masses have always ended by nearly, but not completely, repudiating their redeemer returned from foreign courts.

Herzl, "a prince among princes," and the people had drawn sustenance from each other. But the people used him as only a mirror of its dreams and aspirations. The mirror had been cracked by the East Africa proposals, but now that he was dead, they mourned him deeply. Within a decade Dr. Chaim Weizmann, a youthful leader of the Russian Zionist revolt against him, adopted Herzl's own order of priorities. He negotiated for a charter from Britain with statesmen who had been involved in Herzl's East Africa negotiations, and hence already knew about Zionism. The draft of that first agreement between Herzl

and the British government had been prepared by a young Welsh attorney. His name was David Lloyd George, and he was Prime Minister in the cabinet which published the Balfour Declaration. The Balfour Declaration was a letter addressed to Lord Walter Rothschild, a scion of the dynasty that had alternately been alarmed, enchanted, impressed, and irritated by Herzl, but never, in his lifetime, patently persuaded by him.

EAST EUROPEAN RENAISSANCE

Herzl's odyssey unfolded against the background of one of the great renaissance periods in Jewish history. Its center was Russia, the territories annexed by her, and Austrian-ruled Galicia, known today as the Western Ukraine. The most remarkable phenomenon was the evolution of a Yiddish press, theater and literature. There was a parallel Hebrew awakening, restricted of necessity, to a relatively smaller audience. Yiddish achieved a more thorough demolition of social barriers between the learned and the untutored than had been accomplished by Hassidism, from which it was directly descended.

Until the mid-nineteenth century, Yiddish was regarded superciliously as a language of the lower classes only. The great polemics raging in Jewry since the emancipation were conducted primarily in Hebrew. The lower classes, untutored in Hebrew, were at best eavesdroppers on the debate, as if all the issues raised were to be decided for the people by its elite. This was a very profound disenfranchisement.

Then Yiddish erupted as serious literature. Mendele Mocher Sefarim (Mendele the Book Seller), pseudonym of Shalom Jacob Abramovich (1837-1917), called the "grandfather" of this literature, alternated between the two languages, and by reverently nursing its style, accorded Yiddish new status. A Swiftian social critic of the custodians of Jewish affairs, he made the lower strata his allies, and united the intelligentsia and the people by means of common grievance.

Sholem Aleichem, pseudonym of Sholem Rabinovich (1859-1916) united the people by other means. He pointed out with humor and compassion that all Jewry, irrespec-

253

tive of class, was entrapped in the same dilemma—Czarist persecution.

An important synthesizer was Judah Leib Peretz (1851-1915) whose nostalgic reconstructions of Hassidic mood and folk tale contrasted with the savage caricatures to which the early maskilim, or enlighteners, had subjected Hassidism. He implanted in the younger generation of Jews the same kind of mystique toward Jewish folk custom that populism had earlier engendered towards Russian folkways. Peretz used the common language, Yiddish, to convey both this reverence for the enduring past and for the new European intellectual fashions. Martin Buber later tried to render a similar service with his recasting of Hassidic custom into German, a formal and convoluted language, and for an audience whose socioeconomic cultural experience was wholly removed from the East European milieu.

Chaim Nachman Bialik (1873-1934), the leading poet of the Hebrew renaissance contributed toward synthesis and national unity by versatile means. His folk songs in Yiddish established him with the people, although his major work was in Hebrew; his long poem on the Kishinef pogrom, which he translated into Yiddish himself, and which had been translated into many other languages, bespoke so completely the indignation of the common man in accents they could understand—he summoned Jews to resist violence with violence—that any barriers between him and the people collapsed. He also advocated among the Hebrew intellectual elite the kind of reverence for Jewish religious literature, embracing of course the Talmudic jurisprudence, that Peretz advocated in Yiddish toward Hassidic folk custom.

Although not apparent at the time, a major contributor to synthesis was Rabbi Abraham Isaac Kook (1865-1935), who settled in Palestine in 1904 as a confirmed Zionist when the extremely pious still regarded the doctrine as malignant heresy, and who after the Balfour Declaration became the country's first chief rabbi. He was a mystic, a believer in the incorruptibility of man, the sanctity of labor, the validity of all faiths, the eventual evolution of a universalist faith with Judaism as its base, the immi-

nence of Messianic redemption for all mankind with Jewry as its vessel and Palestine as its stage. He defended the Zionist pioneers in Palestine as divine instruments of God's redemptive will, even if they waived all religious law.

The present-day tolerance of Israel's labor majority toward the excesses of the ultrapietists, who would have denounced Rabbi Kook himself as a heretic, contains perhaps a grain of reciprocity for the late rabbi's affectionate patience with the impious halutzim. He did not evolve a systematic doctrine, but his teachings are brilliant intuitive flashes which mix social justice, religious toleration, and national mystique. As Israel searches for a more profound national identity and purpose than the accoutrements of statehood provide, it may turn to his works for an answer.

DIVISION IN EAST EUROPEAN JEWRY

A sometimes divisive role in Jewry at that time was that of socialism which had then just begun to stir among the East European Jewish proletariat. It broke completely with Jewish religious tradition. In its extreme forms, it renounced the concept of the Jews as a distinct people. In its milder forms, it conceived of the Jewish proletariat as the sole essence of the Jewish people. Yet it was not wholly outside Jewish historical tradition; it was a secular successor to the religious movement of social discontent which arose periodically among the Jews whenever the processes of social mobility seemed arrested. The Karaites, the Sabbatai Zvi upsurge, and Hassidism had been among its eminent religious predecessors. The Baal Shem Tov had quickened the impulse of social responsibility and shored up the self-esteem of the masses. Secular socialism later benefited from this circumstance.

In 1897, the year in which the first World Zionist Congress was convened in Basel, a clandestine meeting in Vilna, Lithuania founded the Yiddish-language Socialist Organization, Bund. Its mass base was the lowest socioeconomic strata in Jewry. Its leadership was drawn from two sources. These were the well educated sons and daughters of the affluent Russified Jewish families (none

other were afforded an opportunity at Russification), and their antipodes, the students of the yeshivot or Talmudic academies who belonged to the lower middle class, and were self-tutored in secular subjects, had found in socialism a more relevant dialectic for their excited minds than rabbinical jurisprudence seemed to offer. Eventually, the proletariat itself produced a leader corps—untutored, but shrewd and intuitive, like the coarse proto-Hassidic miracle healers of the eighteenth century. These leaders, risen from the working mass itself, later discharged an important function in American trade unionism.

Founded to preach socialism to the Yiddish-speaking, the Bund was soon combatting anti-Semitism among the socialists. When the latter projected national fulfillment under the new order for all the ethnic nationalities in the Russian and Austro-Hungarian empires, Bund also demanded a clear-cut pledge to the Jews. The Bundists contended that the Jews were as entitled as any people to full cultural autonomy. Their long history, common mores, renascent Yiddish literature and, albeit enforced, territorial concentration inside the Pale qualified them as a nation, no less than the Poles, Ukrainians, Lithuanians, and others.

Thus, Bund virtually accepted the Zionist concept of the Jews as a distinct people, but it rejected the remote homeland, accused Zionism of superimposing national loyalty over class loyalty in order to deflect the Jewish worker from his class struggle, rejected all Jewish religious custom, and denounced Hebrew as a clerical tongue. Soon there arose socialist parties within Zionism which challenged Bund on its own doctrinal premises, and preached a socialist society in the future Palestine homeland and collaboration with all classes in Jewry toward the attainment of that homeland.

This wide-ranging debate on many issues was carried on in the Yiddish press, from the lecture platform, and even from the stage. All strata of Jewry were informed, engaged, committed. This was education, agitation, and universal suffrage in the most profound sense. As in the days of Sabbatai Zvi, social barriers collapsed, but unlike his time, morals remained firm. The diverse ideologies

each imposed a sense of propriety and obligation on their adherents. Familiar signposts prevented complete confusion. The common threat, Czarist persecution, anti-Jewish violence, compelled unity despite doctrinal schisms.

DISORIENTED IMMIGRANT

Matters were different in America. The East European immigrant had been hurtled into an alien environment which at that particular time had lost its own bearings. The South had been devastated by carpetbaggers, the New England Brahmins were expiring of ennui, rapacious railroad interests were dispossessing the pioneers who had opened the West, gunfire and dynamite decided conflicts between management and labor. Jewish immigrants, who before coming here had been variously disaffected from their own Jewish law, now found themselves in a turbulent America.

AMERICAN ALTERATIONS

The traditional values, rooted in religious injunction, which the Jew maintained through the centuries in many lands, had started to waste away at the time of French Jewry's emancipation. They required translation into new secular terms. Their decline in West and Central European Jewry coincided with the abolition of the autonomous organs of Jewish administration, the medieval type of Jewish "self-government." East European Jewry held out longer because political emancipation there had been delayed. At the time of the great immigration to America, at the turn of the century, the traditional values had already been seriously undermined in Poland, Russia, and the regions of the Austro-Hungarian empire in which orthodox Jewry was congregated. The process was completed with vigor in the immigrant milieu in America.

The last carriers of the old values to America were learned, pious, Jewish middle-class immigrants, vastly outnumbered by the Jewish proletariat. The latter—tailors, cobblers, carpenters, locksmiths, masons—arrived in this country with marketable skills. The middle-class immigrants were business brokers, shopkeepers, and auditors —abilities on which America was not particularly short,

and which, moreover, required a knowledge of the language of the land. Their economic incapacitation on arrival in America led to their social declassment. They became apprentices to the proletariat; the latter, avenging itself for old social slights, reasoned that since the Talmudic scholar had proved himself an ineffectual wage-earner, his reputed erudition and values must also be inconsequential.

Purely physical factors, among which was the housing shortage, contributed toward disorientation. East side tenements were overcrowded. Beds were occupied in several shifts. Someone was always rising from bed sheets on which someone else was about to lie down. Strangers boarded with families whose breadwinner's earnings were insufficient to maintain the household. This proximity and the father's diminished authority were not conducive to familial discipline.

But there were other factors present that worked toward stability. The proletariat adopted the traditional gauges it so vociferously repudiated. Like its betters in Europe, it valued learning, although of a kind that was closer to its needs and comprehension. It turned, for its instruction, to the secularized radical sons of those it had repudiated. These preached socialism, anarchism, and Zionism in crowded Lower East Side meeting halls. Far from alienating the immigrant, these doctrines gave him anchorage in America, prevented him from drifting without designated direction and moral compass.

Some of the immigrant intelligentsia experimented with communal living on farms. They even established communes in the tenements, with all members sharing equally from a common treasury, regardless of the size or amount of their individual earnings.

A group of indigenous American intellectuals had tried this earlier, by establishing Brook Farm near Roxbury, Massachusetts (1841-1847). Their short-lived experiment was based on the Frenchman Charles Fourier's principles of a utopian community. The Jewish immigrant experiments were no more successful than Brook Farm, but their inspiration was not Fourier. They had been conditioned to this kind of living by many centuries. The

ghettos were an extension of ancient tribal reciprocity. The Essenes were Jewry's first Brook Farm. The sixteenth century Safad Cabalists also lived in a commune. The Israeli kibbutzim, also established by East European immigrants, have a successful continual fifty year history.

The landsmanschaften, or mutual aid societies, which the immigrants formed, and which bore the names of the "old home" town or counties, were without ideological pretensions. They were, however, an even more universal extension of the traditional collective commitment. They provided all the benefits of the welfare state—life and health insurance, and low interest loans until "he was able to pay it back." This saved a member from bankruptcy, enabled him to reunite with his family, send a son through college, or establish a son-in-law in business. The landsmanschaften were in a very ancient tradition. The first were formed in Babylonia by the exiles from Palestine. It was to the landsmanschaften, one by one, that the sixteenth century Turkish-Jewish diplomat Joseph Nassi proposed the boycott against the Papal port of Ancona, that very nearly unseated Pope Paul IV.

American society seethed with ugly aggressions. It also burned with a fever of the social gospel. Frontier lawlessness had been transplanted into the East separately by the founders of the country's industrial fortunes and by the "ward" politicians of more recent ethnic vintage. The latter were, in a manner of speaking, Robin Hoods, who waged guerrilla warfare for their people from the city wards under their control, enriching themselves on every kind of vice, yet using a municipal nepotism to compensate their brethren for the many economic opportunities denied them by older American groups.

The ministers of the social gospel, the journalist muckraker and the social reformer, counterpoised the lawlessness from both quarters.

The meeting between the puritan conscience of the social reformer and the social Messianism of the Russian-Jewish immigrant was a fortuitous happenstance. The former learned about the Messianic agony of Russian literature and diverse social doctrines from the Jewish immigrant. The Jew, again a broker of cultures, like his

259

ancestors in Europe on the eve of the Renaissance, learned, in turn, about the mores of American Protestantism, so different from the German, and astonishingly close to his own tradition. German Protestantism, like the Russian Orthodox Church, was mated to the state; American Protestantism was mated to the community. The community has been the base of Jewish self-governance since the days of the first Jewish commonwealth. American culture and Jewish tradition have an analogous predisposition to fluid law, rooted in a firm constitution, but accommodated to new circumstance by amendment and court opinion. Czarist oppression had undermined the Russian Jew's deference for state law. It was now restored to him.

The encounter between the Americanized German-Jewish community and the Russian-Jewish immigrant was vaguely analogous to the confrontation of the Boston Brahmin and the Irish Catholics. But the Christian Protestant was aloof even in his charitable good deeds.

The Jewish "Protestant," the German Jew or Yahudi, was moved by more intimate concern. That amazing autocrat-banker-philanthropist Jacob Schiff was arbitrary and capricious, but never aloof from his Lower East Side wards. He was so accessible to the new immigrants that he resembled a candidate for political office. He had more understanding than others of the East European immigrants' culture. The German Jews as a class never doubted the intelligence of the East European Jewish immigrant. However, they considered him a diamond, albeit rough, and wanted to polish him for social uses. It was over "polishing" and suffrage that tensions arose between the Yahudim and the Lower East Side.

The German Jew felt his status threatened by the growing numbers of new immigrants so distinguishable in manner and wanted them to shed their tumultuous orthodox piety, vociferous political radicalism, and Yiddish tongue. The East Europeans, however, intramurally divided, joined forces—the orthodox and the maskilim, the Zionists and the Socialists—like a nation threatened by the enemy. They were a Judea with a common multiparous culture extending from Russia, Poland, Rumania, and Galicia to New York City. The Reform Temple was

the citadel of the "Roman Legion." To the East European orthodox Jew, any reformer was a near-apostate. To the East European nonbeliever, the reformers were "the bourgeoisie." But some in the Roman camp were enchanted by Judea's energies, fluidity, preoccupation with idea, not status, with law, not protocol. Some defected from the Yahudim to Judea. Foremost among the defectors were Rabbi Stephen S. Wise (1874-1949), the rabbi, and Justice Louis Dembitz Brandeis (1856-1941), "The People's Attorney."

WISE AND BRANDEIS

Wise was to Jew and Christian alike, the personification of America's Social Gospel, and throughout his lifetime, as spokesman for Zionism, a mediator between Goshen and the rest of America. The East Side remembered gratefully that he had rebuffed in 1905 an invitation to serve Temple Emanu-El, where Jacob Schiff worshiped, because it would not guarantee its rabbi the right to speak his mind from its pulpit. The immigrant radicals knew him as the passionate spokesman for all the just social causes of his day, for women's suffrage, the Gary Steel strikers (he inveighed like an ancient prophet against United States Steel), and Negro rights (joining at its founding in 1906, the National Association for the Advancement of Colored People).

A "Prince at Pharaoh's court," an intimate of governors, senators, and United States Presidents, he was the East Side's tongue in hours of woe, his tall, gaunt figure and leonine head leading Jewish multitudes in protest demonstrations against European oppression. Bearded, ear-locked, orthodox Jews turned out in large numbers for mass rallies to listen reverently to his English eloquence. His vocabulary may have been beyond their grasp, but his oratory was never beyond their comprehension. They knew from the tremor in his voice when his heart ached most for the House of Israel, and from his lion's roar when he condemned the evil-doers against the offspring of Jacob. They were scholars, Talmudists, casuists—not a mob swayed by oratorical sorcery. This was not communication, but communion. Wise spoke

261

their thoughts, perhaps because he was descended, on the paternal side, from a long line of rabbis, in an unbroken chain since the seventeenth century. He had been brought as an infant to the United States from Hungary. This one-time Sabbatai Zvi territory had produced Herzl and Nordau. His grandfather had been an ally to the Chatam Sofer in the war on religious reform; his father had been a conservative rabbi. Many of the orthodox avoided the issue of Stephen S. Wise's Reform faith by calling him "doctor."

Louis Dembitz Brandeis' "Jewish" career was brief. Until his appointment to the U.S. Supreme Court he had devoted a great part of his legal career fighting the traction interests, investigating the abuses of insurance companies as unpaid "people's attorney," demanding—in unconscious rabbinical tradition—that the law correspond to the sociologic facts of life.

Brandeis first encountered his "brethren from Goshen" when he was invited to mediate in the New York Cloakmakers Strike in 1910 in which both parties, labor and management, were East Europeans. "What struck me most," he recalled, "was that each side had a greater capacity for placing themselves in the other fellows' shoes . . . that set these people apart in my experience in labor disputes." Yesterday's socialist and anarchist rebels against the Czar and their "landsmen" employers reverted to their people's empirical justice, introduced, for the first time in American industry, impartial arbitration, industry-wide collective bargaining, and the pension plan, and barred prison labor and contract homework.

This one experience was admittedly Brandeis' catalyst. He enrolled as a member of the Zionist Organization in 1912: He became chief of U.S. Zionism in 1914, retired upon his appointment to the U.S. Supreme Court bench (1916) one and one-half years later, and continued to serve Zionism in an ex-officio capacity until 1921 when the East European Zionists renounced him as they had in 1903 repudiated the founder of Zionism himself, Theodor Herzl, another Joseph at Pharaoh's court.

Brandeis' father, a political refugee after the Austrian insurrection of 1848, set himself up as a grain merchant

in Louisville, Kentucky. Brandeis' maternal uncle was the first member of the family to be engaged, albeit, peripherally, in major American history. He was the only delegate from Kentucky to the Republican National Convention of 1860 and one of three who placed Lincoln's name in nomination.

The family on both sides had deep roots in Jewish history. Tombstones with the Brandeis name on in the Prague cemetery date back to 1539. One of his ancestors was the sixteenth century Rabbi Yehuda Aryeh Lowe, the legendary creator of the mythical Golem who adumbrated Justice Brandeis' legal philosophy by stressing social ethics and warning students of the Talmud that legalistic casuistry obfuscates the sages' intent. There were court Jews on both sides of the family—bankers, brokers, army purveyors, pleaders for their people. A Dembitz had joined the followers of Jacob Frank, the false Messiah who ended up in the embrace of the Catholic Church. However, he became a Frankist only after the leader's passing. These sectarians, although spoiled for Judaism, nevertheless did not apostatize. The Louisville uncle was the first Dembitz, however, to revert to orthodox Judaism, even as his nephew Justice Brandeis was the first Dembitz to return through Zionism to the major tradition of Jewish Messianism.

At the time when Brandeis returned to his brethren, there were many, even among the East European immigrants, who defected from Jewish associations—without embracing another faith—because there were no pressures in the pluralistic American society that compelled a Jew in either direction. Yahudim who joined the East Europeans, had like Brandeis himself voluntarily declared their relationship to Goshen. The issue in the conflict between the Yahudim and immigrant East Europeans was not insoluble. The essential issue was franchise and suffrage, the "German-Jews'" arbitrary manner. This came to a head in World War I when the Yahudim yielded to Lower East Side pressure. The American Joint Distribution Committee, which had been founded in 1914 for the relief of Jewish war victims, named spokesmen for the East European immigrants to its board. The American Jewish

Committee, founded in 1906 by solicitous Yahudi notables to defend the rights of Jewries overseas, joined an American Jewish Congress which, speaking for all U.S. Jewry, sent a delegation to the Peace Conference after World War I.

The proposal was advanced by the immigrant multitudes, led by Wise and Brandeis. The American Jewish Committee shuddered at the idea of substituting the impassioned voice of the people for the judicious counsel of its elders. But when 350,000 ballots were cast on January 10, 1917 in a nation-wide election of delegates to the Congress, the American Jewish Committee agreed to join the new body on condition that it dissolve after achieving its purpose. The united American Jewish delegation made a deep impression in Paris and on all Jewry. Like his Roman ancestor, the American Jew wore his toga with confidence and a flourish. He demanded that all treaties with the new European states guarantee civic equality to the Jews, that national minority status be assured the Jews wherever it is accorded to other ethnic minorities, and that Palestine be placed under international trusteeship as a means of facilitating the establishment of the Jewish National Home.

Two young East European labor Zionist pioneers, wartime refugees from Turkish Palestine who were among the catalysts in forming the united American-Jewish front, later rose to signal significance in contemporary Jewish history. They were Isaac ben Zvi, the second President in Israel's young history, and David ben Gurion, who led it in war and peace.

Brandeis and Wise used their influence at Wilson's court for Zionism. Brandeis informally presided over a battery of brilliant Jewish legal counsel which rejected several earlier drafts of the Balfour Declaration before a satisfactory statement was obtained. Directing the over-all Zionist diplomatic effort at the crucial center, London, was Dr. Chaim Weizmann, Russian-born, yeshiva-educated scientist, who doubled at almost the same time as major wartime chemical researcher for the British government.

Both the Allied and the Central powers were concerned

with Jewish public opinion in occupied Poland and the United States before the entry into the war. The Germans at first toyed with a sugar-coated plan to deport Polish Jewry to Turkish territory. As outlined by the German ambassador to Henry Morgenthau, the U.S. Ambassador in Constantinople, it proposed exchanging Polish Jews for the rebellious Armenians who embarrassed also Germany. This was perhaps the seed of Hitler's "final solution." However, the German General Staff soon came up with something infinitely better. It proposed a Turk-Zionist agreement that would accord Jews some measure of autonomy in Palestine and the right to unrestricted immigration. But this recommendation came too late, after Britain had already published the Balfour Declaration.

BRANDEIS–WEIZMANN SCHISM

Having obtained the charter, to which Herzl had devoted all his energies, Weizmann and Brandeis split. Brandeis saw no need for further diplomatic preoccupation, urged concentration of all energies on developing the Jewish National Home economically, opposed the disbursement of philanthropic funds for education and other purposes not directly related to economic development, and argued that the entire development enterprise be placed in competent managerial hands. Weizmann opposed him on all points, although Brandeis' arguments that practical precede political effort corresponded with arguments once used by those Russian Zionists, Weizmann included, who had opposed Herzl. Indeed, after he had won the contest against Brandeis, Weizmann found himself accused of having again reversed course and suspended political work, when he had merely slowed it down.

The true issues between Brandeis and Weizmann were deeper than this formal restatement suggests. They were psychological. It has been within the Jewish historical tradition, since Moses and the desert revolts against him, to welcome the redeemed returned from foreign courts and then repudiate him. Brandeis was also the victim of the continuing revolution in Jewish life, set off by Hassidism which brought the masses to the fore. Rank and file Zionism, in America and elsewhere, was East European,

tumultuous, passionate. American political parties were now courting the East European immigrant's vote, and he no longer felt the need for a Joseph at court. The Yiddish press, addressing hundreds of thousands of readers, sponsored an image, perhaps not entirely false, of the People's Attorney as the great autocrat in Jewish affairs. Even Brandeis' appearance was wrong. Brandeis was colonial American, frugal and trim. Weizmann was baroque; Brandeis' physiognomy was sad and contemplative, which is not unappealing to Jews, but it lacked pleasure which made him suspect to a life-loving people which reveres the innocent, comprehends the sensuous, but is baffled by the ascetic. In 1921, in acrimonious debate, the Brandeis group retired from American Zionist leadership. Departing was a corps of brilliant American Jewish intellectuals—Felix Frankfurter, Benjamin V. Cohen, and others whose kind has never again returned as a group to American Zionism. Individually, they continued to be on call in Zionist emergencies, even when the caller was Weizmann.

Only Dr. Wise, a leader in the Brandeis group, returned almost immediately. His family roots, like Herzl's and Brandeis', were in a land that mixed the Byzantine and the baroque. The East Side multitudes' vigor was too compelling for the passions seething under Wise's exterior.

Brandeis' liquidation from Zionist affairs was the second symbolic regicide in the movement. Its first victim had been Herzl, also an "alien prince." Weizmann was involved in both episodes. The antipode of Brandeis, there was nothing sparse about his manner. Tall, wide-shouldered, and with a slightly Mongolian tilt to his features, he was both imperious and patronizing, with a humorous air about him: East European Jewry's ideal father image, not a Joseph at a foreign court, but a king in his own right and in their own fashion. The myth about him grew. It said that he could still quote pages of Talmudic jurisprudence from memory with the best of the rabbis, and that, a brilliant research chemist, he traded a secret wartime formula for Britain's Palestine pledge. He was both complex and complete; Western Jews and British Prime Ministers saw him in the same light as the

ghetto—the historical Jew, enriched, but unaltered by the Enlightenment, a dark and ancient nobility.

He witnessed the dress rehearsal for the final solution that began almost at once after the peace conferences. With the sole exception of Czechoslovakia, the other new states treated their Jewish citizens as if guarantees had never been solemnized. Perhaps that is why Weizmann soon decided that practical effort in Palestine was more important than reliance on pledges and legal documents. Poland, Hungary, Rumania, Lithuania, and Latvia barred the Jew from the universities, excised him from civil service, assaulted him on trams and trains, invaded his quarters, picketed and looted his shops, and when he defended himself, hauled him into the dock on charges ranging from felonious assault to murder. Even before the Nazis had won a single seat in the German Reichstag, the Polish Socialist Party, member in good standing in the Second International, lapsed into premature Nazism on issues affecting the Ukrainians and the Jews, its two largest minority blocs.

THE AMBIVALENT JEWS

The nations of Western and Central Europe were ethnically closed societies, but unlike their medieval prototype would neither assimilate the Jew nor countenance his separateness. The European Jewish intellectual, squirming in his existential condition, alternately concealed his Jewish origin like a social disease and displayed it as a badge of honor. Marcel Proust, tortured by his twice ambiguous status, coupled the plight of invert and Jew, "their honour precarious, their liberty provisional . . . their position unstable." He wrote: "Like the Jews again (save some who will associate only with others of their race and have always on their lips ritual words and consecrated pleasantries), shunning one another, seeking out those who are most directly their opposite, who do not desire their company, pardoning their rebuffs, moved to ecstasy by their condescenion; but also brought into the company of their own kind by the ostracism that strikes them, the opprobrium under which they have fallen, having finally been invested, by a persecution similar to that of

Israel, with the physical and moral characteristics of a race, sometimes beautiful, often hideous, finding (in spite of all the mockery with which he who, more closely blended with, better assimilated to the opposing race, is relatively, in appearance, the least inverted, heaps upon him who had remained more so) a relief in frequenting the society of their kind, and even some corroboration of their own life, so much so that, while steadfastly denying that they are a race (the name of which is the vilest of insults) those who succeed in concealing the fact that they belong to it they readily unmask, with a view less to injuring them, though they have no scruples about that, than to excusing themselves. . . ."

Proust, only a half-Jew himself, and a citizen of Hellenic Paris, world capital of the expatriate temperament, could contemplate his peculiar state with amused detachment. The German full-Jews, conversely, were bent under a sense of doom—not the only difference between the Teutonic and Gallic moods. Their writings on the German-Jewish relationship had a hysterical pitch even in the early 1920's before Hitler's eminence. The novelist Jacob Wasserman contended in his autobiography that German Jewry was a separate race from East European Jewry, even as Spanish-Portuguese Jews of eighteenth-century Bordeaux differentiated between themselves and German Jews. Wasserman complained that the Germans, however, would not accept the distinction, "Vain to go among them and offer them one's hand. They say: Why does he take such liberties, with Jewish obtrusiveness?"

Walter Rathenau, industrialist, economist, author, diplomat, late model Renaissance man to his fingertips, could not contemplate his origins without losing his exquisite composure. Why could not the Germans be patient, he asked, since the Jews were embracing the church anyway in ever-increasing numbers? He lacked the premonition that even the children of apostates would in less than a quarter of a century later be gassed as Jews by the Nazis. "I have and I know no other blood than German," he wrote. "If I examine myself closely I find that I am hurt more if a Bavarian declaims against the Prussians than if he does against the Jews."

In 1922, when he was in the midst of negotiating agreements with Germany's wartime foes which, if concluded, might have eased her back to dignified normalcy, Foreign Minister Rathenau was cut down by a fusillade of hand grenades and machine gun bullets, the consummation of long nationalist agitation against the "Jew traitor."

EINSTEIN AND FREUD

Zionism left none of the continental Jewish intellectuals indifferent. It either compelled or repelled them. Albert Einstein discovered the physical and spiritual embodiment of Zionism in Dr. Chaim Weizmann. To the scientist, the Jewish problem was a mathematical equation, and he was satisfied that Zionism had solved it. Although he was never sure whether he favored full statehood or a binational state with the Arabs, he was unqualifiedly for Restoration to Palestine. He became a Zionist almost immediately after the Balfour Declaration was published, opened his home for a meeting of the German Jewish elite with Weizmann, and twice in the 1920's suspended his work to join the Zionist leader on a fund-raising mission to American Jewry. Jewish pride vaulted as the two drove side by side in a motorcade through New York's Lower East Side, the personification of disparate qualities that Jewry has always priced highest: Weizmann represented worldly competence, and Einstein, other-worldly preoccupations. Orthodox rabbis greeted them with the ageless Hebrew blessing: "We thank the Lord for having bestowed of his greatness and wisdom upon man."

Although Sigmund Freud never went beyond joining the board of governors of the Hebrew University upon its founding in Jerusalem, in 1925, Zionism haunted him from the very beginning. He mailed to Herzl, then a book review critic, a copy of his first book, *The Interpretation of Dreams*, with the following inscription: "May I ask you to keep this book as a token of the high esteem in which I—like so many others—have held since many years the poet and the fighter for the human rights of our people." His failure to identify Herzl's cause is curious, as is another omission. In his lectures at the University of Vienna, he told of a dream he had of Herzl without

ever having met him in person. However, he deleted this dream from his published lectures. On the other hand, his *Moses and Monotheism,* based on disproved historical hypotheses, is as much a symbolic retelling of Herzl's life-story, the alien prince rejected by his people, as it is a historical monograph.

Freud was of the first generation of his family born outside Galicia, a territory that had been deeply stirred and riven by the folk Cabala, Messianism, Hassidism, and, ultimately, the Enlightenment. In 1930, in a fore-word to a Hebrew translation of *Totem and Taboo,* he made the significant remark that while he was himself not able to unravel the specifically Jewish in his person-ality, it is "probably its very essence . . . some day no doubt it will become accessible to the scientific minds." Two Jewish scholars have since made interesting stabs in that direction. Ernst Simon notes, of Freud's interpreta-tion of dreams, "the relation between a limited text . . . and its wider interpretation brings to mind . . . the mish-nah and the gemara," and that the Talmud's "combination of freedom of expression and a strictly anti-libertine atti-tude (on sex) is precisely what characterized Freud's standpoint towards sex." In 1958, David Bakan, in his book *Freud and the Jewish Mystical Tradition,* advanced guardedly "a hypothesis" on the affinity between Cabalistic and Freudian symbolism, adding "what the Sabbatian (Sabbatai Zvi) movement stood for in terms of emotional and social Messianism, Freud grappled with as a scientific problem." In a postscript in *Commentary* magazine, after his book had been published, Bakan told how he had since learned that Freud's library contained German books on the Cabala and a copy of the Zohar in French. Bakan added, "This new bit of information . . . has made me wonder."

REVOLUTION'S SCAPEGOAT

After the overthrow of the Czar, and even before the Bolsheviks had seized power, Chaim Weizmann wrote: "We are an old nation and must not forego the warnings of history. . . . It is difficult to believe that anti-Semitism,

which had been systematically urged and cruelly practiced in Russia for so long will suddenly disappear."

He was proved right immediately. Russian Jewry was caught on a spigot in the Civil War. In the 1917 elections to the Jewish community councils, the Zionists drew 70 per cent of all votes; most of the remainder went to the Bund, the Yiddish-speaking Social Democratic Party. Both the Zionists and the Bundists opposed Bolshevism on ideological grounds. This did not matter to the anti-Communist forces: the Ukrainians led by Hetman Petlura, successor to the sixteenth century Bogdan Chmielnicki, the guerrillas led by the anarchist Machno, and of course, the several monarchist armies. They branded Communism a Jewish movement, because of some modern-day Hellenists in its party directorate and as a means of solidifying the Russian people behind them. They then proceeded to pillage, rape, and massacre the Jews by the tens of thousands. The Jewish defense units could not endure alternate assaults from these several forces. Some of the Jewish young men then joined the Red Army as a means of retaliation. Red commanders, in turn, quickly checked and severely punished several anti-Jewish spurts among their own guerrillas.

AMBIGUOUS POLICY

Soviet policy toward the Jews in the 1920's was in sharp contrast to Socialist doctrine since Marx. The German Karl Kautsky, Bolshevik "Pope of European Socialism," defined the Jews as "a residue of the feudal Middle Ages, a social ghetto which continues to exist long after the physical ghetto has been liquidated." He echoed Marx, and also Napoleon and the French Assembly debate on the Jews' emancipation (1789-1791). Otto Bauer, Austrian Social Democratic authority on minorities, a Jew himself, offered a similar definition: "nation without history . . . possessing a rootless culture, a fossilized language, and no national literature." Lenin, quoting these "authorities," called the Jews "a caste" and branded as "simply a nationalist philistine" anyone who held otherwise. Stalin called them "a nation on paper," held together by a mesh of "petrified customs and residual psychological reflexes."

271

The three essential characteristics that define a nation, or people, according to Lenin and Stalin, are a common territory, a common language, and a peasantry anchored in the soil. The Jews, they contended, did not universally qualify. The rationale, from Marx through Kautsky, Bauer, Lenin, and Stalin was that the Jews must assimilate.

The Soviet regime, true to doctrine, offered them every incentive to assimilate. Soon Jews were prominent on all echelons of the Party machinery; the civil service, the army, the diplomatic corps, and arts and literature. Underdeveloped Russia was always poor in qualified personnel, and the flight of officials opposed to the regime further depleted its small reservoir. There were interminable vacancies to fill. The Jews were a welcome source. Jews had filled high posts in America and continental Europe since the eighteenth century; Russia under the Czars was an egregious exception. Although this full enfranchisement of the Jews began under Kerensky immediately after the fall of the Czar, its rapid tempo under the Bolsheviks impressed itself on the minds of Jewish youth.

Russia also offered the Jews an alternative to assimilation, the fullest government sponsored autonomy, precisely as the Bund had requested for years. The suppression of religion, Zionism and Hebrew, of course, did not matter to former Bundists who had always opposed these causes. Yiddish was designated one of the official languages of the Soviet Union. The state maintained in the Ukraine, White Russia, and Great Russia itself, newspapers, periodicals, books, theatres, museums, elementary and high schools, and a university in Yiddish. In several towns where Jews were a definite majority, Yiddish was briefly used even in court proceedings and in the conduct of municipal affairs. Like the government schools for Jews established by Czar Nicholas I, these institutions, too, were only a device to accelerate Jewry's assimilation. The majority of the Russian Jewish proletariat knew no other language; hence, it served its uses as a means of propagandizing among the Jewish workers contempt for their tradition and for other classes in Jewry, and obedience to the regime. Many Jews, disgusted by Yiddish newspapers and books that abased their history and convictions,

turned to Russian. Parents preferred to send their children to general schools in which they would be taught nothing about Jews, than to Yiddish schools which instructed them to contemn their people. Thus, the government was not completely lying when it gave diminishing demand as its reason, eventually, for shutting down Yiddish institutions, one after another, when it had become apparent that a majority of Jews could be addressed in Ukrainian or Russian.

In the mid-1920's, the Kremlin seemed to break completely with doctrine by offering the Jews a third alternative to assimilation or cultural autonomy. It offered them Jewish statehood within the frontiers of the U.S.S.R. The number of choices, more than the Jewish people had ever before been offered, confused many Jews, especially young people in the contiguous anti-Communist countries, like Poland, which persecuted their Jews.

First, the Kremlin offered them large scale settlement in Crimea, where Jews had resided since the beginnings of the Common Era. "State" was implied, but not specifically mentioned in the Kremlin's first announcement: "The Jewish people faces a great task, that of preserving its Jewish nationality." Three years later, in 1929, during the war on the "kulaks," all Jewish collective farms were liquidated or fused with non-Jewish Kolkhozes, the Kremlin had ready another territory, Biro-Bidjan, on the Mongolian frontier which was proclaimed an Autonomous Jewish region in 1934. In 1936, in a formal announcement U.S.S.R. praesidium went beyond that, declaring that "the first time in the history of the Jewish people, its burning desire for the creation of a homeland of its own, for the achievement of its own national statehood has found its fulfillment."

Biro-Bidjan's topmost Jewish officials were liquidated in the general purges of 1938, and their successors were disposed of in the final long night of the Stalin regime (1948-1953). Leading Soviet Jewish writers were liquidated during the latter period for allegedly having conspired to sever the Crimea and set it up as a "Jewish satellite" of the United States. Biro-Bidjan is no longer even mentioned in dispatches.

273

Both these projects followed, by historical reflex, the pattern of similarly abortive Czarist offers to settle the Jews on the soil. The Soviet government, like its Czarist predecessors, was each time inadequately prepared for the Jewish settlers, and finally changed its mind altogether. It proposed "Jewish statehood" for very shrewd domestic and foreign reasons. By counterposing a Soviet Zion to the British Zion, it hoped to enlist Jewish sympathies for the Soviet Union, smokescreen its collaboration with the Arab guerrilla war on the Palestine Zionist settlers, and to divert to the Kremlin coffers some of the hard currency which Jewish philanthropists were spending on the Palestine experiment. In fact, without offering Jewries abroad any voice or supervising authority over the proposed Soviet undertaking, it nonetheless addressed a direct appeal to "Jewish capitalists" to help their brethren resettle on Soviet land. The Czar had tried to obtain funds from Baron Maurice de Hirsch under similar dubious circumstances. In fact, several Jewish philanthropic agencies abroad hoped that the Kremlin appeal would possibly offer a solution to the problems of "declassed" Soviet Jews. The "declassed" were a "legion of dishonor," a grab-bag of all kinds of politically unreliable, including all who had engaged in mercantile occupations. Sixty per cent of Soviet Jews, having once been traders and petty shopkeepers, qualified for this social limbo. Denied schooling, housing, and employment through the 1920's-1930's, the sins of their fathers visited upon the sons, these Jews lived on the economic periphery, by their wits, as in Czarist days.

The Kremlin, however, had other Jews in mind for settlement. It hoped to ensnare Communist Party member enthusiasts for Yiddish whose continued presence among the multitudes in European Russia seemed to sustain a "nationalistic ferment," and prevent the rapid assimilation of the Jews under Communism. It also hoped to use Biro-Bidjan as a dam against "oriental infiltration" from Mongolia.

THE NATIONAL HOME

The Palestine Zionist experiment, always a target of Communist attack, drew its pioneers from the European Yid-

dish-speaking centers. There were among them, obviously, men of private enterprise. But the Utopians, the Socialist Zionists, set the style. They experimented with various forms of communal and co-operative living. Some leaned, like the Essenes, to communal societies held together by unitary doctrine, barring all dissidents; others to co-operatives that had a wide ideological range. They conditioned themselves to hard work, and were given to long ideological addresses and to interminable, nocturnal debates. Their societies endure to this day, even though the pace of the country has since been completely altered. Still setting pace for the country, and now also for the underdeveloped African and Asian countries, is Histadrut, the country's unique trade union federation founded in 1920. It has gone beyond the traditional labor union's concern with wages, hours, and working conditions, and has developed its own employment markets, industrial complexes, mercantile co-operatives, sometimes in joint partnership with private investors, which vests social welfare not in government, but in society itself, and subjects it to periodic review not by parliament, speaking with an abstract national voice, but by the labor federation's membership, local by local.

ARAB PROBLEM

The enduring tragic dilemma, the Arab problem, had confronted these pioneers from the start. It resulted in Arab pogroms in 1920, and guerrilla war between Arabs and Jews, in 1929, 1936-1939, and intermittently ever since. The country was the arid, malarial, backroads of a dissolute, decrepit empire, its Arab population indigent, living by custom, not by law, its considerable nomad segment divided into rival tribes, raiding the fellahin with relish, treating all sedentary peoples with contempt. They judged the Jewish colonists as especially incompetent for their environment, until the Shombim, the Jewish Guards, proved their mettle. Their purpose was peace and acceptance by their neighbors. Of romantic disposition, they rode horses with élan, wore the Arab kafia with aplomb, and soon were any Arab's match in the favorite pastime—spinning tall tales with éclat. Arab and

Jew soon began attending each other's communal feasts, and matching their horsemen in fantasias (contests), and in the manner of their common ancestor Abraham, concluding treaties to share grazing grounds and water holes.

The political issues between them did not arise until after World War I. Its source was not the Balfour Declaration but the Arabs' emancipation which occurred under conditions different from the Jews'.

The Jews, mixing nation and religion, and possessing no land, yet having a collective physiognomy, could never accommodate to the formal, modern definitions of nation and denomination.

The Arabs, although never dislodged from their soil, lacked what Jewry dispersed, had always possessed—a national physiognomy, a collective identity. Since the year 900 A.D., they had been under diverse foreign rule, mostly malevolent, intermixed with many nations, and had lost their sense of national identity. Yet living on their own soil and sharing a common language, they qualified for nationhood by the modern definition. Some of their younger men, pseudo-Westerners, began piecing together a national image from European models and their most adverse ancient traditions. The most obtrusive European model was Germany, where Nazism was already stirring. Arab nationalists became involved with Nazis. They also reverted to the spirit of the worst of Muslim laws, which like all law had both enlightened and restrictive features. The latter, which had almost never asserted themselves when Arab power was at its zenith, provide that infidels, especially Jews, be treated as inferiors. Yemen, the most retarded of Arab states, dutifully observed these laws, including the forcible conversion of Jewish children to Islam upon their father's passing, until the Jews departed for Israel in 1948. Arab nationalism, turning on Zionism, struck at the Jew as a foreign intruder, but also as a familiar, contemned, indigenous breed. Because he applied greater celerity to his national undertaking than the Arabs could at that time to theirs, the Jew affronted both modern Arab nationalism and the old tradition which prescribes him an inferior role.

276

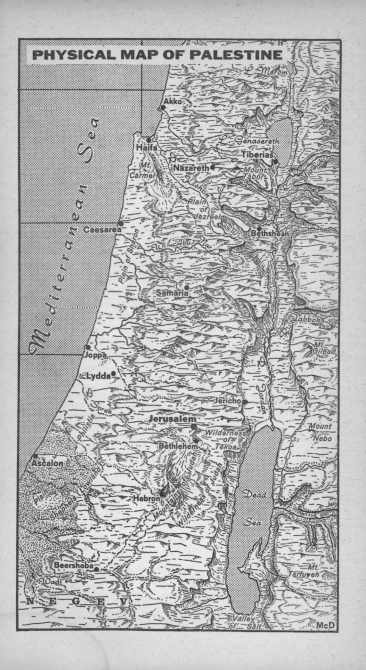

IMPERIAL POWERS

British policy toward the Zionist experiment was compounded of antipodes. The British Colonial Office was against Zionism since the days when it successfully opposed granting an East Africa charter to Herzl. Conversely, the supporters of the Balfour Declaration were centered in the Foreign Office. Underlying all British policy were antithetical impulses: a sincere desire to keep the pledge to the Jews, an intent to scrap the pledge in order to meet Arab protest, and finally a design to keep both parties baying at each other to Britain's advantage.

Moscow-directed Communism looked for a way to dislodge the British and French and establish itself in the region. Its method was to instigate indigenous nationalist leaders to inevitable violence. Its calculated effect was chaos in the area, a bad press abroad that would compel the imperial power to lay down its mandate or any other legal instrument that sanctioned her presence. Moscow's certainty that the Jews would not long prevail in the area over superior Arab numbers and the mating of Zionism and Britain by means of the Balfour Declaration were the most patent reasons for Communism's alliance with the Arabs in the guerrilla wars on Palestine Jews from 1920 through the 1930's. But there were the deeper, the ideological reasons. To Lenin's concept of the Jew as "residual medievalism" that would disappear under socialism, Zionism counterposed the concept of the Jews' historical continuity and their restoration to statehood; Zionist socialism has gone beyond the so-called "purely Jewish" issue by counterposing societal socialism, as demonstrated by the kibbutzim, co-operatives, villages governed by direct vote by their members in open assembly, to totalitarian state socialism, as demonstrated by the kolkhoz whose affairs are governed by an arbitrary government bureaucracy.

The British authorities in Palestine repeatedly restricted immigration; denying political motivations, they contended that absorption of larger numbers was beyond the country's capacity. But Zionism had a legal claim; the charter toward which Herzl had worked was now em-

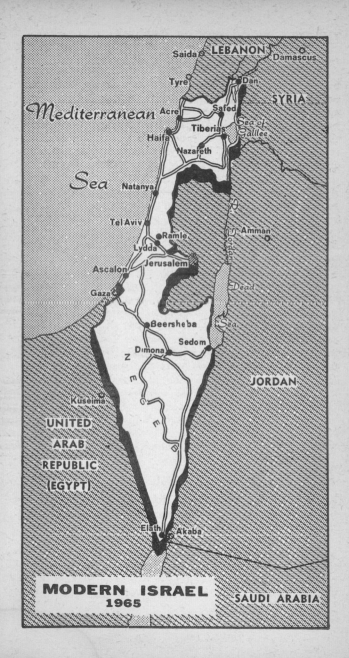

MODERN ISRAEL
1965

bodied in the Balfour Declaration and in a League of Nations mandate. Britain's right to administer Palestine was conditioned on her pledge to facilitate the establishment of the Jewish National Home. Breach of her pledge to the Jews impugned her right to be in Palestine at all. The Zionists repeatedly raised this legal point, and with effect. Meanwhile, the skeletal Jewish National Home constituted itself a shadow government; increasingly capable of defending itself, it turned to its one certain ally, the Jewish people, and primarily the American Jewish community which even in the 1920's, however modest its material wealth, was the most affluent Jewry in the world.

U.S. JEWS VERSUS FORD

American Jews had just experienced several traumas. Proposals to base immigration quotas on ethnic discrimination, hibernating since the turn of the century, were now transfigured into law. Neither mass meetings of the Lower East Side multitudes, nor the impassioned pleas, behind the scenes and publicly, of Jacob Schiff, Stephen S. Wise, and others could prevail against the legislators. Jews seeking respite from Polish and Rumanian pogroms had nowhere to run. The quotas granted these countries were sparse, their distribution lay in the hands of local American consuls who sometimes demonstrated a mean personal bias even beyond the law's intent. Its provision that only husbands, wives, and minor children of American residents may be admitted outside the quota effectively and permanently disunited tens of thousands of East European Jewish families.

There were other disconcerting experiences in the 1920's. The KKK was at its apex. Jewish homes in New Jersey and Long Island were sparse, and their owners would frequently strain behind drawn blinds to watch white-hooded gangs plant the fiery crosses on their lawns. Henry Ford's weekly *Dearborn Independent* purveyed in weekly installment the *Protocols of Zion,* a forgery of the Czarist police, and other material of this type purporting to show that the Bolshevik Revolution was the first stage of a conspiracy of Masons and Jews to dominate the

world. It took ten years, a libel trial, and the threat of a boycott to persuade Henry Ford that he had lent his name to malevolent ends.

His apology was addressed to Louis Marshall, lawyer autocrat, who insisted on dictating policy to rabbis in the Temple Emanu-el pulpit, yet was sufficiently reverent of democratic processes to have led the unified American Jewish delegation to the Peace Conference. He had reportedly been so deeply moved by his experience with Goshen that he reputedly studied Yiddish.

"I deem it my duty as an honorable man to make amends for the wrong done to the Jews as fellow-men and brothers," Henry Ford wrote him, "by asking their forgiveness for the harm that I have unintentionally committed."

Louis Marshall, in the proud tradition of Uriah Levy, and Mordecai Manuel Noah, and Jacob Schiff's intercession with Russia's Count Witte, replied: "The statement which you had sent me gives us assurance of your retraction of offensive charges . . . of your desire to make amends, and what is to be expected from any man of honor, you couple these assurances with a request for pardon. So far as my influence can further this end, it will be exerted, simply because there flows in my veins the blood of ancestors who were inured to suffering and nevertheless remained steadfast in their trust in God. Referring to the Teachings of the Sermon on the Mount, Israel Zangwill once said that we Jews are after all the only Christians. He might have added that it is because essentially the spirit of forgiveness is a Jewish trait."

On the balance, U.S. Jewry had done well through the 1920's. Its campaign against immigration restrictions was unsuccessful within the context, however, of larger American setbacks, the isolationists' triumph over Wilson, America's fateful abstention from the League of Nations. It had won decisively, on the other hand, its contest with one of America's powerful industrial empires, Henry Ford. These two great campaigns, which were indicative of the common danger, contributed to the gradual disintegration completed two decades later of the barriers be-

tween East European and German or Yahudim Jews in the United States.

The economic advancement of the East European immigrant was perhaps the most important solidifying factor. "To Let" signs on hitherto overcrowded Lower East Side tenements implied a great internal migration. Immigrants who had prospered in the garment trades and in realty were moving into the better residential districts, and were developing land values in hitherto underdeveloped boroughs. There was, albeit imperceptible, a diminution of the nightly public forums and lectures. Better housing made evenings at home more pleasurable; the dispersal over several boroughs imposed the burden of travel upon those who wished to attend the Lower East Side forums. The fervent crowds which used to stampede to the night schools to study English were now reduced as a more prosperous Jewish community sent its children through high school and college, and immigration restrictions reduced the numbers of adult immigrants requiring instruction in English.

INTELLECTUALS' EXPATRIATIONS

But there was still in the 1920's a flourishing and intense Yiddish cultural activity in American—more correctly New York—Jewry. The Yiddish theater was at its peak and presented, some four decades before the off-Broadway theaters, the plays of the great continental and Russian masters, while the American theater could barely sustain Eva Le Gallienne's Civic Repertory. Yiddish literary schools flourished. Periodicals multiplied. Poetry evenings still drew their own loyal audiences. Great ideological debates between ranking Yiddish-speaking Zionist, Socialist, and Communist intellectuals drew overflow audiences to historic Cooper Union, where Lincoln once had spoken. All this was part of a great cultural ferment which had its seat in Poland.

Other processes were underway too, quite apart from the secular movements. The Reform and Conservative denominations in Jewry were expanding the faculties of their rabbinical seminaries, the Hebrew Union College and the Jewish Theological Seminary, respectively. They

founded great libraries and attracted ranking European scholars, some of whom became engaged in public affairs, especially Zionism. The Orthodox on the Lower East Side founded the first Jewish parochial schools in twentieth century America, a pattern now also adapted by Conservative Judaism. They also founded the initial institutions which have since burgeoned forth in Yeshiva University. These practical efforts were to have more enduring effect on the evolution of even secular Jewish culture in America than some of the short-term ideologies.

However, amidst this ferment another, a negative development was underway, the dichotomy between public affairs and cultural effort, the expatriation, not into foreign lands, but on native American soil, of the Jewish intellectual. The affluent Yahudim, the East European radicals, and the Zionists alike contributed to this end.

The upper middle-class of German descent was wary of the intellectual ferment, still emanating from the "ghettos" as alien, extremist.

Trade Unionism, founded by socialist intellectuals who had rallied the masses, now came under the domination of tough, hard-bargaining strike leaders who downgraded the ideologian as wholly irrelevant to improving working conditions and raising the living wage. Strangely, this was coterminal with the diminution of the memberships' voice, except during the successful struggle, in the 1920's, against Communist seizure of the garment workers' unions. The seizure of power by the technocrats was not arbitrary. The members satisfied with their gains, simply ceased to exercise their mandate. The unions today have many cultural institutions, are engaged in more diversified commitments than ever before; but these efforts, however costly, are extracurricular, not the integrated essence as when the intellectuals were an influence.

A parallel process was occurring in Zionism. Chaim Weizmann and other Zionist leaders visited the United States periodically on fund-raising missions. The East Side's mass audiences were still essential to their purpose as a demonstration, to Jew and Christian alike, of the vigor of the Zionist mandate. The street corner collections,

in Jewish districts when the over-all revenue for Zionist causes was still small, were both stirring and necessary.

However, Weizmann and his colleagues had their eyes on bigger catch, on the big contributor, both of the older German stock and of the newly rich East European immigrants. Men like Jacob Schiff, while contributing to Zionism's practical effort, disassociated themselves from its political aims which they deemed undesirable and unrealizable. They felt, however, that the Palestinian settlers were no less entitled to philanthropic assistance than other Jewries. Pogroms or government edicts often demolished overnight seemingly enduring assistance rendered East European Jewries by American Jewish philanthropy. The Palestine effort, conversely, although affecting modest numbers, was immeasurably safer because it was under the joint civilized aegis of the League of Nations and Britain.

The newly enriched East European immigrants were an even richer mine for Zionist fund-raising. Their responses were immediate and spontaneous. This wealth bore, however, the defects of the immigrants' too rapid social transfiguration. Much of it was concentrated in the former lower strata—the artisans who by skill, ability, and energy had advanced to contractor, manufacturer, and realtor. They reciprocated with generous contributions to the Palestine cause, for the distinction of having Weizmann to dinner, but they were also conceited about their real importance to his effort. There was not much real place in this scheme for the majority of moderate means and none at all for the intellectual. As in the trade union movement, the alienation of the intellectual and the disenfranchisement by default of the masses occurred simultaneously.

The intellectuals' ouster began in November 1921, when the Brandeis group was ejected from Zionism. Its significance was lost, however, because it was wrapped in the larger conflict between East Europeans and notables, and because the Brandeis faction was temporarily replaced by the intellectual of the Yiddish press and lecture platform. By the late 1920's, these had been ousted by the technocrat, the fund-raiser, as tough and cunning as his targets, the newly rich.

THE NINETEEN-THIRTIES

This brought disastrous effects in the 1930's when the community needed intellectual leadership. The Jews suffered from the great depression perhaps sooner and more intensely than most Americans. Both as employer and employee he drew his livelihood, as he still does, from consumer goods and services, peculiarly sensitive to economic precipitation and pinched by even the mildest recession.

He suffered the classic misadventures that have always, everywhere been his fate in times of economic dislocation and political distress. That the Jew, economically, was a victim rather than a perpetrator of economic and social injustice in this country did not seem to matter. Nazi Germany's anti-Semitic propaganda found resonance among isolationists and the organic residues of populism and Know-Nothingism. The Irish-American immigrant had been the primary target of these movements in the nineteenth century, but some of his heirs enthusiastically joined their war on the Jews in the 1930's. Respectable German-American organizations were distressed by the exhibitionism of jack-booted Yorkville Storm Troopers of recent German American immigrant vintage, but in their own circumspect way they too helped enlist sympathies for the Fatherland arisen to new glory under Hitler.

None of this surprised the Jew. What distressed him was the comportment of more august American quarters. Theodore Dreiser, a card-carrying Communist at the time, proposed the mass deportation of Jewry to "cleanse" the American blood stream. Eugene O'Neill also made some biting remarks. Barbed disquisitions, clothed as dispassionate opinion, were published in *The Atlantic Monthly* and *The Saturday Evening Post*. The State Department concluded reciprocal trade agreements with Nazi Germany, informed Jewish delegations of its distaste for anti-Nazi mass demonstrations, and apologized to Berlin for scathing remarks about Hitler by Mayor LaGuardia.

All Jewry turned to its American brethren as the Jews of Ancona had once turned to Joseph Nassi of Constantinople. The Yiddish intelligentsia offered bold initiative through its press; then still addressing hundreds of thousands it proposed a world-wide boycott of German goods

285

and services. Upper-class Jewry opposed the boycott on the grounds that it would provoke the Nazis, and embarrass the U.S. Government. The bold and wonderful autocrats were gone: Jacob Schiff who interceding for his brethren had angrily stalked out on a President of the United States and shook an admonitory finger at a Czarist minister, and Louis Marshall who could treat a chastened American industrial empire builder with withering condescension. One of the sage bold men was still around. Dr. Stephen S. Wise reports in his autobiography, *The Challenging Years*, of his meeting with Louis D. Brandeis, then seventy-seven, several days after Hitler had been named Chancellor of Germany (January 30, 1933):

"Categorically and almost too dogmatically, as it then seemed to me, Justice Brandeis . . . said, 'The Jews must leave Germany: There is no other way.' I interposed the question, 'how can 585,000 people be taken out of Germany?' Before I could again record my doubt about the unlimited difficulties, he more fully and less categorically added in explanation, 'I would have the Jews out of Germany. They have been treated with deepest disrespect. I urge that Germany shall be free of Jews. Let Germany—' and these were his only stern words, self-respecting rather than vindictive—'share the fate of Spain.' Once again with an equal sternness he repeated, 'No Jew must live in Germany.' "

Stephen S. Wise's leonine roar still stirred the lower middle-classes, once the passion of all Jewish public effort, but now shunted aside for the big contributor. They responded dutifully to his summons, marched doggedly in protest demonstration, filled Madison Square Garden with thundering indignation, and tenaciously picketed stores selling German merchandise, but their custom rendered or withdrawn could in no way affect the size of German exports to America. The trade union movement and the Zionists both joined in supporting and sponsoring the boycott. But the tough realists who had built the Jewish unions were immersed in their primary concern, the urgent labor affairs of those tumultuous years, and American Zionism was preoccupied with its overriding task—raising funds (Jews from Germany were

reluctantly moving to the Jewish National Home; few other countries would have them), protesting British restrictions on Jewish immigration to Palestine, supporting the Jewish National Home under assault by Arab gangs simultaneously but separately sponsored by Moscow and Berlin.

A new dimension was added to American Jewish life: the defense agency, today called human or community relations agency. Old ones that had long functioned modestly now began to extend their apparatuses. New ones grew like barnacles or announced themselves with sirens screaming. Although their semantics ranged from vulgar to subtle, their common purpose was simplistic—refutation of anti-Semitic libel, exposure of anti-Semitic groups, solicitation of "character affidavits" from prominent Americans confirming the Jews' continued usefulness and loyalty to American society. Like the Zionist effort in Palestine and the organizations for the relief of Nazi victims, these too revolved around the fund-raising dinner whose dais was dominated, as was the audience, by the big contributor and the big name politician who gave—and still gives—status to such events.

Bedeviled by the many ominous portents, and unable to detect a central design or elucidation of their dilemma in the manifold effort of the Jewish organizations, some Jewish college youths turned elsewhere for salvation. The Communist front organizations offered a seventeen day economy tour to universal messianism, which would deliver the Jew with all humanity.

GENOCIDE IN WASHINGTON

Dr. Chaim Weizmann used American Jewry as a supply base. Policy was decided primarily in London and Jerusalem. The Zionist high command was thinking along the lines of Brandeis in respect to evacuating German Jewry. An agreement to exchange German goods for Palestine oranges resulted in the release of Jews and their assets.

When the war broke out, Zionist youth operated rescue missions in German-occupied Europe. It was in America that the apparatus stalled. Decisions were taken by a wide spectrum of American Jewish leadership, who were by dis-

position and class disinclined to radical measures. They also had a delusion that the Roosevelt administration was as deeply concerned as they with the fate of European Jewry.

The above estimate is supported by a depressing chronology of events, revealed in Dr. Wise's autobiography and the diaries of U.S. Secretary of the Treasury Henry Morgenthau. On August 28, 1942, Wise received circuitously the incredible information that the Nazis were about to begin the mass extermination of Europe's six million Jews. He was asked by Under-secretary of State Sumner Welles to withhold the information until it was checked. American Jewish leadership withheld the information until November, 1943 when the Undersecretary of State reported that more than two million Jews had already perished.

The first report had reached Wise through the British Foreign Office. The U.S. Legation in Bern, after three weeks, returned the message to the sender, explaining that its facilities could not be used for this purpose. Welles now instructed the Legation to relay all messages for Wise without delay, yet when weeks passed without them, Welles queried Bern. Bern promptly replied that it had withheld them in accordance with Welles' cabled instructions not to transmit "any more stories of atrocities which might provoke more mass meetings and more public protests." His name had been signed without even consulting him.

"Early in 1943" Wise received a Nazi official's offer to release seventy thousand Jews for a set ransom to be deposited in a Swiss bank which was not to pay out the monies until the war's end. An application for permission to transfer the funds was promptly filed with the U.S. authorities. Months passed with no word from Washington. Dr. Wise on July 22, 1943, called the White House with the result that the application was approved. It was only on December 18, 1943, that the clearance actually came through. By then it was too late.

In January, 1944—the year when he ran for his fourth term—President Roosevelt formed the War Refugee Board to facilitate heterodox Jewish rescue efforts. It performed

well, but too late for effectiveness or excellence. Six million Jews had perished by then.

When the war ended, American Jewish leadership, shaken by what had occurred while it deliberated, hesitated, vacillated, and trusted, girded its energies for a prodigious effort. It mobilized enormous financial resources to reclaim for secure and normal life the hundreds of thousands who had survived and were still penned-in in DP camps in Germany. It marshalled vigorous political pressure to compel the British to permit these survivors to settle in Palestine. American Jewry resorted to extralegal measures. It bought vessels to run the British blockade. It bought arms which were smuggled to those who were to defend the illegal immigrants against apprehension and all of Jewish Palestine from Arab attack. Bold and imaginative initiatives were required for this task. But most of these came from the Palestine Zionist leadership which worked in accordance with a grand design, to compel Britain to lay the mandate down, and to restore Jewish sovereignty in their ancestral home.

The emergence of the State of Israel is the most dramatic segment on a broad canvas of changes that have occurred in Jewry since World War II.

At the outset of World War II, American Jewry numbered less than five million; today it has passed the 5,510,000 mark. Poland at that time had three million Jews; most of them vanished in Hitler's gas chambers, representing half of the six million Jews Germany had so destroyed. Of the survivors, only some thirty thousand Jews have remained in Poland. Palestine had a Jewish population of 650,000; Israel today has a Jewish population of over two million.

Barring Russia's three million Jews, whom Soviet authorities have isolated from all contacts with other Jewries and involvement in Jewish affairs, the two great poles of Jewish life today are Israel and the United States. This represents an obvious geographic shift. Israel is the first globally important Jewish center on Asian soil since the sixteenth century.

Eastern European Jewry created a culture as distinctive as that of Babylonian Jewry. Its language was Yiddish,

and there is no greater repository of the genius of a people than its language. It contains both a people's ethos and myths. For several centuries East European Jewry was the most active segment of the Jewish people. It produced Talmudic academies, with their own exegeses and their own pedagogy. It produced Hassidism. Mendelssohn may have begun the revival of Hebrew, but in German Jewry's custody, it would have been the possession of pedants in libraries and museums. East European Jewry revived Hebrew as a spoken tongue. It produced Yiddish literature and the Yiddish theater, pioneering Zionism and Jewish socialism, a very distinctive Jewish secularism and, of course, that mass immigration which formed American Jewry.

With the passing of Polish Jewry and the three million European Jews, most of whom were also East Europeans, the Yiddish-based culture has passed. American Jewry, although of East European origin, is not the successor to that culture. Neither is Israel. American Jewry lives in an environment that is, from a Jewish historical view, analogous to the Greco-Roman. East European, like Babylonian Jewry, was self-contained, albeit communicating with the general culture. Secondly, eighty per cent of America's Jews are native-born. They don't have any memory, any direct knowledge of East European Jewish culture.

Nor can Israel be the successor to the East European Jewish tradition. About one-half of Israel's population is of Afro-Asian origin. East European Jewish culture succeeded Afro-Asian. Are we seeing a reversal of roles? Eventually, perhaps, not immediately. The European (not East European) Jewish tradition began to emerge long before the decline of the Afro-Asian. Rashi, in France, preceded Maimonides, in the East, by a half century. The Afro-Asian Jewish populations have been in stagnant waters for the past several centuries; hence, it will take long before they can, in Israel, assume the succession, and if they could it would have no relationship to what has immediately preceded them. The Yiddish-based tradition is entirely alien to them.

The sabra (native-born) youth of East European parentage is almost equally uncommunicative with East

European culture. His pioneering parents, as a matter of principle, had taught him to abhor everything about the "Diaspora," because the Diaspora was a two thousand year old badge of shame. Yiddish was a Diaspora tongue, hence part of this horrible humiliation to which Jewry had been subjected. The Jews must be reborn as a people in their ancestral land, and part of the rebirth involves the reacquisition of Hebrew as their living tongue. That is how the pioneers felt and reasoned. Now that they have aged, and become parents and grandparents, and Yiddish was so horribly eradicated in the Nazi genocide crusade, they have become penitent. They would like to stir in their offspring respect for that culture. But it is too late. The children have been conditioned by contempt for East European Jewish culture. The same is true, to some extent, of the East European Jewish immigrant in America. Some of these immigrants were ideologically fervently committed to the perpetuation of Yiddish. They were a small segment. But even among that segment were some whose subconscious dictated a behavior contrary to their convictions. They somehow did not labor vigorously enough to keep Yiddish alive among their offspring. They subconsciously feared that this might prevent their children's "Americanization."

Bernard Malamud, Saul Bellow, the cult of the Yiddish writer Isaac Bashevis Singer, the success of such plays as *Fiddler on the Roof* and *The Zulu and the Zayda* are proof, however, that the Yiddish myth is reasserting itself in new guises.

The same is evident also in some sabra writers. Their first instinct has compelled them toward archeology. The Bible, which they study at school, has been their guidebook. Its language is their daily speech, and they walk the soil on which most of its events occurred. Thus, they are able to reconstruct their myth almost layer by layer. But it ends somewhere in the first century of the Common Era. There follows a compelling two thousand year gap in their myth.

The most serious dilemma that faces the modern Jew, particularly in America and Israel, is that of self-definition. Who and what is the Jew? What is the kinship

291

between one Jew and another? This self-questioning almost always corresponds to a crisis of confidence among the gentiles in whose midst he resides. The struggle between the Pharisees and the Sadducees, within the larger framework of universal Hellenism, would seem to have been over the issue of the Jew's self-definition. It was certainly the issue between the Nazarenes and Paul. It arose very sharply in the days of Saadia Gaon when Muslim civilization was torn by heresies. It compelled Maimonides to write the *Guide to the Perplexed*.

Its root is whether the Jew relates best to the world by enduring as himself or assimilating. It is a guilt-ridden dilemma compounded for the modern Diaspora Jew by the fact that he does not fit tightly into any of the contemporary categories. The Jewish peoples predate by several thousand years all modern definitions of religion, people, nation. The Jew has endured because his historical answer has been that he can only relate himself to the world by being himself. That which ceases to be ceases to relate, obviously. The problem facing the modern Jew is how he may continue being. It is perhaps no problem at all for the Israeli Jew, although he is as obsessed with the issue as any other Jew. He is in control of the instruments by which his society functions. That society becomes the receptacle of his ethos. He can set its compass in the direction of his four thousand years' historical experience although distillation of its essence is a herculean task. A member of Israel's high courts, for example, has suggested that Israeli law shift from its present Anglo-Saxon to a Talmudic base, of course after revising the ancient law by which the Jew has lived, more or less, up to two centuries ago.

We now reach a most serious point in this summation. Endurance suggests permanency. The question has been raised as to how permanent, or more bluntly, how secure American Jewry and the State of Israel really are? At their present stage, in the excellent definition of historian Ben Halpern, the American Jew is emancipated, the Israel Jew is liberated. The emancipated community is a minority that has been accorded equality by the majority. The liberated community is a people settled on its own

land that has acquired political sovereignty. How enduring is Israel's liberation and American Jewry's emancipation?

Israel is surrounded by Arab foes who are supported by the two Communist Goliaths, the U.S.S.R., and Red China. Israel's leaders openly concede the Arab threat to its existence. Conversely, American Jews, insist that "America is different" and that their emancipation is forever. To prove that the repetitive pattern of Jewish exilic experience has been broken they cite the astonishing gains of the American Jew since World War II. Before then medical and engineering schools maintained secret quotas against Jewish applicants, and there was no place for the Jew in American basic industry. Today, Jews staff the faculties of the very schools that had barred them as students, and Jewish engineers, chemists, and all manner of experts occupy dignified posts in American basic industry, although still barred from the top management hierarchy. Of course, there are many reasons for this. American industry needs talent. Most states have passed anti-discrimination laws which, in themselves, are testimony of an altered climate in the land. The country is prosperous. The sated are too self-centered to digress into violent social action. Christian society has not yet purged itself of its guilt over the six million Jews who perished in gas chambers in a Christian-dominated world. The Negro, having ceased to be docile, has replaced the Jew as society's whipping boy, or victim-hero. But the Jew has not yet been dismissed from class. There hangs over the United States the threat of compounded tragedy, rising technological unemployment and mounting racial conflict; should the vise of these two complementary threats tighten, the American Jew might find that it tightens around him. This is improbable, perhaps, but not impossible. There have been white Christian complaints, not only from Southern segregationist quarters, that the Jew is too deeply involved in what is "not his business." Conversely, although American Jewry has even produced two CORE martyrs, who actually gave their lives for this cause, there have been Negro complaints that the Jew, who should know better, has been stand-offish on the issue.

293

This leads to some arithmetic on the subject of Jewish-Negro relations. Some thirty-one per cent of all American Negroes, according to Charles Silberman's *Crisis in Black and White*, are concentrated in thirteen major American cities. By coincidence, the majority of American Jewry is concentrated in half of these cities. "To the Negro in the black ghetto the Jew is highly visible," C. Eric Lincoln writes, "consequently the negative image . . . is likely to be extremely exaggerated." What has made the Jew so "highly visible"? By what chemistry or magic has the Negro singled him out from among 170,000,000 white Americans of many ethnic origins and faiths? First, because the Jews, in Leslie Fiedler's phrase, "inhabit at one remove or another the region between (the Negro ghetto) and the neighborhoods which mean real belonging." Their faith makes them distinct from all other Americans, white and Negro alike. His Christian faith conversely, is the Negro's strongest single bond with the white majority. It is incomprehensible, the Negro reasons, that the Jewish minority should enjoy greater rewards than he, the Christian, albeit his skin is black; it therefore follows that Jewish gains have been achieved at his expense. The ubiquity of the Jewish businessman in the Negro ghettos provides "support" for this thesis. The Negroes are peculiarly the People of the Book. They are torn between the Old Testament, through which they identify with the Jew, and the New Testament which poses them against him. They cannot regard the urban Jew they know as the Hebrew who fled from bondage. He is more accurately Pharaoh's favorite, Joseph.

Their contiguity in the major cities is very crucial. The Negro demands his share and better of economic opportunity and political office. The Jew has not yet really impressed himself on the heartland of the American economy —the utilities, finance, and the automotive and steel industries. At best, he hovers on the periphery of these. U.S. Jews' primary affluence is drawn from the essentially precarious consumer goods and services and the professions. This is true also of other ethnic minorities concentrated in these cities. The Negro breaking out of his ghetto

will make his first claim upon these middle-class economic sinecures.

To a large measure, then, the comfort of the Jew in American society relates to the Negro-Jewish symbiosis. By historical coincidence, Israel is also largely dependent on Negro peoples. It cannot place its reliance on white Western states alone. These may soon be outnumbered. They are remote from the area. They are torn between Israel and the Arab states, and it may be hard for them to break the historical habit of thinking of the Jew, as an individual and as a people, in mythical terms, as the ever-present sacrificial Christ. At best, association with the Western states exclusively would place Israel in the anomalous position of being an intruder in the dust basins of the Middle East as the Arabs allege. Israel, isolated by the Arab states, leaped across them and reached out for friendship to other African and Asian states. Its unique co-operative labor economy has especially impressed Africans. Its technical aid, on a minute scale, although the maximum Israel can afford, has been highly instructive, because it is based on experience that roughly corresponds to the Africans'. It is adapted to circumstances that roughly correspond to Israel's. The secure existence of Israel is considerably dependent on its continual acceptance as a member by the Afro-Asian nation complex.

We now focus attention on several phenomena that are perhaps no less astonishing than the restoration of Jewish sovereignty on Palestine soil after a hiatus of two thousand years.

For the first time since the Moors were beaten back from Spain, the major body of the Jewish people, represented by American Jewry and Israel, has re-established vital rapport with races other than the white. There have occurred equally astonishing alterations in Jewry's interfaith relations. For centuries, major Jewish history unfolded in countries under Catholic domain. Between World War I and II, American Jewry, in a Protestant society, outnumbered Polish Jewry, but it was the latter that generated the literature, the ideas, and the incentives that shaped the Jewish image. Today, the only large Jewish community on Catholic soil is the Latin American. It

numbers approximately one million. There is no evidence
that it shall ever achieve dominion in Jewry's arena. The
Jews of Russia, notwithstanding residual Christianity
there, live in a non-Christian society. The two million
Jews of Israel live geographically outside the largely
Christian sphere. Israel's present generation is still very
conscious of the universal Christian presence. The native
Israeli of European parentage has had no direct personal
experience with Christianity as a force determining the
fate of the Jews. The Oriental element in Israel is certainly
devoid of any Judeo-Christian complex. Within a decade
or so, Israel will be dominated by a Jewish generation
that will deal with Christian powers, of course; but it
will be a relationship stripped of centuries-old attitudes.
Israelis of the next generation will become aware, instead, as Jewry of old had been, of Islam and of the so-
called pagan faiths within whose framework Israel's culture will unfold. Even America, although the churches
fight a rear guard war, is so highly secularized that some
Christian theologians admit it is a post-Christian society.
Thus, altogether, Jewry is terminating its long, seemingly
interminable relationship with Christendom.

READINGS: CHAPTERS TEN AND ELEVEN

Political and Sociological Works

Adler, Cyrus and Margalith, A. M. *With Firmness in the
Right, American Diplomatic Action Affecting Jews, 1840-
1945.* New York: American Jewish Committee, 1946.

Bein, Alex. *The Return to the Soil, A History of Jewish Settlement in Israel.* New York: The Youth and Hechalutz
Department of the Zionist Organization, 1952.

Ben Gurion, David. *Israel: Years of Challenge.* New York:
Holt, Rinehart and Winston, 1963.

———— *Rebirth and Destiny of Israel.* New York: Philosophical
Library, 1954.

Bentwich, Norman. *For Zion's Sake, a Biography of Judah L.
Magnes.* Philadelphia: Jewish Publication Society, 1954.

De Haas, Jacob. *Louis D. Brandeis.* New York: Bloch Publishing Co., 1929.

Fineman, Irving F. *Woman of Valor, the Life of Henrietta Szold.* New York: Simon and Schuster, 1961.

Glazer, Nathan, and others. *The Characteristics of American Jews.* New York: Jewish Education Committee, 1965.

Halpern, Ben. *The American Jew.* New York: Herzl Foundation, 1956.

Hofstadter, Richard. *Age of Reform: From Bryan to FDR.* New York: Alfred A. Knopf, 1955.

Janowsky, Oscar J. (ed.). *The American Jew, a Reappraisal.* Philadelphia: Jewish Publication Society, 1964.

Manuel, Frank E. *The Realities of American-Palestine Relations 1832-1848.* Washington: Public Affairs Press, 1949.

Voss, Carl Herman. *Rabbi and Minister, Wise and Holmes.* Cleveland: World Publishing Co., 1964.

Weizmann, Chaim. *Trial and Error*, his autobiography. New York: G. P. Putnam's Sons, 1949.

Wise, Stephen S. *The Challenging Years*, his autobiography. New York: Harper and Bros., 1949.

Literary Works

Asch, Sholem. *Three Cities.* New York: G. P. Putnam's Sons, 1937.

—— *Uncle Moses.* New York: E. P. Dutton and Co., 1920.

Fiedler, Leslie. *The Jew in the American Novel.* New York: Herzl Institute, 1959.

—— *Waiting for the End.* New York: Stein and Day, 1964.

Halkin, Simon. *Modern Hebrew Literature.* New York: Schocken Books, 1950.

Heschel, Abraham Joshua. *The Earth Is the Lord's, the Inner World of the Jew in East Europe.* New York: Henry Schuman, 1959.

Howe, Irving and Greenberg, Eliezer. *A Treasury of Yiddish Stories.* New York: Viking Press, 1954.

Samuel, Maurice. *The Prince of the Ghetto.* New York: Alfred A. Knopf, 1948.

—— *The World of Sholem Aleichem.* New York: Alfred A. Knopf, 1943.

Singer, I. J. *The Brothers Ashkenazi.* New York: Alfred A. Knopf, 1936.

Singer, Isaac Bashevis. *The Family Moskat.* New York: Alfred A. Knopf, 1950.

Wasserman, Jacob. *My Life as German and Jew.* New York: Coward McCann, 1933.

Zweig, Stefan. *The World of Yesterday.* New York: Viking Press, 1943.

Others

Glueck, Nelson. *The River Jordan*. Philadelphia: Westminster Press, 1946.
——— *Rivers in the Dust*. New York: Farrar, Straus and Cudahy, 1959.
Hertzberg, Arthur. (ed.). *The Zionist Idea, a Historical Analysis and Reader*. New York: Meridian Books, 1960.
Scholem, Gershom. *Major Trends in Jewish Mysticism*. New York: Schocken Books, 1946.

INDEX

Note: Page references to maps are in *italics*.

ABOUT THE AUTHOR

JUDD TELLER is Executive Vice-Chairman of the American Histadrut Cultural Exchange Institute. Previously, he was a consultant on minority problems and a foreign correspondent at the United Nations. As a trilingual writer, he has contributed to such periodicals as *Commentary, Commonweal, American Reporter Magazine, The Nation, The New Republic* and to a number of Hebrew and Yiddish newspapers and periodicals.

Judd Teller came to the United States at the age of nine from Poland. He has since traveled widely in the U.S.S.R. and other Communist countries, Central and Western Europe, Asia and Africa.

From Moses to Maimonides, from Isaiah to Louis Brandeis, from Judah the Maccabean to Theodor Herzl—rebels, wanderers, workers, fighters—statesmen, generals, artists, prophets, writers, leaders—

PROFILE OF A PEOPLE

Here is a remarkable profile of the Jews in their constant migrations from continent to continent, across the centuries. Here is the quintessence of the Jewish personality as exemplified in the rare genius of its leaders and thinkers.

THE JEWS:
BIOGRAPHY OF A PEOPLE
BY JUDD TELLER